STAY ALIVE ALL YOUR LIFE

By Norman Vincent Peale

A GUIDE TO CONFIDENT LIVING
THE NEW ART OF LIVING
THE POSITIVE PRINCIPLE TODAY
SIN, SEX AND SELF-CONTROL
STAY ALIVE ALL YOUR LIFE
ENTHUSIASM MAKES THE DIFFERENCE
THE TOUGH-MINDED OPTIMIST
FAITH IS THE ANSWER (with Smiley Blanton)
POSITIVE IMAGING
INSPIRING MESSAGES FOR DAILY LIVING
THE AMAZING RESULTS OF POSITIVE THINKING
TREASURY OF JOY AND ENTHUSIASM
THE TRUE JOY OF POSITIVE LIVING
HAVE A GREAT DAY
WHY SOME POSITIVE THINKERS GET POWERFUL RESULTS
POWER OF THE PLUS FACTOR
THE POWER OF ETHICAL MANAGEMENT
(with Kenneth Blanchard)
THE POWER OF POSITIVE LIVING
THE POWER OF POSITIVE THINKING
YOU CAN IF YOU THINK YOU CAN

STAY ALIVE ALL YOUR LIFE

by

NORMAN VINCENT PEALE

"May you live all the days of your life."
Jonathan Swift

FAWCETT COLUMBINE • NEW YORK

A Fawcett Columbine Book
Published by Ballantine Books
 Published in the United States by Ballantine Books, a division of Random House, Inc., New York, and simultaneously in Canada by Random House of Canada Limited, Toronto.

http://www.randomhouse.com

Library of Congress Catalog Card Number: 96-96626

ISBN: 0-449-91204-3

This edition published by arrangement with Prentice-Hall, Inc.

Manufactured in the United States of America

First Ballantine Books Mass Market Edition: June 1983
First Ballantine Books Trade Edition: August 1996

10 9 8 7 6 5 4 3

To my wife

RUTH STAFFORD PEALE

with appreciation for her wise advice, enthusiastic support, and constant helpfulness in the writing of this book

To the reader

Dear Friend:

I appreciate your interest in this book. It was written with you in mind. Its purpose is to help you enjoy a more satisfying life. I like to think that by reading and, more important still, by practicing the suggestions the book contains, you will have a greater sense of well-being, increased vitality, and a keener interest in living.

This desired result is achieved through applying certain simple formulas. But these are not easy. There is no easy road to a happy life. But neither is that goal impossible.

I believe the Lord intends us to be filled with energy and enthusiasm; to have dynamic health of body, mind, and soul. Vibrant life is surely God's intent. We can come to no other conclusion if we read the Bible. Life glows from its pages. One of its most characteristic statements says, "I am come that they might have life, and that they might have it more abundantly." (John 10:10)

This volume goes further than my previous book, *The Power of Positive Thinking,* in emphasizing how to achieve well-being, vitality, enthusiasm and effectiveness in life. My former book outlined how to *think* positively about your problems. The present volume attempts to show you how to put these positive thoughts into *action,* and by believing and having faith in their power, succeed in achieving what you want out of life.

I am sorry that I cannot promise all the answers. Who can? But some of the answers to effective living are outlined here. I base this judgment upon the experience of many who live by the principles described in this volume, and some of whose inspiring stories are mentioned. I sincerely trust that through this book you, too, will learn to live dynamically and happily all your life.

I wish to express appreciation to my daughter, Margaret Ann Peale, for her valuable secretarial assistance in the preparation of this manuscript. Acknowledgment is made to *Guideposts Magazine,* Carmel, New York, for permission to quote from various articles.

Norman Vincent Peale

CONTENTS

HOW TO USE THIS BOOK xi

I. THE MAGNIFICENT POWER OF BELIEF 1

II. ENTHUSIASM CAN DO WONDERS FOR YOU 23

III. HOW TO CONQUER YOUR FRUSTRATIONS AND BE CREATIVE 45

IV. KILL WORRY AND LIVE LONGER 65

V. YOU CAN HAVE POWER OVER YOUR DIFFICULTIES 86

VI. YOU CAN HAVE LIFE IF YOU WANT IT 105

VII. STOP BEING TIRED—LIVE ENERGETICALLY 121

VIII. LEARN FROM MISTAKES—AND MAKE FEWER 137

IX. WHY BE TENSE? HOW TO ADJUST TO STRESS 157

X. YOUR LIFE CAN BE FULL OF JOY 172

XI. LIFT YOUR DEPRESSION AND LIVE VITALLY 193

XII. PEACE OF MIND—YOUR SOURCE OF POWER AND ENERGY 212

XIII. HOW TO FEEL WELL AND HAVE VIBRANT HEALTH 231

XIV. SELF-CONFIDENCE AND DYNAMIC ACHIEVEMENT 247

XV. LIVING ABOVE PAIN AND SUFFERING 264

XVI. LIVE FOREVER 284

How To Use This Book To Help Solve Your Problems

Publisher's Note: This short section has been specially designed to aid you in solving some of the difficult problems you face in the course of your daily social, business and personal life. It also will refer you to specific chapters in the book where more detailed help is available.

Below you will find a number of such problems stated. Along with each is a brief comment by Dr. Peale on the subject and a reference to a particular section in the book where the problem is fully discussed by him. We hope this special section will prove useful to you in suggesting solutions to some knotty problems, and that you will look to this section whenever you feel the need of Dr. Peale's help.

❖ ***How can I stop worrying about things I can't possibly do anything about?***

"The basic secret of overcoming worry is the substitution of faith for fear as your dominant mental attitude. Two great forces in this world are more powerful than all others. One is fear and the other is faith; and faith is stronger than fear . . ."

See Chapter IV, "Kill Worry and Live Longer," page 69.

❖ ***I get keyed up so often and cannot seem to relax. Is there anything I can do about this?***

"The Biblical prescription for energy calls for 'waiting' upon the Lord . . . The secret of a continuous power-flow is in adjusting yourself to God's controlled pace and tempo. Synchronize your thinking and living with God's unhurried timing . . . The absence of tiredness depends upon being in the natural rhythm of God."

See Chapter VII, "Stop Being Tired—Live Energetically," page 124.

❖ ***I've always thought peace of mind was a good trait. But lately I've been hearing that it just "lulls" people into a false sense of security. Is peace of mind really a valuable thing to acquire?***

"A great value of peace of mind is that it increases intellectual power. The mind is efficient only when it is cool—not hot. In a heated state of mind, emotions control judgment, which may prove costly. Power comes from quietness . . ."

See Chapter XII, "Peace of Mind—Your Source of Power and Energy," page 212.

❖ ***Why do I so often seem to be* wrong *about things? Is there some formula for not making so many mistakes?***

"A successful life depends upon developing a higher percentage of wisdom than error. Then you will do fewer things wrong and more things right. In improving your right-decision percentage, the knowledge of *how* to make a decision is very important. And more and more people are learning that the highest percentage of right decisions is attained when spiritual methods are employed."

See Chapter VIII, "Learn from Mistakes—and Make Fewer," page 146.

◆ ***How can I control my temper and keep from flying off the handle when frustrating things happen?***

"A rudimentary fact that many miss is that there are some people and things in this world that you just have to get along with, and no amount of resistance or railing will accomplish anything except to increase your frustration . . . A quiet and urbane philosophy . . . is most important in eliminating frustrated feelings."

See Chapter III, "How to Conquer Your Frustrations and Be Creative," page 48.

◆ ***I am a moody person; how can I develop a more positive and happy outlook on life?***

"Your mind may try to block you in your desire to become a joyous and harmonious individual by telling you that 'thinking doesn't make it so.' But thinking CAN make it so and often does, if at the same time thinking is implemented by diligent effort and by scientific and persistent practice."

See Chapter X, "Your Life Can Be Full of Joy," page 177.

◆ ***How can I be expected to accomplish things that I feel are beyond my limitations? Maybe I'm not as smart or talented as other people?***

"The amazing untapped power you have within you is of a force and quality that you cannot fully comprehend. Therefore, do not let yourself be a victim of the dismal concept of self-assumed personal limitation . . . Even if your ability, training, and experience are less than others', you can compensate for almost any lack by dynamic enthusiasm."

See Chapter II, "Enthusiasm Can Do Wonders for You," page 26.

❖ ***How can I conquer boredom and that "half-alive" feeling in regard to my daily work?***

"Put animation into your daily work. Your life's vitality can be increased by taking an immense pleasure in all that you are doing. Practice liking it. By this attitude tedium and the distinction between labor and pleasure is erased . . . you will get enjoyment out of your activity because aliveness stimulates the sense of excitement."

See Chapter VI, "You Can Have Life If You Want It," page 110.

❖ ***What is it that makes me so tense at times and what can I do about it?***

"Tension can and does have deeper causes than pressure and hard work. Tension may arise from old and seemingly buried feelings that originally caused hurt and may have deepened into resentment. We seldom put two and two together to see the connection between our present tension and old antagonistic attitudes . . . but you should explore this possibility . . ."

See Chapter IX, "Why Be Tense? How to Adjust to Stress," page 169.

❖ ***I can manage to handle the "little" things in life, but I'm just afraid to tackle the big ones. Can you help me?***

"I believe that when you plan something big you are actually thinking the way God intended men to think . . . Big faith equals big results. Big dreams, plus big thinking, plus big faith, plus big effort—that is the formula by which big things are done . . . and by which big difficulties are overcome."

See Chapter V, "You Can Have Power Over Your Difficulties," page 91.

◆ ***I constantly doubt my ability to accomplish the things in life I really want. How can I fight this self-doubt?***

"Every individual forms his own estimate of himself and that basic estimate goes far toward determining what he becomes. You can do no more than you believe you can. You can be no more than you believe you are. Real belief helps to make your faith come true. Belief helps stimulate power within yourself . . ."

See Chapter I, "The Magnificent Power of Belief," page 12.

◆ ***I wish I could believe in a life after death, but I can't. Is there any* proof *of immortality beyond what religion teaches?***

"One of the most significant facts about modern thinking is the new conviction that the universe is spiritual. The old materialistic conception is fading . . . Current scientific investigation seems to lend support to our intuitions and faith. Recently an eminent scientist expressed as his personal belief that the soul theory has been proved according to the minimum standards of science."

See Chapter XVI, "Live Forever," page 287.

◆ ***Is it really true that emotions can cause sickness, and, if so, what can be done about it?***

"A real cause of ill health is ill will. Having allowed ill will to accumulate and its inevitable accompaniment of guilt to clog the mind, naturally your vital powers are depressed. Sick feeling results. The cure of this condition is good will . . . This may be accomplished by a shift to the attitude of love and the healing qualities which it generates."

See Chapter XIII, "How to Feel Well and Have Vibrant Health," page 238.

❖ ***How can I rid my mind of depressing thoughts?***

"Study your thoughts, write them down on paper and analyze them, whether they are creative or destructive . . . replace every weak thought with a strong one, each negative thought with a positive one, a hate thought with a loving one, a gloomy thought with a lifted one . . . You will find this literally a magic formula."

See Chapter XI, "Lift Your Depression and Live Vitally," page 204.

❖ ***How can I cope with my problems when I feel so alone in facing them—so alone that I lose confidence in solving them?***

"There is a text in the Bible that is so powerful it can change your life . . . 'If God be for us, who can be against us?' Personalize these words so that they apply directly to you . . . Now bring a picture into your mind of God facing your obstacles. Can they stand against God . . . ?"

See Chapter XIV, "Self-Confidence and Dynamic Achievement," page 248.

❖ ***How can I have faith in life, or even in God, when I am so frequently distracted by pain?***

". . . faith becomes an instrument for getting insight into the fundamental meaning of suffering and for bearing it. Even as pain may be removed by faith, so it may be endured by faith."

See Chapter XV, "Living Above Pain and Suffering," page 267.

STAY ALIVE ALL YOUR LIFE

CHAPTER I

THE MAGNIFICENT POWER OF BELIEF

"Every individual forms his own estimate of himself and that basic estimate goes far toward determining what he becomes. You can do no more than you believe you can. You can be no more than you believe you are. Belief stimulates power within yourself. Have faith in faith. Don't be afraid to trust faith."

ONCE, WHILE I WAS DINING WITH FRIENDS in a Southwest Texas hotel before giving a lecture, a man entered the restaurant and asked for me.

In the conversation he startled my friends and me by saying, "I came to this town a bum." Noting our bewilderment, he continued, "I mean it—a bum, a hobo." This statement was so unbelievable, considering the obviously fine person who spoke, that we listened intently.

He told us that back in West Virginia, a few years before, he began drinking heavily. He lost one position after another, each new job being further down the economic scale, until finally he hit bottom. Dirty and unshaven he shuffled the streets, only halfheartedly looking for work which he did not get. Finally, in desperation, his wife left him. Homeless, broke, and defeated he left town and aimlessly "bummed" west. He slept in haystacks, barns, and alleys. Meals were begged from door to door.

One day a kindly lady gave him a handout on her back porch and stood watching him wolf it down. "You look like a nice young man," she observed. "You shouldn't be in this condition. I am going to give you something which can change your life if you will use it."

She went into the house and returned with a book. "Read this," she said. "Do what it says and you can be a useful person again."

Our friend shuffled on west with the book in the pocket of his ragged coat. Having nothing else to do and much time on his hands, he read every word of it dozens of times. Often, to escape the winter cold he would go into libraries and there read his book.

Gradually, its simple message began to penetrate his dark thoughts and permeate his consciousness. "Get in harmony with God, change your thoughts and your way of living; believe and succeed; through faith you can; believe you can, and you can." So ran the emphasis of the book.

Finally, by practice, he learned to pray and to have faith. He sincerely tried the spiritual technique suggested and the change began. Presently he came to this Texas town where he had been told a certain man would give him a job. "As I approached his home a beautiful young woman was sweeping the walk. Will you believe it when I tell you that she is now my wife?" he asked with a smile.

He worked at a number of small jobs, each better than the last. Then he felt a desire to be an accountant, having a liking for figures and some experience with them in the pre-drinking days. One day a company dealing in pipe for the oil fields asked him to figure a job estimate. He had never undertaken so complicated a proposition, but he prayed for guidance, studied hard over the problem, and finally figured costs quite accurately. This was a remarkable achievement considering his lack of experience. From then on he went steadily forward and became successful as a person.

Finishing his remarkable story he pulled from his pocket the soiled and ragged book which he had carried on his wanderings and tenderly laid it on the table with the remark, "Anybody can do as I did, and most will not have as far to rise. The secret is, have faith, believe, and practice."

This man's experience demonstrates a law which is stated succinctly in the dynamic and creative teachings of Jesus Christ. "If thou canst believe, all things are possible to him that believeth." (Mark 9:23) As you train your mind to believe, defeat tendencies are reversed, and everything tends to move out of the area of the impossible into that of the possible.

First, become a believer in God, not merely academically, but believe confidently in Him as your guide, and actually practice spiritual principles. Second, believe in yourself, in people, and in life itself. Have a sincere desire to serve God and mankind, and stop doubting, stop thinking negatively.

How do you have faith? Simply start living by faith, pray earnestly and humbly, and get into the habit of looking expectantly for the best. This type of thinking will presently cause an actual reversal in the flow of your life, for life is always in a state of flow one way or the other. Failure factors will move from you and success factors, by a magnetic attraction, will move toward you. The dynamic and positive attitude is a strong magnetic force which, by its very nature, attracts good results.

This, of course, does not mean you will get everything you want. When you live on a faith basis your desire will be only for that which you can ask in God's name. But whatever you should have, whatever is good for you will be granted. There is no limit to what God will give to those who practice His laws.

By success, of course, I do not mean that you may become rich, famous, or powerful for that does not, of necessity, represent achievement. Indeed, not infrequently, such individuals represent pathetic failure as persons. By success I mean the development of mature and constructive personality.

Through the application of the principle of constructive thinking you can attain your worthy goals. The natural outcome of living by creative principles is creative results. *Believe and create* is a basic fact of successful living. You can make your life what you want it to be through belief in God and in yourself.

Frank Lloyd Wright, the famous architect, who has been called one of the most creative geniuses of all time said, "The thing always happens that you really believe in. And the belief in a thing makes it happen. And I think nothing will happen until you thoroughly and deeply believe in it."

The Biblical law, "According to your faith be it done unto you," (Matt. 9:29) expresses the truth that the extent to which you receive God's blessing depends precisely upon the degree to which you believe.

Many illustrations of the operation of this principle might be given. For example, a woman told me that for years she depreciated herself as "the plain one" of four sisters. The other three so-called more charming sisters had always told her she was plain and unattractive and she came to believe that untruth.

Then one day a friend said, "But you are not plain. Try picturing yourself as the sincere and attractive person you are. Charm," she continued, "is not procured from a bottle. It comes from right thinking and radiant living. So, decide what you want to be, then paint a picture of yourself as being that. Humbly believe that, with God's help, your picture of yourself will come to pass."

This friend asked her a direct question, "What do you really want from life? You will need to answer that question specifically, before you will have any chance of getting it." It was a wise question, for goals are never reached unless they are first specifically formed in the mind.

"If you really would like to know," said the other with embarrassment, "I want a husband and children and a good home." (Her sisters, all married and having homes of their own, had assured her that she was too plain and could never hope for marriage.)

"Do not be embarrassed by such a normal desire," said her friend. "To accomplish this worthy goal hold a mental picture of the home and husband and children you want. Then put the wish in God's hands to give or to withhold. If it is His will, He will grant it. Ask Him to develop your personality in preparation for wifehood and motherhood. Ask God to make you beautiful, charming, and good."

This woman painted and held her mental picture, affirming it by unremitting perseverance into reality, and this Cinderella story came true.

Some people complain that only the gifted or the accomplished may successfully employ these creative techniques. Such thinking is a dangerous form of rationalizing failure. The more jealousy one has in his nature the more critical he is of those who have accomplished things.

If you are critical and mouthing negativisms it could be that your own failures are caused by a mixed-up, hate-filled mind. A sign of mental health is to be glad when others achieve, and to rejoice with them. Never compare yourself or your achievements with others, but make your comparisons only with yourself. Maintain a constant competition with yourself. This will force you to attain higher standards and achievements. Do not defeat yourself by holding spiteful or jealous thoughts. Think straight, with love, hope, and optimism and you will attain victory in life.

A demonstration of these facts is described in a letter I received several years ago from a man who applied them in a difficult situation.

Dear Dr. Peale,

A week and a half ago I was ticket collector and doorman at a theater in the Bronx. Then the boss told me business was slow and I was laid off. In my heart and soul, however, I had no fear because faith had entered into my life.

In a week my money was about gone, and I still had no job, so I went to the New York State Employment Service and filled out an application for a hotel job. I pictured myself getting a good job. A day later the man called me and gave me a good job at a hotel for more money; $42.00, when I had only been getting $27.56.

Now, I learned all this in the Marble Collegiate Church by going to the services on Sunday. My life is improved and I am improving. My life is turning to light, and goodness, and the darkness of ignorance is being blotted out of my life. I know how to get ahead and keep going. I love the church and I will help the church out as much as I can and I am going to give the church one dollar every Sunday.

He loves the church and he wants to give to God. Why not? The church taught him the great secret of positive faith, which opened new vistas of hope for him. This man, lacking in education and struggling on a poverty level, had nevertheless become sensitized to that electric atmosphere that develops in church when spiritual power is released. He listened to the message about getting in harmony with God and learning to live by faith.

He believed that message and practiced it. It did not free him from difficulty. It was never promised that it would. But that message did give him the know-how and power to handle his difficulties and master them. The validity of his experience is attested by the fact that, having received, he wanted to share with God. It is a subtle and important fact that if we seek spiritual values only for ourselves they will turn dead in our hands; but when we receive and give, they replenish themselves.

I have seen transformations in people, under the influence of spiritual power, that are almost unbelievable. I have watched people come to the church as one sort of person and depart altogether different. In church creative living techniques are taught and specific methods are outlined for using dynamic principles to overcome failure, cast out fear, and heal sorrow. Something may happen to you in church that can completely change everything in your life for the better. You will be very wise, indeed, if you get alerted to the possibility.

To the Marble Collegiate Church every Sunday come people of all creeds, or no creed. Among them are old and young, sophisticates, the poor, the rich, the mighty, and the defeated. They are all there, mixed with the happiest crowd of people you ever saw, people whose lives have been changed. You should hear them sing. Their enthusiasm is infectious. They have a happy religion, because it is to them the symbol of victory over themselves and every wrong and defeating thing that previously took the joy out of life. Dynamism is in the very atmosphere.

Let me tell you about another man who, like our theater doorkeeper from the Bronx, found the answer; only this man was a banker. Spiritual laws are not respectors of persons. They are available to all who will believe and practice and live on a spiritual level.

I stood with this banker one summer Sunday outside a small, country church where we had both been worshipping. "What a great place the church is," said Bill. "If people only knew what they can get in church, they would flock there by the thousands." (Perhaps that is why immense throngs are now pouring into churches every Sunday.)

He was speaking of something he knew to be true through personal experience, the surest of all verifications. Several years before he had been president of a bank but, due to a feud, he had been ousted and found himself, at fifty-two, with no job. His first reaction was one of panic, for he had two children in college and other financial obligations. He was flooded with hatred for the men responsible for his dismissal. Finally he yielded to the sinister despair that he was finished.

It was at this point that he came to church, desperately looking for a way out. He heard about the simple, dynamic, creative principles of faith. Then Bill and I had a conference. How could religious faith help him, he wanted to know.

I said, "First you must empty out all that hate. Pray for those men. Ill will corrodes the soul and impedes the channel through which spiritual and creative power flows."

"That is hard," he said, "but I'll try."

"Then," I said, "fear must come out. Put your problems confidently in God's hands and believe that He will guide you."

He followed these directions and continued to practice this new way of thinking even though things grew much worse. His finances actually got so low that he was forced to resort to blueberry picking to buy groceries. This would be enough to discourage most men completely, and previously it would have done so for him, but his new faith was working in him. He felt strangely peaceful and was able to see the creative values in his hard experience.

"Formerly my wife and I were so busy we became almost strangers to each other. Picking blueberries on opposite sides of a high bush helped us really to know each other. Her smile, the loveliness of her soul, the wonderful things she said, and the loyal way she stood by me built me up. We found God and each other in a blueberry patch," he said tenderly.

Today Bill is head of a small town bank, but more important, he is a constructive factor in his church and community. And when people consult him about business matters he goes further and gives them some helpful thoughts on how to believe and succeed. In his own practical way he gives people the simple, dynamic, creative philosophy of Jesus Christ.

One thought you must always hold is that you can attain a higher level for your life. Few people realize their real possibilities. Many believe that "ordinary" persons must remain ordinary all their lives. That concept is false and a slander on human nature and on the God who created you. One of the chief functions of spiritual truth is to reveal and release the extraordinary possibilities in so-called "ordinary" persons. Personally, I do not believe any human being is ordinary. I like the statement of Dr. Harold C. Case, President of Boston University, that "The spirit of democracy is to believe everyone into greatness."

Why do some people seemingly have the touch of failure? Why do things go so wrong for them, and so often? Why do they experience an ever accumulating series of irritating frustrations, their projects and plans so frequently going badly? In most cases, analysis reveals that ineptness is inherent in the individual, rather than in the circumstances. If things continually go wrong for you, perhaps the psychology of wrongness is in you and should be corrected.

Do not waste time complaining about conditions or about other people. Honestly face the possibility that your thinking may be wrong; that your trouble may be within yourself. It isn't that you lack ability, but rather that your mental slant and approach is tinged with failure thoughts and, naturally, failure follows. Also, your attitudes may be harsh, critical, and unfriendly toward other people, with the result that they withdraw from you without themselves understanding the reason. In subtle ways a lack of personal inner harmony is quickly reflected in inharmonious personal relations. And your relationship with other people is profoundly important to your own successful living.

It is also important to emphasize that a basic factor in successful living is not how much you know or how hard you work, although neither is to be minimized. The most important factor is what you believe and how sincerely you believe it. This law was stated by William James, one of the greatest thinkers in American history, who said, "In any project, the important factor is your belief. Without belief there can be no successful outcome. That is fundamental."

At a high school commencement a large banner stretched across the stage proclaimed the class motto in huge letters, "They Conquer Who Believe They Can." High school graduates who go into the world with that truth printed on their minds, will do something constructive, provided they continue to hold the concept. Whatever your goal, you can attain it if you believe you can and then keep on believing even when it is hard to believe.

This truth is so dynamic that even the most unlikely persons often demonstrate its power. For example, a janitor's helper in a big city railroad station had a job pushing a mop. At forty-five he was only a mop-pusher. It would seem that a man so situated would not have any great future.

However, there was a railroad conductor, a man of faith, who came in and out of that station. He liked this mop-pusher and one day said to him, "You ought to have a better job than this."

"How?" the man asked dully. "I have a wife and three children and an aged mother and I never had any education; and besides, a man can't get ahead like they once did in this country. Those days are gone forever." So he mouthed the cynical, negative philosophy we have heard so much in late years.

But the conductor made him believe in his country and himself and reminded him of all that God can do with a person who is surrendered to God's Grace. He painted a picture of something better, until that picture began to form in the man's mind. This set in motion dynamic forces that stimulated events. One day the conductor told him that in a near-by town a man wanted to sell a hamburger stand. He inspired the mop-pusher to go and look over the opportunity.

When he arrived in that town he found the price asked for the hamburger stand was three hundred and fifty dollars, and our prospective restaurant man had but twenty-five in cash to invest. But now he had something worth more than money. He had positive thoughts. He had developed real faith, and the sustained visualization of a better opportunity had already made his personal reactions dynamic. With this fresh, new quality of mind he was unwilling to accept defeat. So, carefully and prayerfully, he considered the situation and submitted to the owner a proposition that he purchase the place without down payment, but agreeing to pay, within a year, the sum of five hundred dollars. Ordinarily the owner would have impatiently brushed aside such an offer, but something in the spirit of this man impressed him and he accepted. Then this man arranged with the grocer and butcher for the daily purchase of supplies on credit, with the stipulation that they be paid for each morning from the previous day's receipts.

From that desperate beginning the erstwhile lethargic and defeated mop-pusher worked, believed equally hard, and today owns a very nice restaurant. Printed on his menus are these lines which nourish the spirit of his customers as his good food strengthens their bodies.

If you think you are beaten you are;
If you think you dare not, you don't;
If you want to win but think you can't
It's almost a cinch you won't.
If you think you'll lose you're lost;
For out in the world we find
Success begins with a fellow's will;
It's all in the state of mind.
Life's battles don't always go
To the stronger and faster man,
But sooner or later the man who wins
Is the man who thinks he can.

"I can do all things through Christ which strengtheneth me," (Phil. 4:13) is the statement of a spiritual law, which expresses the result that comes when a believing person establishes a real working partnership with God.

It is most important to have faith in faith itself. Cultivate the conviction that, as you think constructively in terms of faith, you can successfully handle any situation that may confront you. Emerson warned that "no accomplishment, no assistance, no training can compensate for lack of belief." The late Mr. Justice Cardozo of the United States Supreme Court said, "We are what we believe we are."

Every individual forms his own estimate of himself and that basic estimate goes far toward determining what he becomes. You can do no more than you believe you can. You can be no more, than you believe you are. Real belief helps to make your faith come true. Belief stimulates power within yourself. Have faith in faith. Do not be afraid to trust faith.

The parents of a sixteen-year-old boy entered him in a preparatory school which they could scarcely afford, but they wanted their son to have advantages they had not enjoyed. The boy appreciated his opportunity and determined to justify it. He set his heart on winning the scholarship prize to compensate for his parents' sacrifice. He worked diligently and began to ascend to dizzy heights of scholarship that he had never attained previously.

Up and up went his marks—80, 85, 90. He had never received such grades and, like a person climbing a high place, became frightened at his own achievement. Then came a destructive thought. "This scholastic level is too high for me. I am out of my depth. I cannot hold this standard." Thus, he began to doubt and to disbelieve. Soon his mind accepted his lack of faith in himself. Then, since his ability was no longer challenged, his mind closed up and he could not seem to remember his lessons as well. The quality of his work fell off. Soon he was doing poorly in his studies and his marks declined. He became very discouraged and was even ready to quit.

"But one night," said he, "I opened my Bible in the hope of some encouragement, and happened upon the verse which said, 'With God all things are possible.' (Matt. 19:26) That made me think, 'My parents believe in me and, for awhile, I was able to get high marks. Since I did that well once, why couldn't I do it again. I believe that God will help me.' All of a sudden," he said, "I knew that I could do it." And he did do it. His grades crept up again. He became top boy in scholarship. When he recovered faith in faith his personality focused and power flowed through.

So, practice every day the act of casting all doubt out of your mind. Never settle for anything less than all that you want to be. Perhaps you are getting older and you say to yourself, "I have done all I will ever do; I have reached my limit." Never say that. Never entertain such an unworthy or false thought. You are not entitled to write yourself off as through. Do not impose self-created limitations upon yourself. Keep on believing as long as you live and your effectiveness will be prolonged.

Academically and theoretically most people believe that

God helps people, but not always do they actually seek that help in specific situations. "What can God do in this particular instance?" they ask dubiously. Let us answer that negation with the question, "What can't God do?" Thousands of sincere people have demonstrated that, through faith, a power and wisdom beyond all human ingenuity may be brought to bear upon specific situations.

When Bob Richards, world's champion pole vaulter, received an award as the amateur athlete of the year he was asked by reporters for the secret of his athletic powers. "I owe my achievements to the power of the Lord," he replied. When the athletic sportswriters interrogated him further he explained, "Oh, don't get the idea that some metaphysical power comes down as I start to vault, and lifts me over the bar. It isn't that way at all. When I speak of the power of the Lord, I mean the psychological influence which He exerts over all those who search their souls and find there the strength to perform wonderful things."

So conclusive is all the evidence that spiritually constructive thinking can determine the outcome of our lives that an intelligent person cannot wisely ignore this scientific law of living. First, get your life right in terms of God's laws. Be a dedicated person. Next, be sure your goals are spiritually sound. Then, think success, believe in success, visualize success and you will set in motion the powerful force of the realizable wish. When the mental picture or attitude is strongly enough held it actually seems to control conditions and circumstances.

An example is that famous story of a tense moment in a World Series baseball game some years ago between the New York Yankees and the Chicago White Sox. In the fifth inning the score stood 4 to 3 in favor of Chicago with Charlie Root on the mound for Chicago. At the plate stood the mightiest batsman of all time, Babe Ruth. But the pitcher did not fear him, for Ruth had hit a home run in the first inning and surely that was the only home run he had in his system for that day.

The pitcher put the ball straight across the plate. Babe Ruth held up one finger in derision. Straight as an arrow the second ball came whizzing across. Ruth held up two fingers of derision. Pandemonium reigned. Was it possible that, like the mighty Casey, he would strike out in this crisis? Then Ruth did a strange and almost contemptuous thing. He raised his finger and pointed straight across the fence to indicate where he proposed to hit the ball.

The pitcher went into his windup and sent the ball once again whistling straight across the plate. There was a sharp crack and in a beautiful arc the ball sailed straight and true just where Ruth had pointed over the fence. It was an electric moment, an unforgettable episode in the history of American sport.

After the game somebody asked Babe Ruth, "But suppose you had missed that final strike?" A look of genuine surprise overcame the Babe's face. "Why," he said, "I never even thought of such a thing." Which may be precisely the reason he did not miss the ball.

This illustrates a profound law; namely, that when you take into your mind the thought of impossibility, you tend to create the conditions of impossibility. Prior to the formation of such a negative thought your entire being, body, mind, and spirit, works as a unity in perfect harmony. The powerful positive forces of the universe are flowing through your personality. But when you change the cast and slant of your mind so that you hold the idea of the impossible, you tend to block off in yourself the continued flow of coordinated power.

As a result the fine balance of personality is lost. You become rigid and tightened up. The easy flow of harmonious power is interfered with. In the case of a baseball player his all important timing is affected just enough to make that fraction of a difference whereby the bat will pass over or below the ball rather than meet it squarely. Similarly, in your life skill will be lacking when the doubt idea becomes uppermost.

I am not sure that positive thinking extends to fishing, but I witnessed what seemed a demonstration. I went fishing one day, in the inland waterways at Sea Island, Georgia, with two men and my daughter Elizabeth, then about eleven years old. None of us were catching anything except Elizabeth, who hauled in two fish.

"How come, honey?" I asked. "Our lines are in the water right alongside yours and yet we catch nothing and you've got two."

She looked at me with a twinkle in her eye. "Oh, Daddy," she explained as she pulled in another, "I practice positive thinking."

The army engineers corps has a suggestive motto: "The difficult we do immediately—the impossible may take a little longer." Since God and you form a strong combination and "with God all things are possible," then it may be assumed that God and you can do the impossible even if it does require a little time. Make that the dominating thought of your mind—God and you are undefeatable. As this thought takes real hold of you then things which heretofore you considered impossibilities will move into the area of the possible.

Though these assertions may perhaps seem extravagant, nevertheless, the principle works when you believe and practice it as countless persons have demonstrated. The secret, of course, is daily to practice filling your mind with possibility thoughts. Continue until belief firmly takes hold of your mind. One simple method for doing this is to avoid saying, "I don't believe I can do it," and instead affirm, "Perhaps I cannot do it alone, but God is with me and with His strength I can do it." Affirm in this manner a dozen times a day until your negatively trained mind accepts the positive point of view. Remember, always, that you can if you think you can, and do not allow doubts to clog your mind.

I had an appointment for luncheon in Washington and, having a short time to wait, went into a pleasant garden adjoining the hotel. This garden has a fountain with a bird bath. A few elderly ladies were taking the sun.

I noticed a young sparrow perched on the edge of the bird bath. All the other sparrows came down, got themselves a drink, gave themselves a bath, then flew away, but he remained hesitant. Then two or three of the women came up and said, "What's the matter with the poor little thing?" One said, "I think we had better take him into the house; there is something wrong with him."

But a man standing nearby said, "Let him alone. What do you want to do, destroy his self-confidence?"

"But," they argued, "the bird is sick."

"No, he is not sick," said the man. "He is just getting a start in life; leave him alone."

I became very interested and watched carefully. Finally the sparrow got up enough courage to fly a few feet. His mother and father came around and encouraged him and all his relatives gathered around and urged him on. I watched him learning to fly and marveled at his spirit. It was an object lesson in perseverance and confidence.

That evening, by curious coincidence, I happened to read in my paper a letter to the Editor about a robin which had hurt its wing. "Even though his wing droops," the writer said, "the robin sits up in an old cherry tree and sings. But," he added, "I am worried about his wing, what shall I do about it?"

The Editor answered, "Let his wing alone. A robin's wing is of gossamer texture proportionately stronger than much material of greater density. And," he continued, "remember a good, old doctor named Mother Nature. If you refrain from applying human methods to that wing, the robin, because he has no academic knowledge to hamper him, will have faith enough to let his wing droop until nature restores its strength.

"The robin," he continued, "is wiser than humans because, not knowing so much about the difficulties of life, he does not become discouraged. In this the robin is helped, without doubt, by his lack of human intelligence." Then the Editor concluded with this penetrating observation: "In the case of the robin, the channels of immortal help are not blocked by thought."

It is true of people no less than robins that the inflow of Divine power is blocked by thought, negative thought. Our failure lies in not being naïve enough to practice the power of faith. Perhaps the importance of this quality of naïveté explains why the greatest of all Teachers emphasized the value of becoming as a little child, since by the childlike attitude we are able to have faith and not doubt. It is indeed a searching thought that we may block the channels of immortal help by wrong thinking. You may know so much about your difficulties that your mind can see nothing but those difficulties. Too much emphasis upon difficulty will fill you with complete defeatism.

The head of a sales organization told me that one of their salesmen reported it was impossible to do any business in a particular section of the city where he was working. A baseless legend to this effect had developed and he accepted it. So, he was defeated before he began. A few setbacks and he just knew that sales were impossible in that area.

The company then transferred him out of town and put another salesman into his territory without informing the new man of his predecessor's defeatist ideas about that particular section of the city. The new salesman's first report showed more business out of that area than from any other. He had the advantage, actually, of an unworked section and, due to his lack of a defeatist feeling toward that area, proceeded to make the most of it. The new salesman had success simply because he did not know there was supposed to be no business in that section. Doubt did not have opportunity to affect his sales.

The principle of believe and succeed is no bright and easy panacea. Certainly it is not advanced as a method for gaining material things. And it is difficult to master. But it is an amazing formula for achieving goals, and for overcoming failure.

That this dynamic thinking is closely related to the basic truths of this world is demonstrated by the fact that it sets powerful forces in motion which stimulate accomplishments in even the most difficult circumstances.

People who insist upon failing tell me that while these principles may work in easy situations they do not apply in difficult ones. But just remember that the Bible, from which these creative ideas are taken, was not written for easy situations. Its teachings were meant to apply under the most difficult conditions.

Some years ago I met a couple who told me "how poor" they were. They reiterated this dismal complaint several times in that one conversation. They had two attractive young daughters whom they wanted to send to college. They were hard working, upright people, but were very negative. They emphasized, repeatedly, how little they had and that their girls would doubtless be denied a college education for that reason.

"I have read your philosophy of positive thinking," said the father, "but that is not for us, only for the more fortunate. Tell me how I can send my girls to college by thinking positively? My wife is a college graduate. I'm not, but our greatest ambition is to give our girls this advantage. But how can we?"

I started figuring some way to get the money for them,

but the father quickly said, "I don't want money from anybody. I want to do it on my own."

I admired him for his independent attitude and said, "Let's start by affirming now that, by the help of God, the girls are going to have a college education. Repeat the affirmation daily. Believe you will be shown how to make your faith a reality.

"The second step," I continued, "is to paint a mental picture of your daughters receiving their diplomas. Hold that picture firmly in consciousness. Establish it as a fundamental thought in your mind, your wife's mind, and in the girl's thoughts, also. Then, put the picture in the hands of God and go to work.

"You will need to work hard, think hard, and believe hard. Adopt the principle of believe and succeed. Believe and picture constantly that the college graduation already is an accomplished fact in the projected scheme of things."

He grasped this concept and began to shift from his defeatist "poor" thoughts to a thought pattern of creative accomplishment. Not only did his daughters graduate from college but, also, the economic level of the family has risen. These people have become dynamic and vital and are making a real contribution to their church and community.

Asked to explain these accomplishments the father declares, "I simply learned to believe. I kept on believing at all times even when everything seemed most difficult." And he added, "I also got busy and worked instead of wasting time and energy in complaining and feeling sorry for myself."

By such a sound formula of thought and action he was able to meet difficulties and, instead of being defeated by them, they merely helped strengthen his faith. His belief put him in harmony with the law of supply and, as a result, new and creative sources of support opened.

Another example of the creative power of belief is the experience of my friend, Dr. Frank L. Boyden, famous headmaster of Deerfield Academy, one of the finest of American preparatory schools. When Dr. Boyden came to the school years ago its future was precarious due to inadequate financial support. Today it has a beautiful campus, outstanding plant and equipment, and a superior faculty.

I asked Dr. Boyden how he created this splendid school from such unpromising beginnings.

"Well," he replied, "I think the banks in our town had their doubts. Probably they felt many times like writing us off; yet, whenever I needed help it was always available. I just kept on believing that we would come through." And he added, "I believe in the law of supply. When everything seems to be against you, even when there seems little hope, fill your mind with faith, do your best, work hard, and put the results in the hands of God. If sincerely you endeavor to do God's will, the law of supply will operate and it will supply your needs. This school was built upon the spiritual law of supply."

Of course the plus to that formula is Dr. Boyden's own dedicated personality and amazing understanding of boys. And not least in importance was his willingness to work hard and give his best. When this is done the law of supply operates effectively.

Any human being can do more with his life than he is presently doing. To begin with, you must desire to do so. The second step is to surrender yourself to God and live by His will. Then take God as your spiritual guide and partner in life. Next, pray without ceasing and have faith always. Be sure to hold positive pictures of achieving worthily and unselfishly. Finally, expect the cooperation of events, work hard, and think creatively, forget self, keep a heart full of good will, hold no resentment. And always remember—with God's help you can if you think you can.

❖ ❖ ❖

How to Believe

1. Believe.
2. As you train your mind to believe, everything tends to move out of the area of the impossible into that of the possible.
3. Never compare yourself or your achievements with others, but make your comparisons only with yourself.
4. A sign of mental health is to be glad when others achieve, and to rejoice with them.
5. Failure lies in not being naïve enough to practice the power of faith.
6. Make your life what you want it to be through belief in God and in yourself.
7. Start living by faith, pray earnestly and humbly, and get into the habit of looking expectantly for the best.
8. Get your life right in terms of God's laws.
9. Be sure your goals are spiritually sound.
10. Think, believe, visualize success.
11. Keep on believing as long as you live.

CHAPTER II

ENTHUSIASM CAN DO WONDERS FOR YOU

"When you cast out pessimism and gloominess and cultivate the attitude of optimism and enthusiasm, amazing results will be demonstrated in your life. Even if your ability, training, and experience are less than others', you can compensate for almost any lack by dynamic enthusiasm."

ARE YOU AN ENTHUSIASTIC PERSON? Do you eagerly anticipate each day? Are you excited about life? If not, then at all costs get real enthusiasm into your personality, for enthusiasm can do wonders for you.

My own mother was one of the most enthusiastic persons I ever knew. She was alive to her finger tips even though forced to cope with physical difficulty a large share of her life. She got an enormous thrill out of the most ordinary events and happenings. She had the ability to see and enjoy romance and zest in everything.

She travelled the world over. Years ago in China, during a revolution, she complained that she encountered so few bandits. Once, when her party was halted by fierce-looking brigands, she seemed actually disappointed that they did not kidnap her and her companions and cause some thrilling international incident.

I recall an experience with her one very foggy night while crossing from New Jersey to New York on a ferry boat. To me there was nothing particularly beautiful or interesting about the fog, but my mother excitedly cried, "Norman, isn't this thrilling?"

"What is thrilling?" I asked rather dully.

"Why," she enthused, "the fog, the lights, that ferry boat we just passed. Look at the mysterious way its lights fade into the mist."

Just then came the sound of a fog horn, deep-throated in the "heavy-padded whiteness" of the mist. That phrase, "heavy-padded whiteness," is my mother's, and I thought it particularly picturesque. Her face was that of an excited child. Up to that moment I had no feeling about that ferry boat ride except that I was in a hurry to get across the river; but now its mystery, romance, and fascination began to penetrate even my dull spirit.

She stood by the rail and eyed me appraisingly. "Norman," she said gently, "I have been giving you advice all your life. Some of it you have taken, some you haven't; but here is some I want you to take. Realize that the world is athrill with beauty and excitement. Keep yourself sensitized to it. Never let yourself get dull. Never lose your enthusiasm."

Wherever in the great beyond she is today, I am sure she is having the time of her life. Being what she was and is, she is as enthusiastic over there as she was here. I determined to follow her advice and have practiced keeping enthusiasm alive. Therefore, I can assure you from personal experience that it does wonders for you.

Ruth Cranston in her *Story of Woodrow Wilson* says: "Woodrow Wilson's classes at Princeton were the most popular ever known in the history of that University, and they were far from being snap courses. Year after year the students voted Wilson the most popular teacher. And the reason, he radiated enthusiasm.

"'He was the most inspiring teacher I ever sat under.' 'He made everything he touched interesting!' 'There was about him an aliveness, an enthusiasm that was infectious.' Such were some of the comments of his students, though he was lecturing on subjects that could be obtuse and dull; international law and political economy."

The President of a large company states: "If I am trying to decide between two men of fairly equal ability, and one man has enthusiasm, I know he will go farther than the other because enthusiasm acts as a self-releasing power and helps focus the entire force of personality on any matter at hand. Enthusiasm is infectious; it carries all before it."

That, of course, is understandable, for a man with enthusiasm gives the job his full potential. He throws everything into it. Enthusiasm is constantly renewing and releasing him, bringing all his faculties into play, utilizing his best.

Those who do the most and the best in life invariably have this quality of enthusiasm. So amazing are the achievements of such persons that it may be said that optimism and enthusiasm can actually work miracles in people's lives.

Emerson, considered by some to be the wisest man who ever lived in the United States, is an advocate of enthusiasm. "Nerve us up with incessant affirmatives," he says. "Do not waste yourself in rejections nor bark against the bad, but chant the beauty of the good." When you cast out pessimism and gloominess and cultivate the attitude of optimism and enthusiasm, amazing results will be demonstrated in your life. Even if your ability, training, and experience are less than others', you can compensate for almost any lack by dynamic enthusiasm.

In the light of this, how foolish to accept the depressing

and uninspiring doctrine of personal limitation. If asked how far they can go and how much they can do, some say, "Not very far and not very much. You see," they negatively explain, "I am not as gifted as others." To that assertion I would answer by a question and a statement: "How do you know you have limited ability? You do not know that for certain; you have merely accepted the concept, and by so doing, have actually limited yourself."

As a matter of fact, the amazing untapped power you have within you is of a force and quality that you cannot fully comprehend. Therefore, do not let yourself be a victim of the dismal concept of self-assumed personal limitation. Without being immodest you can and should be enthusiastic about yourself. Remember what William James, one of America's greatest psychological thinkers, said about your possibilities if you practice belief: "Believe that you possess significant reserves of health, energy, and endurance and your belief will help create the fact." Such is the power of dynamic and enthusiastic faith.

Many persons are paralyzed, not in their limbs, but in their thoughts. They have sold themselves on a constricted view of themselves; but such self-appraisal is a false opinion of their own personality. Most people underrate themselves. To counteract the crippling effect of such downgrading of yourself, practice optimistic enthusiasm about your own possibilities. When you vigorously reject the concept of personal limitations and become enthusiastic about your own life it is astonishing what new qualities will suddenly appear within you. You can then *do* and *be* what formerly would have seemed quite impossible.

An outstanding example of the infectious power of enthusiasm to bring out new capabilities was demonstrated by the old Boston Braves when, by transfer of franchise, they became the Milwaukee Braves. In Boston, the team had been drawing small crowds, had no support, stirred no enthusiasm, and did very poorly their last season in that city. Then they were transferred to Milwaukee. It had been fifty years since Milwaukee had boasted a Big League Baseball Club and the enthusiasm of the citizens for their new team was positively unbounded. They crowded the ball park, twenty to thirty thousand for each game. All Milwaukee, it seemed, took the Braves to their hearts, were proud of them, and wanted them to win. Indeed, all believed they would.

As a result, that former seventh-place team played as never before. A newspaper article stated that one could sit in the stands and actually feel optimism, confidence, and faith flowing from the spectators into the players. The same team that finished in seventh place one year, pushed almost to the top of the League the next year, and has been one of the most dramatically successful teams ever since.

They were the same men as before; the same, yes, but with a difference. They were now experiencing and drawing upon a new power, a power sparked by enthusiasm. And that power worked miracles by releasing abilities hitherto unrealized. They were now superb athletes, whereas before they had been ordinary, faltering, and defeated.

You, too, can draw on new power. If you are now defeated by your weaknesses, your tensions, your fears, and your inferiorities, it is only because you have never taken into your mind this glorious, radiant quality of enthusiasm. While the change to this new quality of life is not easy, no profound change in character ever is, yet the method is clearly and simply defined. There are two steps, psychologically and spiritually sound, which you can take to increase your enthusiasm. One is to change the character of your thoughts, the other is to revamp the existing pattern of your attitudes. This is best accomplished by practicing the basic principles of religious faith and psychological understanding.

Enthusiasm cannot live in a mind filled with dull, unhealthy, destructive ideas. To change this condition, practice deliberately passing a series of enthusiastic thoughts through your mind every morning. Look in the mirror and say something like this: "Today is my day of opportunity. What fine assets I have—my home, my family, my job, my health! I have so many blessings. I will do my best all day and God will help me. I am glad to be alive." Repeat this same thought-conditioning technique as you retire at night. This daily process of ridding your mind of gloomy and depressing thoughts which, of course, are profoundly unhealthy and self-defeating, is very important since your prevailing pattern of ideas can affect your whole impact upon life. Unhealthy thoughts can make you unhealthy. Defeatist thoughts can defeat you.

I hailed a taxicab in New York City on a sunshiny morning, saying in merry fashion to the driver, "Good morning. How are you?"

He looked at me wearily and answered coolly, "So what?"

Despite this chilly response I persisted, "Sure is a great morning!" He glanced at me again, "I don't see anything great about it. It's going to rain after awhile and the weather's going to get bad."

"Well, what is wrong with rain?" I asked. "Good old rain."

But that didn't affect him either. There was another man with me who kept calling me "doctor," so after awhile the taxi driver turned to me and said, "Say, doc, I've got some pains in my back. I feel terrible."

"A young fellow like you shouldn't have pains," I replied. "How old are you?"

"Thirty-five," he answered, then added plaintively, "what do you suppose is the matter with me?" Apparently he took me for a Doctor of Medicine.

"Well," I replied thoughtfully, "I think I know what you've got, although I am not accustomed to practicing in taxicabs." Continuing the physician fiction I said, "I think you have psycho-sclerosis."

"What's that?" he demanded with a startled look.

"Did you ever hear of arteriosclerosis?" I asked.

"Yes," he said doubtfully, "I guess so."

"Well," I explained, "that is hardening of the arteries. Perhaps, instead, you have hardening of the thoughts, psycho-sclerosis, and it can be very serious."

"What can I do about it?" he asked apprehensively.

"Well, I have been riding with you in this cab for only a few minutes, but your gloomy and pessimistic thoughts and expressions would depress any passenger, to say nothing of yourself. Perhaps if I rode with you very much I would develop psycho-sclerosis, too!"

By this time we had reached the Marble Collegiate Church, my destination, and I got out and said, nodding in the direction of the church, "I'm not the kind of a doctor you are thinking of. I'm what you might call a spiritual doctor and while I do not want to preach to you, I believe spiritual treatment would help you." I then explained various spiritual treatments, mentioning the method of passing happy and enthusiastic thoughts through the mind, indicating my belief that such practice might help reduce his pains. I did emphasize that he should see his physical doctor as well. The taxi driver was quite bewildered by the diagnosis that his trouble might be mental and spiritual, but a look of understanding came over his face and he said, "I get you. You think I am feeling badly because I am thinking badly."

"Yes," I agreed, "that is a good way to put it. I have known that to happen, and if I were you I would really go to work on my thoughts. Get your mind full of enthusiasm and optimism." I invited him to consult our counseling experts at the church clinic, which he did; and to attend services, which he also did. He was given religious and inspirational literature to read, study, and practice and he proved a cooperative "patient" in psychological and spiritual therapy.

The practice of enthusiastic ideas and attitudes may come hard to an individual whose tendencies veer toward automatic negative reactions. The development of an instinctively enthusiastic outlook begins with a positive affirmation, as previously described, even though at the start that may run counter to actual feelings. The very use of the affirmation itself commits one to the positive attempt and when real effort is made to affirm enthusiasm however feeble it may be, a start is made toward becoming an enthusiastic person. Success depends upon resolutely keeping at it until the positive pattern of enthusiasm takes firm hold. I must reiterate that the formula I am advocating is not easy, but if you try and keep trying, you will get wonderful results.

How this method changes conditions by changing individuals is illustrated by the case of a man who telephoned me from a hotel in a nearby city one night. "I just don't know what to do," he said desperately. "I can't sleep I'm so discouraged. In fact, I'm just about sunk. Tomorrow afternoon at three o'clock I have to meet the greatest crisis of my whole business life," he went on gloomily, "and if things don't go right tomorrow, I'm finished." In addition, he said, "I've just received word that my wife is ill and may have to go to a hospital and all in all, I'm in such a bad way that I thought I would phone you. I hope you don't mind."

I assured him that I didn't mind and then said, "No doubt you have survived many crises and you will get through this one, also. You seem awfully tense," I suggested. "I imagine you are sitting in your room hunched over the telephone, clutching the receiver very tightly, and your free hand is probably clenched too. Am I right?"

"I guess you are," he mumbled.

"Well, please hold the receiver loosely and unclench the

other hand." Then I asked, "Is there an easy chair in your room?" He replied that there was. "Well, pull it up, sit back in it, stretch out your legs, put your head against the headrest of the chair, and talk to me easy-like."

I detected that he was slightly bewildered by all this. Finally, he said, "O.K., I'm sitting in the easy chair. My head is resting on the chair back."

"Now," I said, "put your feet up on a desk or another chair." He sort of laughed at that one and said, "O.K., you've got me pretty well eased up now."

I then explained that it is very difficult to force a creative idea up from the subconscious as long as the surface of the mind, the conscious part, is in a rigid state. "You must get yourself relaxed so that the fresh and vital thoughts which you need can come through. What have you been thinking about lately?" I asked.

"Mostly about myself, of course. What else is there to think about?"

I suggested that he shift his thought emphasis from himself to other people, that he cease projecting inwardly, and start cultivating an outgoing attitude. By this he would bring to bear the subtle spiritual law that, as you give yourself, you find yourself. He happened to have a passing knowledge of the Bible and was aware of the law to which I referred. For your information it is stated in the following words: "For whosoever will save his life shall lose it: and whosoever will lose his life for my sake shall find it." (Matt. 16:25) And let me add, it is one of the most subtle laws applicable to human experience.

Then I asked, "Have you done anything unselfishly for anybody lately?"

"No, I haven't," he admitted. "I've been too tied up with my own anxieties."

"All right, tomorrow morning, first thing, go to the Salvation Army, in person, and ask them to give you the name of some needy person. Then go and personally do something for him. By that means you will start forgetting yourself. In fact, you will get better results if you do something for several people. Make a real sacrifice. Go out of your way to get interested in somebody and help him; then note how much better you feel. That will prove a releasing device and will get life to flowing properly. But remember, you must not do these things for what you may get out of it, but rather you must try to have a sincere desire to help other people.

"Then," I continued, "after we stop talking immediately start offering a prayer of thanksgiving. Stop asking, and start thanking. Give thanks for everything you can think of—all positive factors of good that are yours; and continue to offer thanksgiving. It might help to list them all on paper.

"Next, put the problem of tomorrow in the hands of God and confidently believe that He will give you a good night's sleep. Then tomorrow go into that interview, peacefully and confidently, believing that you are being guided by God, and that God is with you. Conceive of Him as actually taking charge of the situation, guiding you in what you shall say. Meanwhile, calmly think everything through in a constructive manner. Above all," I concluded, "be optimistic and enthusiastic—no gloom, no negativism, only faith and gladness. Practice this technique and I am sure things will go well."

It was several weeks before I heard from him. Then he telephoned to say that while everything had not turned out exactly the way he wanted, he was now convinced that the outcome had been for the best. He was amazed by the manner in which the situation had clarified.

"I have certainly learned my lesson," he said. "I have discovered that gloominess and depression destroy creative capacity and therefore block off the ability to handle things. I realize that I still must do a powerful reconstructive job on myself. But I have been practicing enthusiasm and already it has made such a difference in me that I am going to make enthusiasm a habit. And," he added, "I have adopted as a policy your suggestion about doing something for somebody every day. Believe me, you've got something there."

He concluded with this observation "I wonder why I never realized before that Christianity really works as a practical program."

To sum up the formula he used:

1. Practice calmness and quietness.
2. Do something everyday for somebody.
3. Pray with thanksgiving.
4. Flush negatives out of the mind with enthusiasm and optimism.

A good Bible text to repeat everyday is "O give thanks unto the Lord; for he is good." (Psalm 106:1) Never doubt that the creative power of enthusiasm will do wonders for you. It is a powerful factor in the art of living dynamically all your life.

Enthusiasm also has a powerful effect on well-being. A noted New York State physician said "people can actually die because they lose their enthusiasm. The physical organism cannot handle the mental attitude of uselessness." Recently I asked a physician to appraise the psychological advantages of optimism over depression, and this was his answer: "Depressive thoughts, habitually held, increase the possibility of infection by at least tenfold. Optimism, real faith, and enthusiasm taken together, are powerful agents in burning out infection. I have noticed that people who maintain a confident attitude show greater healing power in the presence of sickness and disease. Enthusiasm is one of the greatest sources of health." So said the physician.

That this is a practical fact is illustrated in a letter from

Mary Alice Flint. Ten years ago, she says, she was habitually tired and lacking in energy and enthusiasm. Today she is spiritually vigorous and physically well. In my opinion she and her husband Maurice Flint are two of the most spiritually influential persons I know. She is a vital and vibrant personality. She says she can work all day without tiring. After returning from a recent trip where she held meetings and talked to customers in the stores where the jewelry which she and her husband manufacture is sold she wrote this dynamic letter:

"My trip was terrific and stimulating. It gave me some fresh new ideas. I used to spend a lot of time dreaming of the things I would like to do, but I never went so far as to dream of the things that have actually come about in the last few years.

"Whether I have been reborn or only released, I do not know. But I do know that at my age, when my energy should be waning, I have experienced a renewal of strength beyond anything I ever had before. The marvelous part of it is that I know, so long as I am needed to do the work God intends me to, this strength will continue. If this isn't one of the modern miracles, then it is mighty close to it.

"My husband and I realize that the source of this revitalizing is in God and in enthusiastic faith in Him."

Every day this woman passes through her mind, by a process of prayer, meditation, and surrender of self, a series of enthusiastic faith thoughts. This has revamped her whole slant on life, renewed her interest in living, brought out the best in her personality, and has given her a flow of energizing health, both spiritually and physically.

A second effective way to develop enthusiasm is simply to act enthusiastic until you become so. It is a psychological fact, often demonstrated, that you can be freed from an undesirable feeling by assuming the exact opposite feeling. For example, if you feel afraid, you can make yourself courageous by acting courageous. If you are feeling unhappy, by deliberately acting happy you can induce happy feelings. In similar manner, if you are lacking in enthusiasm, by simply acting enthusiastic you can make yourself enthusiastic.

A fascinating illustration of a man who demonstrated this principle is told in the first chapter of Frank Bettger's book *How I Raised Myself from Failure to Success in Selling.* This one chapter is a classic in the techniques of enthusiasm. Bettger was playing baseball on the Johnstown, Pennsylvania team. Though young and ambitious, he was fired from the team on the ground of being lazy. Bettger knew that he was not lazy, only nervous. The manager explained that if he expected to get ahead he would have to put more enthusiasm into his work.

Finally, the New Haven team gave him a tryout. He said: "My first day in New Haven will always stand out in my memory as a great event in my life. No one knew me in that league, so I made a resolution that nobody would ever accuse me of being lazy. I made up my mind to establish the reputation of being the most enthusiastic ball player they'd ever seen in the New England League.

"From the minute I appeared on the field I acted like a man electrified. I acted as though I were alive with a million batteries. I threw the ball around the diamond so fast and so hard that it almost knocked our infielders' hands apart. Once, apparently trapped, I slid into third base with so much energy and force that the third baseman fumbled the ball and I was able to score an important run. It was all a show, an act I was putting on. The thermometer that day was nearly 100°. I wouldn't have been surprised if I'd dropped over with a sunstroke the way I ran around the field.

"Did it work? It worked like magic. Three things happened: 1. My enthusiasm almost entirely overcame my fear. 2. My enthusiasm affected the other players on the team, and they too became enthusiastic. 3. Instead of dropping with the heat, I felt better during the game and after it was over than I had ever felt before."

Bettger says his greatest thrill came the following morning when he read in the New Haven newspaper, "This new player Bettger has a barrel of enthusiasm. He inspired our boys." Then the newspapers began calling him "Pep" Bettger, the life of the team. It is an exciting demonstration of the power in acting enthusiastic.

The significant fact is that two years from the time he was discharged by Johnstown, he was playing third base for the St. Louis Cardinals and had multiplied his income 30 times. "What did it?" he asks. "Enthusiasm alone did it. Nothing but enthusiasm."

Later, when he went into life insurance, he put into effect the same principle of demonstrating enthusiasm and became an outstandingly successful man in that field.

Walter Chrysler stated a powerful truth when he declared: "The real secret of success is enthusiasm. Yes, more than enthusiasm, I would say excitement. I like to see men get excited. When they get excited they make a success of their lives."

So, to become enthusiastic, practice deliberately forcing yourself to act enthusiastic. By this procedure you can actually become enthusiastic. In a short time you will no longer need to force enthusiasm as it will become natural to you.

Real enthusiasm, not the synthetic or assumed kind, the enthusiasm that bubbles up from deep inner sources, is spiritual in nature. The word "enthusiasm" is derived from two Greek words, "en" and "theos," meaning "God within you," or "full of God." Therefore, you will have enthusiasm, force, and power to the extent that God is actually present within you. God gave you life; God can and will renew your life. When you get out of harmony with God, life declines, vitality ebbs, and then enthusiasm leaks away. When enthusiasm is low, vitality, energy, and power are also low.

Therefore, get full of God and your enthusiasm will rise and as it does, you will experience new vitality, energy, force, and effectiveness. Always remember that enthusiasm was built into you by Almighty God in an original creative process. And God not only creates, He also recreates unless, by living in a nonspiritual manner, you interfere with His natural renewal processes. But if you keep in harmony with God, recreative enthusiasm and vitality will continue to renew you indefinitely.

Enthusiasm is an important factor in the vibratory pattern of life. The entire universe being in vibration, it is important to be in harmony with the vibrations that come from God. At this very minute you are being bombarded by millions of vibrations. You are receiving vibrations from people and objects surrounding you. They strike upon you and unconsciously you respond to them. It is important to cultivate sensitivity to positive vibrations from God, the source of your life.

There are varying grades of vibrations. For example, on a rainy day you get different vibrations than on a sunny day. People have vibrations, too. Some people leave you cold, and others make only a moderate impression upon you. And then you encounter people who are surcharged with vibratory power. They thrill and captivate you, they fascinate you, move you, draw you to them.

I attended a high school play, a very good one. Everybody in the cast was excellent, but there was one boy who appeared on the stage for not more than three minutes. He was a slight boy of about sixteen, and yet he was a bundle of dynamic vibration. What he will be at twenty-five is not hard to imagine, for that boy has the Divine gift of vibratory transmission. He swept in upon the stage so briefly, and yet he lifted and captivated the audience. Days later I was still under the spell of that boy who was surcharged with enthusiasm and, therefore, was in harmony with the vibratory powers of the universe.

So, to have enthusiasm affirm, and believe as you affirm, "I am now in harmony with the spiritual vibrations that flow from Almighty God. I will now live as though I have enthusiasm. I do have enthusiasm. I am now in God's vibration flow and am receiving enthusiasm from God." You can demonstrate to yourself by practice the absolute reality of such affirmation. This technique is practical because it works. Deepen your faith, affirm enthusiasm, forget yourself, serve God and people, and you will attain new and higher levels of life. And you will have deeper satisfaction. When the power of enthusiastic faith is constantly maintained you will have a perpetually fresh interest. Life will never get old or stale. You will become and remain vital and effective.

We sometimes hear people complaining: "There is no future for me in this business or in this town. Everything is against me." Such complainers actually make their own unhappy situations. What you picture tends to actualize in fact if you hold the picture long enough, continuing to emphasize it. Such people do not realize what great things would happen in their lives if they would quit complaining and saturate their minds with creative enthusiasm.

People who go ahead constructively in life are those who pour boundless enthusiasm into what they are doing. They never minimize their work or opportunities but on the contrary, they take hold enthusiastically and, therefore, stimulate the forces of successful accomplishment.

Recently, while recording radio talks I became aware that the engineer with whom I was working, Hal Schneider, seemed to get an unusual thrill out of his work. He kept stimulating me with his own enthusiasm. I was helped by his enthusiastic spirit. It seemed to draw me out of myself.

After the recording and while he was gathering up his equipment I said, "You really like your job, don't you?"

"I sure do, I love it," he replied, and at my urging proceeded to tell me about himself.

He came of a poor family that lived in an under-privileged section of New York City. His first job was that of elevator boy in an apartment house. It was not much of a job, but he never thought of it that way. It spelled opportunity to him and he gave his whole self to it with enthusiasm. He was ambitious to do something with his life and he said, "I tried to become the best elevator boy they ever had."

But his real ambition was radio engineering. He studied that subject in his spare time. He was most enthusiastic and haunted the radio studios until finally he got a small job. But that job was not a small job to him. He went at it so enthusiastically, studying and thinking and working, that in due time he became one of the National Broadcasting Company's top engineers. In fact, he was good enough to get the assignment of traveling with General Eisenhower during his 1952 campaign.

"On that train," he said, "I wonderingly reminded myself that I was that poor little elevator boy. And here I was, actually putting a famous General, now candidate for President of the United States, on the air. I just couldn't get over it, I was so thrilled.

"But my greatest experience came," he said, "after the General was elected. It was at a huge meeting in New York City. Thousands were present and the whole nation was waiting to hear what the new President would have to say. It was a tremendous moment.

"There stood the President ready to speak, and there I was ready to put him on the air. The President waited at the podium. They were a bit slow coming through with the cue. I stood for fifteen seconds with my finger poised and you could hear a pin drop in that big auditorium. Then all of a sudden it came over me, think of it, even the President of the United States could not begin until I pointed my finger and gave him the go-ahead. Sure I love this job, it's full of thrills." He glowed with the enthusiasm that made him a top-flight engineer.

This man's experience proves once again that any job may become more than a job when you have the imagination and the enthusiasm to make it so. This young man had enthusiasm within him and he let it come out. So can you. You want your life to be different, you want to rise above humdrum routine. You want to render a real service. You can have it different, but you do not need to change your job in order to change your life. Just change yourself. Change your thoughts and attitudes. Become enthusiastic and the old job will become a new one, and your life will fill up with power. In this way you will start up the path that leads to greater things.

I have seen the combination of enthusiasm and prayer do so much in the lives of so many that I must write with enthusiasm about what enthusiasm can do for you.

I can tell you with enthusiasm, soundly based on the facts, that every idea, every suggestion, every technique described in this book will work. I have seen them operate in the lives of hundreds of people. Therefore, you can, with confidence, believe in the practicality and workability of the principles which are presented in this and other chapters.

One man who achieved a rebirth of enthusiasm through these methods was formerly a sleepy, dull salesman. As a result of his lethargic thinking and uninspired work, he was living from hand to mouth. When he heard about the achievements of other salesmen, he could always tell you wherein their methods were wrong. The habit of criticizing other people who are doing constructive things in life is one sure sign that basically you are a failure. At heart you are not very big, and no man is a true success unless he is big at heart and generous. Whenever you find yourself criticizing others in this way, it would be wise to make a thorough and honest analysis of your jealousies and resentments.

This salesman had sold nothing in many days. He was constantly telling his wife of the mistake he had made getting into selling in the first place; he didn't like it, he didn't like people, people didn't like him. Whenever he went into an office to see a prospect, people froze. So ran his dismal complaints.

One real asset which this man had was a wise and spiritually minded wife. She did not argue with him, but instead, with positive faith, prayed for him. She prayed and believed that guidance would be given. When you ask for God's help and at the same time negate your prayer by doubting that you are going to get it, your prayer will be answered by denial. How could the answer be otherwise for obviously the real prayer is one of doubt.

But this wife prayed with positive faith that her husband's native enthusiasm and ability would be reasserted. Finally, she persuaded him to pray with her. Their joint prayer took the form of an affirmation that their life was being renewed and they visualized a change as taking place within them.

This kind of praying always has an effect, and one morning the husband said to his wife with a new firmness, "Let me pray this morning" and this was his prayer: "Lord, fill me with enthusiasm for my product (naming it). Fill me with enthusiasm for all the good I can do through my work."

That may seem a strange prayer, but remember the selling of that product was his work in the world, his livelihood; that is to say, his life. Through prayer, he had gotten the creative idea that the purpose of selling a good product is not only to make a living but primarily an opportunity to serve God and man. He went out that day in an outgoing and self-forgetful frame of mind, his emphasis shifting to a sincere interest in the people he called on.

That very day he sold two small orders. Day and night he continued to affirm creative enthusiasm. Naturally he did not change all at once; people seldom do. They sometimes make spectacular and instantaneous reversals, but personality change is usually gradual. But his new attitude gradually reshaped him until he became one of his company's most effective producers. "I am a man of only average ability," he told me, "but I have discovered that when an ordinary man believes enthusiastically in God and in his work and in people, he can do his job in an extraordinary manner." And how right he is!

The application of enthusiasm to occupations which seem drab and uninspiring often proves the magic touch that turns the ordinary into the extraordinary. Any aspect of life is only as drab as you conceive it to be, only as commonplace as you think of it. But you can, by your thoughts, lift it out of drabness, out of the commonplace, and cause it to be extraordinarily worthwhile. It all depends upon how much enthusiasm you generate and sincerely maintain within your mind and how spiritually dynamic is your motivation. A real sense of purpose plus enthusiasm will enhance your job, whatever it may be.

Successful living may be measured by the extent of your enthusiastic participation in life. I watched a football game on television. Two men in the backfield of one team were dynamos of enthusiasm. Everywhere the ball went, there they were. They seemed to cover the entire field, so eager and fast and enthusiastic were they. Their extraordinary effectiveness was explained by a simple fact, they were filled with enthusiasm. They gave it all they had.

If you are not getting on as well as you would want—and we should never be satisfied regardless of achievement—

try giving more to your work, to your family, to your church, and to your community. Notice how the giving of yourself draws people to you. One of the surest of all truths is that life will give you no more than you give it. Go all out for life and it will go all out for you.

Enthusiasm carries all before it. Enthusiasm can do wonders for you.

❖ ❖ ❖

Enthusiasm is so important that I wish to conclude this chapter by summarizing some steps which will help you to cultivate this essential quality.

1. Look for interest and romance in the simplest things about you.
2. Enlarge your view of your own God-given capacities. Within the limit of humility develop a good opinion of yourself.
3. Diligently practice eliminating all dull, dead, unhealthy thoughts so that your mind may be freshened up and capable of developing enthusiasm.
4. Daily affirm enthusiasm. As you think it, talk it, and live it, you will have it.
5. Practice daily relaxation to keep your mind and spirit from getting tired. Enthusiasm is a characteristic of the vigorously alert.
6. Act enthusiastic, for as you act you tend to be.
7. Allow no sense of guilt to take the luster off your spirit. It's the greatest of all causes of ennui.
8. Keep the creative channel open between God and yourself, remembering that enthusiasm is "entheos" meaning "God within."

9. Keep spiritually virile and alive.
10. Give all you've got to life and it will give its greatest gifts to you. It will never grow dull.

CHAPTER III

HOW TO CONQUER YOUR FRUSTRATIONS AND BE CREATIVE

"There are levels of the mental life to which no exasperation or frustration can ascend. And peaceful thinking brings you to that mental level where nothing can bother you unduly."

TO LIVE with dynamic aliveness all your life you will need to keep from feeling frustrated. And, of course, you can.

People react curiously and quite differently to frustration. A California woman, exasperated by her inability to keep her house in a neat and tidy condition, decided to get rid of the place. So she set it afire and burned it to the ground. That was her startling way of coping with frustration.

A man returned home after an absence of twenty-five years. He had walked out, a quarter of a century earlier, because his wife was a nagger and he couldn't take it any longer. His wife said she was glad to have him back and he found her much quieter than before. That was his way of dealing with his frustration.

A business executive, fifty years old, was found dead at his desk, revolver in hand. He left a note explaining that tension and exasperation were "driving him mad," and he could stand it no longer. So he simply blew his brains out. That was his way of meeting frustration.

One evening in a hotel lobby, I encountered a man who was quite intoxicated and noisy. Knowing him, I was aware that he had a well-developed inferiority complex which usually kept him quiet, even shy, when sober. But liquor always transformed him into a rather unpleasant extrovert.

"I suppose you wonder why I'm drunk," he demanded. "Well, I get so exasperated it drives me crazy. When I get drunk I forget my frustration, for a while at least."

"Does frustration return after you sober up?" I questioned.

"Sure, always. Perhaps I should stay drunk all the time." That was his method of handling his frustration.

When frustrated we may not burn down our houses, walk out on our families, shoot ourselves, or become alcoholics; but in many subtler ways we allow frustration to dominate us and destroy our happiness and effectiveness.

Obviously, none of the above methods is an adequate answer to frustration. What then is the answer? One very good method is simply to do the best you can about everything, and then do nothing further. If you rush feverishly, doing your work with tense anxiety, never feeling that anything is finished, you arouse the hot and irrational emotion of frustration. Try substituting cool emotions by emphasizing deliberateness and organized efficiency. Quietly affirm that you are doing all you can. Practice entertaining quiet thoughts, rather than excited thoughts or hot thoughts or nervous thoughts. Picture yourself as "pouring" coolness on your heated tension. This, of course, is easier said than done, but you can do it by just doing it.

My good friend, the famous psychiatrist Dr. Smiley Blanton, author of the important book *Love or Perish,* declares that St. Paul's statement, ". . . and having done all, to stand," (Ephesians 6:13) is one of the greatest of all methods for healing frustration. That is to say, when you have done all you can do, just stop; do no more, let the matter rest. There is nothing further that can be done, so do not do anything further. Leave it with God. Let Him handle it from there on.

When you cease your nervous and feverish efforts to do more than you can or need to do, calmly realizing that there must come an end to anxious concern and nervous effort, then you will be delivered from the disorganizing effects of frustration.

I met a New York business man on the veranda of a resort hotel. I had known him for years as the hard-driving type, and had rather formed the opinion that he was an over-tense, frustrated individual. But here he was sitting with his feet on the porch railing, hat pulled down over his eyes, just sitting.

Somewhat astonished I said, "I'm very interested in seeing you relax so efficiently."

"Well," he drawled, "I was about as frustrated a person as you could find, but I learned to get over it. And it's quite simple; I just decided to do all I could about everything, and when there is nothing more to do I just don't do it."

In modern language, he was agreeing with St. Paul's anti-frustration technique. Relieved of frustration he could relax effectively, and have adequate and well directed energy when it was needed.

A second procedure for avoiding frustrated feelings is to practice peaceful thinking with the objective of making it your permanent mental slant. And this is an acquirable ability. The curative effect of peaceful thinking on frustration is illustrated by the experience of a woman who over-frequently consulted her doctor. And she always got around to talking about her daughter-in-law, habitually using the phrase, "She is driving me crazy. I simply cannot stand her." This monotonously reiterated statement of annoyance with the younger woman was not unlike a record needle stuck in a groove.

The doctor noticed that she had developed a peculiar physical symptom, that of moving her head constantly from side to side. He suspected that his patient's trouble was caused by some deep frustration, which he shrewdly felt was tied in with hate. He pointed out to her that there was nothing she could do about the marriage of her son to the young woman; that her daughter-in-law was, in fact, her daughter-in-law and that she would just have to learn to get along with her.

A rudimentary fact that many miss is that there are some people and things in this world that you just have to get along with, and no amount of resistance or railing will accomplish anything except to increase your frustration. Therefore, the quiet and urbane philosophy of accepting persons and situations, and of learning to think about them peacefully, is most important in eliminating frustrated feelings.

Such was the philosophy the doctor outlined to this woman. As a prescription he gave her what he called a "therapeutic formula," not in the form of medicine but rather a medicinal mental pattern. He assured her that, by the "injection" of peaceful thoughts into the depths of her mind, she could overcome her frustration and perhaps, also, the physical symptom of the nervous head movement. His instruction was simply to repeat over and over many times daily these affirmative words: "God is giving me peace." In addition, she was to speak about her daughter-in-law in a kindly fashion as frequently as possible each day.

Improvement did not come easily, but after some days of this "spiritual medication" the head motion noticeably lessened and finally ceased altogether. Her spirit of frustration diminished gradually, and in due course she was able to accommodate herself to her daughter-in-law. The doctor presently tells me that he believes a genuine good-will relationship is developing between the two women. This skillful and effective religio-medical healing of frustration was brought about by the acceptance and practice of peaceful thoughts, accompanied by elimination of hate.

Another doctor tells of a young man who was constantly saying, most explosively, when anything annoyed him, which was often, "That burns me up." The doctor pointed out that the expression used by this patient was, in fact, a true picture of his inward state, both emotionally and physically.

The young man was running a persistent fever of approximately 100°, and at night he suffered cold sweats. The doctor at first thought these symptoms might indicate tuberculosis, but upon further analysis concluded that they were due to a "burning frustration." This physician, who is very accomplished in applying not only *materia medica,* but healing thought therapy as well, suggested to the young man that he go regularly to church. He directed him to a church where the therapy of quietness is an integral part of the worship service.

The first result was a profound feeling of quietness experienced by the patient. As he grew more skillful in the practice of quietness, he saw clearly that the chief values of his life were being lost in the hectic intensity of uncontrolled emotion. The healing therapy of spiritual peace presently got through to his mind. The doctor reports that in time he learned to apply spiritual technique to his everyday problems; and gradually the temperature became normal and the night sweats ceased. The therapy of applied quietness, penetrating to the deep center of his frustration, had a healing effect.

We need quietness as we need food and water, as we

need sunshine and restful sleep. And we do not half appreciate the cumulative effect on our frustrations of peaceful thoughts deliberately employed.

I addressed the annual convention of the National Automobile Dealer's Association in the civic auditorium at Miami Beach, Florida. The audience consisted of some five thousand men engaged in one of the most competitive enterprises in America. And since the meeting came at a time when this particular industry was under considerable economic pressure, there was, in that group, not a little concentrated tension and frustration.

That morning, before going to the auditorium to give my speech, I was in my hotel working on a manuscript, and ideas were not flowing too well. In fact, at that moment I had to deal with some personal tendency toward frustration. Finally, I became aware that the mounting tension within me was blocking the flow of creative ideas. So, I relaxed in my chair and looked out at the beach where the sea was washing softly on the sandy shore and the ocean breezes were moving gently among the palm trees.

Have you ever noticed the utterly relaxed and graceful manner in which a palm tree lies over against the wind or moves with its motion? If you get the chance it might pay you to study palm trees for their secret of real relaxation. Their fronds move with a dignified sweep and rhythmic gracefulness and there is complete absence of rigidity.

I left the room and went to the beach which was deserted at that hour and location. I was alone with the sea and the sky and the winds and the sun and the palm trees. I sat with my back against a tree and looked at the sky which Emerson so aptly called, "the daily bread of the soul." As I listened to the deep roar of the sea I began to feel quiet, relaxed, and peaceful. What healing there is in the sea, sand, sun, and wind! As I watched and listened and communed with nature and with God, the frustration feelings left me.

Then I went to the auditorium to speak to the Automobile Dealers. The two speakers who preceded me told how difficult it would be to get business that year. They described all the trouble that was in store for the dealers, and you could sense the deepening gloom and frustration in that great crowd of American business men.

When my turn came to speak I felt moved to ask how many of them in the four days they had been in convention at Miami Beach had gone apart and communed with the great ocean that lay before them and which dominated their environment. I told them of my experience before coming to the meeting and quoted a verse from Masefield's poem:

> I must go down to the seas again, to
> the lonely sea and the sky,
> And all I ask is a tall ship and a star
> to steer her by.

I suggested that each man go down to the sea, preferably alone, and spend a little time with the sky and with the vast waters and with God. While making this suggestion, I noticed that a curious hush fell over that great audience. I believe we could all sense a deep and healing power. These men, important to the economy of our country, needed strength from a deeper source.

On the plane coming north I met a man who said, "I was sitting in that convention nervous, exasperated, frustrated. I heard you make that statement about your experience by the sea and it appealed to me. So, after the meeting I went to a lonely spot on the beach. I did not even take my wife along. I walked along the shore and observed the sandpipers running near the edge of the water. I picked up some shells and listened to the roar of the sea. I sat there a long time watching twilight come and the long shadows fall across the waters."

He hesitated, then continued with some embarrassment, for obviously he was deeply moved. "I happened to remember that story in the New Testament about Jesus being on the sea with His disciples and how they were frightened by the storm and He quieted the sea. And I remember particularly where it said, 'And there was a great calm.'

"Suddenly I felt peaceful and quiet. It was one of the most moving experiences of my life. So, I have come away from that convention, not discouraged, but with hope and optimism; I know that I am going to have a good year not only in selling, but in living as well." It was evident that he had experienced a spiritual, mental, and even physical rejuvenation.

Frustration is a combination of heat and stress; and the healing of heat is coolness and the healing of stress is peace. When one receives deeply into his being such an experience as this, he can thereafter work with vigor and energy. He will no longer work in a feverish and tense manner, plagued by exasperating frustration. There are levels of mental life to which no exasperation or frustration can ascend. And peaceful thinking brings you to that mental level where nothing can bother you unduly.

In overcoming frustration, another important technique is to desire and practice emotional control. I emphasize desire because one must first decide, honestly, very honestly, whether he really wants emotional control. People often say they do, but really they do not want it at all. They do not want to give up the "luxury" of letting themselves go emotionally.

I was watching a baseball game on television with my daughter Elizabeth, then ten years old. One of the players flew into a heated controversy with the umpire and reacted violently. "He's getting nowhere acting like that," I commented.

"Oh, yes he is," Elizabeth replied. "He certainly is getting somewhere. He's getting out of the game."

If that player could have seen himself as millions of people saw him, neck muscles distended, mouth stretched wide open, he might have regretted making such a spectacle of himself. It is curious indeed that people are actually willing to experience failure, unhappiness, even the sickness that comes from emotional upset just to have a temporary, sadistic satisfaction of flying off their control center. So, to have the emotional control that overcomes frustration feelings you must really want it, and when you do want control you can have it.

This was demonstrated by a hotel room clerk who revealed such remarkable imperturbability and self control that he quite fascinated me. I checked into his hotel early one morning. Just ahead in the line of people waiting to register was a woman to whom he was saying that he was sorry, but unfortunately no room was available at the moment, but would be within a short time.

At this she became very irritated and began to berate the clerk in a loud and complaining tone, which could be heard by practically everyone in the lobby. Yet, never by a flicker of an eyelash, or by rising color, or by any change in tone of voice did this imperturbable clerk indicate that the conversation was anything other than pleasant. He was very kind to the woman. He explained the situation in detail. He was most patient and courteous.

Meanwhile, the waiting line was growing. Finally grumbling, still obviously annoyed, and with a rather crude parting shot or two, the woman turned from the desk after being assured by the clerk that she would be accommodated satisfactorily.

When my turn came to register I could not help commenting, "I observed this incident with interest and I admire your emotional control."

The clerk smiled and said, "I believe in the principles you teach, and I try to practice them for they really work."

I knew there was an interesting story back of this man's attitude, and later sought him out. He told me that formerly he had been very easily upset. This weakness had brought him humiliation and failure in several instances so that he realized how important emotional control was to his success in life. And he evolved a plan for developing it which seemed most interesting.

He explained: "I learned that much irritation and frustration result from unrelieved muscular tension. So, every morning and night I practice relaxing my muscle tensions. My method is to mentally 'feel' the healing touch of Jesus Christ as starting at my head and in turn resting on every muscle. I conceive of Him as actually removing from my mind all tension.

"Then I ask for automatic emotional control. This is important for irritation may burst through when least expected. But, if like a thermostat on a heating system, you can set your emotional check valve at a certain point and maintain automatic control, then you can be sure of yourself, no matter what the provocation. But to do this requires the arduous practice of spiritual control," he concluded.

This man was able to master such control since he knew very well that to succeed in his line of work he must do so. Therefore, he really wanted control enough to make himself work at it and finally he achieved it. Through these effective methods he was able to overcome the volatile explosiveness of frustration. I was not surprised to learn, only recently, that he has advanced well up the ladder in the hotel industry.

People who fail in life are often those who give way to annoyance, make the sharp retort, the mean comeback, and who show the irritated reaction. These supersensitive, uncontrollable people go unhappily from one job to another because they cannot get along with people. They are always in some personality clash or personal-relation difficulty.

You can become a very great asset to yourself by mastering the art of being urbane and philosophical, by always having your reactions under control, and by demonstrating inner peace through the practice of the techniques outlined in this book. And how vital this is! Doubtless more people have muffed their opportunities, perhaps even destroyed their future, by the display of irritation and exasperation resulting from frustration than for almost any other reason.

A man who was consulting me about his problem of frustration said, "I cannot understand it. Anger surges up within me and before I know it I fly to pieces. Then I throw discretion to the winds and let them have it. But," he explained, "fortunately, people understand that I am a nervous type and they overlook what I say and do and everything is all right again."

But if that easy outcome were true he would not have felt the need for consulting anyone. The actual fact is that people do not understand and usually they do not overlook and basically nothing is quite the same again. People just do not like such a person and he does not have their respect or regard.

Deep exasperation is so difficult to master that, as previously stated, the only certain way to overcome this liability is through God-control of frustration. God changes alcoholics, thieves, liars, and cheats. The reason these types are changed, many times, and the emotional cripple is not, is that the latter is less likely to admit defeat. But God can change people whose trouble is uncontrolled emotion just as He changes individuals with moral defeat.

There is a waiter who works on a train which I take occasionally for a long, overnight trip. He and I are good friends. I will never forget the first night I met him. He served me, along with several others, and I watched him; he had a glowering look on his face.

As I paid my check he leaned down and asked me, "May I come and see you after awhile?"

"Sure, come along," I replied.

And when he was off duty he came and sat with me in my compartment. "I don't know how much longer I can hang onto this job, Doctor," he said, and I could read desperation in his face.

"What is wrong?" I asked.

"I am getting so everybody annoys me," he said. "I keep myself under control, but one of these days I am going to bust out and ruin myself. I want to know what to do."

"What is your problem?" I asked.

"Well," he said, "I'm in the dining car and along comes one of these fellows who is always throwing his weight around, and he says, 'Come here, Boy.' Now, I ask you, am I a boy? I'm fifty years old!"

"Remember," I said, "we are all boys until the very end. And there are people," I continued, hoping to help him lift his problem from the emotional to the intellectual plane, "who want to compensate for their own feeling of inferiority by depreciating somebody else."

"There's another kind of trouble," the waiter continued. "I'll bring a man his order just the way he's written it down on that piece of paper, and he'll say it isn't what he ordered. According to the rules I have to say, 'Yes, Sir, I'm sorry, Sir,' and take it back." The waiter showed me his tray which he had brought with him. "Look at that tray," he said. "One of these days I'm going to crown one of those people with it." But his voice was milder than his words.

"Let us talk about the man who calls you 'Boy.'" I really went to work on that waiter's problem; I could see it was serious. "He is an infant. Back home he doesn't amount to much and so he actually has a deep inner sense of inadequacy and tries to compensate for it by assumed extrovertish actions. Be sorry for him. Think of him as you would of a child and let it go at that.

"And that fellow who complains about the order you have brought him. Instead of hitting him over the head with your tray, I'll tell you something you can hit him with that will really get results."

My waiter friend became very interested. So I told him about Frank Laubach and his spiritual genius for shooting prayers at people. "You will get so that the person at whom you are shooting prayers will turn and smile at you," I assured him.

My friend was really thoughtful and promised, "I'll try."

At breakfast next morning I watched him. He looked at me over the head of a complaining dowager he was serving, and winked. When he passed me he leaned down and whispered, "I've got to shoot more 'n one prayer at her before she starts smiling."

And here is proof of my thesis that we must try to understand people instead of being irritated by them. This same woman stopped me in the vestibule of the car before I got off the train and asked me to pray for her. "I am going to Miami for the funeral of a loved one," she said.

When I had the opportunity to tell my waiter of this he said, soberly, "I guess you never know the trials and troubles of people." He had made a good start in his war with irritation. "In your patience" you shall possess your soul, when, like the hotel clerk, you are master of yourself; when, like this waiter, you start shooting prayers instead of striking back.

From the standpoint of both efficiency and health it is extremely important to keep frustration and emotion always under control. In his famous bestseller, *How to Live 365 Days a Year,* Dr. John A. Schindler points out that we have within our system the greatest of all health forces, the power of good emotions. The "medicinal" value of good emotions cannot be overestimated. Good emotions make us well, bad emotions make us ill.

Dr. Robert C. Peale says, "The greatest and most efficient pharmacy is within your own system. But so far we have not learned to regulate our mental and emotional reactions in order to make the maximum use of it."

This means that the elements for healthy living are within you. It only remains for you to keep yourself in harmony with them. God gives us what we need, but it remains for us to learn to use these gifts.

A neurologist states that in his personal practice frustration is a predominate cause of many cases of nervous breakdown. "People become so frustrated," he says, "that personality cannot stand the pressure and gives up."

Doctors tell us that anger disturbs the rhythmic action of the small muscle fibers of the stomach and the intestines, causing a spastic condition in the intestinal tract. It can raise the heart rate as high as one hundred sixty and the blood pressure from a normal one hundred thirty to over two hundred. There have been many cases of strokes under anger, caused by a burst blood vessel in the brain due to a sudden jump in blood pressure. If you carry a low grade seething anger in the form of resentment it can actually create a disturbance of the glandular secretions with an accompanying disorganization of the body chemistry. It is understandable, therefore, why the Bible advises, "Let not the sun go down upon your wrath." (Ephesians 4:26) Flush out of your mind the bad emotions: anger, fear, and hate, and you can develop definite feelings of health and vitality.

If you are not actually made ill by frustration, it may at least be reflected in loss of energy and tiredness. A man worked in an industrial plant under a foreman who mistakenly thought the best way to command respect was to bark orders in a top sergeant tone. And in other ways the tough foreman humiliated and annoyed his workmen. Each day this employee came home so nervous and fatigued that he thought of asking for lighter work or transfer to another company. His doctor found no physiological reason for his fatigue. Then the surly foreman was replaced with a more reasonable man who enlisted the cooperation of his workers, and treated them with consideration.

Almost at once this employee had a complete change of reaction and could work without tiring. Obviously, his exhaustion had been caused not by eight hours toil, but by a seething annoyance and frustration caused by his boss's manner and attitude.

The Bible, having the greatest number of those good thoughts which lead to good emotions, is therefore a source of prescriptions for healing frustration. Practice committing to memory some of its many therapeutic or healing passages. An excellent one is this: "In your patience possess ye your souls." (Luke 21:19) Patience is a very great word, implying maturity, urbanity, and mental health.

As you grow in patience you will react not merely with your feelings, but with your intelligence. You will not respond with uncontrolled emotion, but rather, your motivation will be on a spiritual basis. In this way, you will become a person of philosophical and patient control. You will not easily be upset as are some who have not mastered this spiritual skill.

I watched a man trying to put through a telephone call. He got the busy signal several times. What did this great business executive do? He slammed the receiver down so hard that it bounced off the hook and slapped against the side of his desk. It was an exhibition of plain unadulterated infantilism. The man's face was red, his breath came hard, doubtless his blood pressure shot up. Such a person isn't grown up. Emotionally he is still in the infantile state, but since his blood vessels are of his physical age, such emotional outbursts often develop more pressure than they can handle.

A golfer had trouble sinking his ball in the cup. With the perversity inanimate things sometimes show, the ball just would not go where he wanted it to go. Of course the trouble was not in the inanimate object, but in the man. What did he do? He coldly restrained himself until, finally, he got the ball into the cup. Then, with a look of hate, he took the ball out, placed it on the ground and drove it with his club deeply into the earth. I do not know what score he had on the next fairway, but losing his temper could deprive him of that fine sense of timing necessary to good golf shots.

Jimmy Durante, commenting on frustrating irritations, says, "Dem is de conditions dat prevail." That is indeed a wise observation. Situations do just prevail, and you have to get along with them. But if you approach them urbanely, philosophically, and spiritually you will control situations instead of having situations control you.

The human mind can develop the ability to block out frustration. A doctor told me of a woman who was forced to wear a hearing aid. She hated it and constantly complained of a roaring in her ears. "I just can't stand it," she said.

"You can stand it," the doctor replied, "if you discipline your mind. You can actually train yourself no longer to hear that noise. There is a faculty in the human brain that can block out any annoyance if you determine that you want to block it out."

Naturally, this does not come easy. It requires patience and effort and time. Nothing worthwhile in this life is easy. Disciplinary action and an exercise of will are required. Keep your mind focused on irritations and you will build them up. But by focusing your mind power on blocking them out you can successfully do so.

Prayer is a chief aid in the blocking out process. Try the experiment of praying in an outgoing manner, affirming good will toward those who irritate or frustrate you, and discover for yourself that you have the amazing power of eliminating frustration.

I demonstrated this for myself while staying in a beautiful hotel at Stresa on Lake Maggiore in Northern Italy. This is one of the loveliest places in Europe. The lake and the great hotel resemble an old painting, serene and tranquil. The village is a colorful riot of flowers. The placid lake stretches away toward the hazy, towering hills in a charming vista. The fascinating little island villages, which seem to float in the lake, give the illusion of being out of a medieval picture book.

I went to bed that night expecting a restful night's sleep in that idyllic spot. But the hotel is on the main road which skirts the shore of the lake, and a constant and unending stream of noisy Vespas and Lambrettas (motorcycles) turned the night into bedlam. I lay in bed listening hopefully for just one brief interlude of quietness between the racing motorcycles and strident horns, but none ever came. The noise was always either trailing off, or coming up, or bursting upon me in devastating power.

Soon I found myself getting into a state of agitation. Then I realized that I was actually getting mad at those motorcyclists. I arose and shut the windows, but the heat was more than I could bear. It was either heat, or noise, or both, for the sound was so penetrating that it came through the windows, even though they were double ones. I tried plugging my ears with cotton, but this was uncomfortable. I tossed restlessly on my bed and with mounting asperity told my wife what I thought of people who would race with open cutouts through the still night with a total disregard for people who were trying to sleep.

I gradually worked myself into a state of frustration where sleep would be quite impossible. Then it occurred to me to practice, in this situation, the simple principles of Christianity. And when one does practice, one gets results, as I demonstrated on this occasion. I decided to send good will thoughts toward the motorcyclists. Why were they riding those motorcycles? Simply to get some joy and happiness out of life. Or perhaps they were on their way to some destination that was important to them. Life, with its many interests and hopes and problems, was riding those motorcycles along that lake, lying misty and lovely in the silvery moonlight. Therefore, every time I heard a motorcycle approach, which seemed about every half minute, I prayed specifically that the person riding it would have a wonderful life, that God would guide and bless him.

I became so positively engrossed in my spiritual contact with those nice Italian people speeding along on those ear-shattering motorcycles that I forgot my irritation, the frustration left me, and the next thing I knew it was seven-thirty in the morning. Those Vespa riders did not bother me from that time on throughout my entire stay in Stresa. It is a fact, that by prayer, if you really mean it and actually believe in it, you can block out frustration.

Learning to apply a scientific attitude in personal relations also helps to overcome frustration. By scientific I mean to take an objective and impersonal attitude toward people rather than to react emotionally. When someone does something that hurts or irritates you, the scientific, objective method is to say, calmly, "Well, now let's analyze him to see why he does this." Then develop a strategy designed to correct the relationship.

For example, a man consulted me who was very upset about another man's actions. Noting that he was in a state of frustration I explained this scientific attitude and recommended its use to him. But he protested vehemently. "It is all right to talk about being scientific, but it is I who am suffering this insult. What do you think this man called me?" he demanded.

"What did he call you?" I asked.

"I hate to tell you," he answered, "it is so terrible."

"Well, never mind, tell me what he called you."

"Why," shouted the man, "he called me a skunk. He is going everywhere telling everybody that I am a skunk."

"Well now, let us apply the scientific method," I said. "Are you a skunk?" I asked him.

"Of course I'm not a skunk!" he exclaimed, outraged.

"Well then, does his calling you one make you one?" I pursued.

"Of course not," he replied. "I'm no skunk and he knows it. What he says about me doesn't make me a skunk."

"Then," I said, "what he is saying is a lie, and a lie, according to an old German proverb, 'cannot run very far because it has short legs.' So, let him keep on saying it. It isn't so and after a while people will know that you are not a skunk and they may even conclude that he is one. You will come out of this all right."

By the practice of scientific objectivity, though not without difficulty, I observed this man rise to a high level of judicial impersonality. Actually he became quieter and less agitated. Then he began to apply the objective method to himself, to discover what there might possibly be about him that made the other person dislike him so much.

As a result of his honest, objective analysis he saw and eliminated certain unattractive personal qualities. He straightened out a few things he had done that needed adjusting. He developed an outgoing friendly attitude. His ability to take criticism and hatred quietly, without fighting back, and his genuine kindliness toward his enemy, finally drew the sting out of the other's feelings and the attacks ceased. In due course a pleasant relationship actually developed between the two men. It is a simple but powerful truth that you can pray out, love out, and think out any kind of frustration. And your ability to live successfully will be immeasurably increased thereby.

❖ ❖ ❖

To conquer frustrations:

1. Decide that you honestly want emotional self-control.
2. Practice peaceful thinking. With practice you will find it easier, more natural.
3. Instead of letting frustration irritate you, try to understand other people objectively, what makes them the way they are.
4. Set apart a period of quietness daily.
5. Each day practice relaxing muscular tensions.
6. Before going to bed, flush out of your mind the bad emotions.
7. Look to God for help in substituting calmness for irritation.
8. Do the best you can and leave the results to God. Then it will work out for the best.

CHAPTER IV

KILL WORRY AND LIVE LONGER

"The basic secret of overcoming worry is the substitution of faith for fear as your dominant mental attitude. Two great forces in this world are more powerful than all others. One is fear and the other is faith; and faith is stronger than fear."

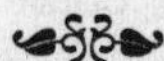

ONCE, IN LOS ANGELES, I delivered a public lecture using as a title the subject of this chapter, "Kill Worry and Live Longer." A newspaper misprinted the title to read, "Kill Worry and Love Longer." No doubt this mistake unconsciously represented the Hollywood influence.

Upon reflection, however, perhaps the garbled version wasn't too wide of the mark. For if you kill worry you will love longer. You will love your wife and children longer. You will love life longer. Kill worry and you will live longer and love longer, either way you take it. Fortunate, indeed, is the person who has learned to live without worry.

One glorious May day Mrs. Peale and I were driving in West Virginia. We came down a wide highway to a crossroads where a little road meandered off up a valley and into the mountains. At the intersection was a sign pointing to the smaller road. Intriguingly, it read "Sunshine Valley."

I turned to Mrs. Peale and asked, "Shall we go up Sunshine Valley?"

And she answered, "Let's go up Sunshine Valley."

I am glad we made this side trip because it was there we met Tommy Martin. We left the car and sat by one of those clear, rushing mountain streams coming down out of the blue misty hills on its way to the sea. We were listening to the music of water singing over the rocks and watching it swiftly disappear under a bridge, when Tommy came into view. He was about twelve years old and was sauntering down the road wearing a slouch hat, high boots, and well-worn trousers. He was chewing bubble gum and had a fishing rod slung over his shoulder. He looked us over with level gaze and apparently liked us, for he said, "Hi."

And then he turned to me, as though to an old friend, "Haven't you a pole? Well, come on, I'll fish for both of us." He took me to where two streams met. There, he declared, the best trout were to be found. He waded into the stream, cast his line and, in a brief moment, up came a beautiful trout. As he took it off the hook, I asked whether he was using dry flies or lures.

Chewing mightily he answered, "No, just plain old worms. They're better than fancy lures." Then he explained that the trout he had just taken was a brook trout and added, "I shot a deer in these woods last winter."

I asked him one of those stupid adult questions: "How come you're not in school?" It was Thursday, after all.

He made some sort of answer which I didn't get, but it sounded vague. And that day, as I sat on the bank watching this twelve-year-old boy fishing in a sunspeckled trout stream, I fell to wondering which of us knew more about living, he or I? And I asked, "Tommy, do you ever worry about anything?"

He looked at me with big brown eyes and answered in

his mountain twang, "Worry? Shucks, there ain't nothin' to worry about!" Presently I went back to Mrs. Peale, wondering if I could ever again be like Tommy Martin.

Well, of course, the truth is that adult life brings certain responsibilities which are inescapable facts of maturity. And we have to live in a world that requires much of us. But isn't it possible, no matter our lot or how heavy our duties, to retain a gay and youthful spirit? I firmly believe that it is, and a purpose of this book is to help you recapture that spirit of joy and trust.

When I say you can leave worry behind, I do not imply that you should be indifferent to human suffering or have a careless disregard for the problems of society. Indeed, the elimination of worry will help you be a more effective citizen of the world. It is very important to acquire that sense of peace and confidence which makes you so much more adequate as a person.

The word *worry* is derived from an old Anglo-Saxon word meaning to strangle or choke. If someone were to place their fingers around your throat and press with full strength, cutting off your vital supply of air, he would be doing to you, dramatically, what you do to yourself if, over a long period of time, you are a victim of worry. You block off your own flow of power. Worry frustrates your best functioning.

I hope, therefore, you can develop Tommy Martin's philosophy: "Shucks, there ain't nothin' to worry about." And there isn't—not as long as we have God. And that is for always.

The ill effects of worry are well known to doctors. A New England physician wrote me saying, "I have noted in my practice over a good many years that fear either causes or accelerates many maladies. And," he added, "the best antidote I know is simple faith."

Dr. Walter Clement Alvarez of the Mayo Clinic is reported to have said, "We little realize the number of human diseases that are begun or are affected by worry." Dr. Seward Wood, of the University of Oklahoma Medical School, in an address before the nose and throat section of the American Medical Association on the relation of worry to the common cold and to infection of the sinuses and asthma said, "One young woman patient can turn asthma on and off by turning worry on and off."

A physician asked me to see a patient who had been admitted to the hospital with seemingly genuine symptoms of a heart attack, including shortness of breath and pains in the chest. "But," explained the doctor, "I am inclined to suspect that it is not a real heart attack but rather an anxiety heart. Will you talk to him and explore the psychological and spiritual basis of his anxiety?"

After counseling, it was ascertained that the patient did, indeed, suffer from acute anxiety. I discovered that this man, now in his sixties, had committed several sex sins in earlier life. As far as I was able to determine such incidents were limited to that early period and his conduct, subsequently, had been impeccable. He had lived in constant fear, however, that his wrongdoing would be discovered.

Those old sins had created a deep sense of guilt and had hatched a flock of fears and tensions that had haunted him for years until now they actually had him back in a hospital, with symptoms of a heart attack. His illness was entirely due to these long-held anxieties. We were able to help him find forgiveness and to achieve healthy-mindedness about the entire matter. His physical symptoms gradually disappeared, and he returned to normal health. The doctor expressed the opinion that, had the guilt-worry complex continued, the man could actually have died of the physical condition which it stimulated.

Frequently you hear people say, "I'm sick with worry," or "I'm worried nearly to death." There is more truth in these statements than you might suppose, for worry can indeed make you sick and has even been known to cause death. It is a fact that by killing worry we can, in all probability, live longer and certainly live much better.

The basic secret of overcoming worry is the substitution of faith for fear as your dominant mental attitude. Two great forces in this world are more powerful than all others. One is fear and the other is faith; and faith is stronger than fear. Basically, then, the method for overcoming worry is deliberately and consistently to fill the mind with faith until fear is displaced.

Of course, normal fear is a healthy mechanism built into us by Almighty God for our protection. Abnormal fear, on the contrary, is a pattern of unhealthy thinking that is both destructive and disintegrating. It is one of the most potent enemies of personality. Abnormal fear seems to possess the inherent power to cause ill health and even disaster.

A doctor felt this so keenly that when called to a home where he found members of the family clustered anxiously and apprehensively about his patient, projecting to him their fear thoughts, he took direct action. He told them, vigorously, that they were filling the patient's room so full of "fear germs" that his healing efforts were valueless. To dramatize his concern, the doctor threw the windows open wide. A strong gale whipped the curtains straight out. "I've got to fumigate this room of fear germs," he explained brusquely. "Unless you people start thinking faith instead of fear you are going to make it very hard for me to help. As that strong wind blows through this room purifying it, let the power of faith purify your minds of this destructive apprehension. You must stop surrounding my patient with the virus of fear." This may seem a curious procedure but it was no doubt an effective way to dramatize the influence of fear in sickness.

Worry may be described as a spasm of the emotions in which the mind takes hold of a thought or obsession, clutches it spasmodically, and will not let it go. To break its hold one must gently, but forcibly, insinuate a healthier and stronger idea into the mind's convulsive grasp. This stronger idea is that of faith in God. When faith, rather than fear, becomes your obsession you will master worry.

And how does one fill the mind so completely with faith that fear will be displaced? It is not easily done. One method is to read books about people who have overcome their fears. Do not read about weak, disorganized, and mixed up people except as it may show you how to find constructive answers. Much fiction today deals with unhappy, blundering, conflicted, and defeated people. Many current novels contain the pathetic accounts of those who have never found themselves, who really do not know what life is all about. These books have the air of sophistication, but actually they are not sophisticated at all. The word sophistication means worldly wise, to know your way around. The unhappy characters in these books are certainly not very wise, judging from the astonishing lack of solution they demonstrate.

But tremendous stories are available about people who have overcome every manner of difficulty and fear by applying the skills of faith. Saturate your mind with such biographical material and it will help recondition your life and free you from worry.

An important technique is to fill your mind with the fear-eliminating words of the Bible. There is an enormous power in the words of the Scriptures. The Bible says, "If ye abide in me, and my words abide in you, ye shall ask what ye will, and it shall be done unto you." (John 15:7) Read and study the Bible, underlining every passage that has to do with faith. Assemble a great collection of such passages and, each day, absorb at least one into consciousness. That is best done by committing it to memory. Repeat the passage many times during the day, conceiving of it as dropping from your conscious into your unconscious by a process of spiritual osmosis. Visualize your unconscious as grasping it and fully absorbing it into your personality.

The following day commit and absorb another faith-passage in the same manner. At the end of one week, seven life-changing passages should have become a definite part of your mental equipment. On the seventh day, go over the seven verses you have absorbed. Meditate on each one, seeking to understand their deeper meanings.

You now have seven powerful faith concepts lodged in your mind, any one of which is well able to overcome fear thoughts. At the end of a month you will have received into consciousness thirty passages of faith and hope and courage. If you truly absorb these and live by them, you will definitely gain control over worry.

Still another method is to make use of freshly conceived and unhackneyed symbols which may, in themselves, seem extraordinarily simple, but which have the power to direct the mind into new attitudes of faith.

In a radio talk I used the phrase, "Trust God and live a day at a time," and some weeks later received from a woodcraft company an attractive sign upon which, in raised letters, were these same words, "Trust God and Live a Day at a Time."

Accompanying was a letter which said: "I heard your radio talk. My business was going badly and I was filled with overwhelming fear and anxiety. I had come to believe that success in my little business was absolutely impossible; but when you used that phrase, 'Trust God and live a day at a time,' it struck me forcibly. So I had it made up in wood and placed it at the foot of the stairway in my home. Every night on my way up to bed I would look at it and affirm, 'Trust God and live a day at a time.'

"I said over those words the last thing before falling asleep. It helped to put the day behind me. Then I would ask God to give me a good night's sleep. In the morning, coming down to breakfast, that sign would remind me to trust God and live that day only. I felt more peaceful and confident.

"Presently I began to take the attitude that just one day was all I had to worry about and so I would give that day all I had of faith and effort. I began to believe that God would be with me all that day. And He was, too." The letter concludes by saying, "My business isn't out of the woods yet, but it is on the way and I see light ahead."

By the practice of this simple device, this hitherto worried man changed his outlook and his motivation from one of fear and anxiety to one of faith and hope. I find it helpful, also, for I placed the sign in my office where I can see it daily.

Another technique for destroying worry is to set against it the contrary attitude of boldness. Obviously, the worrier is not a bold person; but boldness can be cultivated. This again is not easy, but nothing worthwhile can be attained without persistent effort. The first step is to start thinking in terms of boldness. Undertake some constructive thing that frightens you; but think boldly about it.

Picture yourself as boldly attacking and overcoming your fears. Picturized concepts in the conscious mind will, if reiterated, impress themselves deeply within the subconscious. But assumed boldness must not be mere cockiness. It must be soundly based on faith as expressed by the words, "Fear not: for I am with Thee." (Isaiah 43:5) By this method of boldness your fear will disintegrate, for it cannot long maintain itself in the atmosphere of spiritual courage. Emerson advises, "Do the thing you fear and the death of fear is certain."

Steel yourself, by an act of will, to do that which you fear, whereupon you will discover that the feared thing is not as strong as you thought it to be. My dear friend, the late Grove Patterson, one of America's greatest newspaper editors, said, "When a man has quietly made up his mind that there is nothing he cannot endure, his fears leave him." We need to emphasize the importance of will power, for in many it has become flabby. It can become strong through use, however; so use yours.

Boldness will reveal to you that you are stronger than you have imagined. Fear will diminish and courage rise in direct proportion to the effectiveness with which you put boldness into effect. Practice first, the bold thought and second, the bold act. This will stimulate supporting spiritual forces that will enable you to overcome fear.

The well known writer Arthur Gordon, contributed an article to *Guideposts* magazine which I regard as a classic in the literature of overcoming fear:

"Once when I was facing a decision that involved (I thought) considerable risk, I took the problem to a friend much older and wiser than myself. 'I'd go ahead,' I said unhappily, 'if I were sure I could swing it. But . . .'

"He looked at me for a moment, then scribbled ten words on a piece of paper and pushed it across the desk. I picked it up and read, in a single sentence, the best advice I ever had: 'Be bold—and mighty forces will come to your aid.'

"It's amazing how even a fragment of truth will illuminate things. The thought my friend had written was inspired by a book, I discovered later, by Basil King.* It made me see clearly that in the past, whenever I had fallen short in almost any undertaking, it was seldom because I had tried and failed. It was because I had let fear of failure stop me from trying at all.

"On the other hand, whenever I had plunged into deep water, impelled by a momentary flash of courage or just plain pushed by the rude hand of circumstance, I had always been able to swim until I got my feet on the ground again.

* *The Conquest of Fear*

"Be bold—that was no exhortation to be reckless or foolhardy. Boldness meant a deliberate decision, from time to time, to bite off more than you were sure you could chew. And there was nothing vague or mysterious about the mighty forces referred to. They were the latent powers that all of us possess: energy, skill, sound judgment, creative ideas—yes, even physical strength and endurance in far greater measure than most of us realize.

"Boldness, in other words, creates a state of emergency to which the organism will respond. I once heard a famous British mountaineer say that occasionally a climber will get himself into a position where he can't back down, he can only go up. He added that sometimes he put himself into such a spot on purpose. 'When there's nowhere to go but up,' he said, 'you jolly well go up.'

"The same principle works, less dramatically but just as surely, in something as commonplace as accepting the chairmanship of some committee, or even seeking a more responsible job. In either case, you know you'll have to deliver—or else.

"Some of the mighty forces that will come to your aid are, admittedly, psychic forces. But they are more important than physical ones. It's curious actually, how spiritual laws often have their counterpart in the physical world.

"A college classmate of mine was a crack football player, noted particularly for his fierce tackling although he was much lighter than the average varsity player. Someone remarked that it was surprising that he didn't get hurt.

" 'Well,' he said, 'I think it goes back to something I discovered when I was a somewhat timid youngster playing safetyman. I suddenly found myself confronting the opposing fullback who had nothing but me between him and our goal line. He looked absolutely gigantic! I was so frightened that I closed my eyes and hurled myself at him like a panicky bullet . . . and stopped him cold. Right there I learned that the harder you tackle a bigger player, the less likely you are to be hurt. The reason is simple: momentum equals weight times velocity.'

"In other words, if you are bold enough, even the laws of motion will come to your aid." So concludes Arthur Gordon's inspiring article.

But since fear is composed of shadows and ghosts it tends to become sinister and overpowering. Boldness helps to project the light of truth through the fog which fear creates in the mind. Then, by common sense and complete realism, you know that fear is, very largely, the product of fevered imagination.

So the method is first, get a clear, straight view of your fear. Second, meet it boldly, head on; and third, with God's help resolutely have done with it.

A friend told me that for years he was a confirmed worrier. "But one New Year's Eve," he said, "I was scheduled to go to a party and had an hour of leisure before I was due to leave for that event. So, the year's end being an appropriate time for taking personal stock, I decided to write on paper all my worries so that I could adequately appraise them."

He found that he was able to remember his worries of that particular day, December 31st, and also December 30th, 29th, and 28th; but he had a less clear definition of his worries through the preceding week. And he could scarcely recall what he had worried about back in November. By the time he had worked back as far as September he found that his worries were just a hazy jumble in his mind.

"I was so disgusted," he said, "at this proof of the foolishness of worry that I rolled that paper up in a ball and threw it hard against the wall. It caromed off and appropriately lodged in the wastebasket. Then," he continued, "I asked forgiveness for being so lacking in faith. God had watched over me in the past; I knew I could count on His watchful care in the future. I decided I would more diligently live the life of faith. I became more diligent in analyzing any new worry as a result of these tactics. Worry is no longer a problem," he concluded. This man saw his fear for what it was; he stood up to it, and so he defeated it.

In this incident please note the emphasis upon diligence. It reminds me of an interesting remark by my friend Walter Annenberg, publisher of the Philadelphia *Inquirer*, "Diligence is entitled to a come-back." It is a virtue Americans once valued very highly. Today, no less than formerly, real achievement is impossible without it. And diligence is important in eliminating personality defects.

So, stand up to your fears, diligently do the thing you fear, and in this manner kill your fear. Some years ago I addressed a dinner meeting at which another speaker was a United States Senator who surprisingly claimed that he "hated to make a speech." He was a huge, athletic man and in his early days had been a prize fighter. He told me that one reason he entered public life was because he feared making a speech and he realized that as a public man he would be forced to make speeches.

"I wasn't afraid of the man I faced in the prize ring," he said, "but I was afraid of standing before a crowd and trying to talk to them. So, I just had to learn to make speeches because I was not content to live in fear of something." Senator Warren Barber did the thing he feared and so he put his fear to death. Incidentally, he became an accomplished speaker.

I repeat, fear is a conglomeration of sinister shadows, and a shadow has no substance. It is usually only a magnified reflection of something very small. That is why, in standing boldly up to a fear, you often find it inconsequential. An illustration of this truth comes to my mind which, I am sorry to say, does not reflect particular credit on the author. On our honeymoon my wife and I went to a delightful, but isolated cabin in the North Woods of New York State. A friend who had kindly offered us the use of this cabin said, "You should go off alone with your bride so that you can get to know each other." Well, my wife learned some things about me which were not very inspiring.

We arrived at the cabin, deep in the woods, after dark. I built a fire while my wife cooked dinner. Meanwhile, I sat by the fire and read the newspaper. It contained the report of a murder in Utica, not many miles distant, and stated that the killer was loose in the North Woods. The fearful thought flickered across my mind, "I hope he doesn't come near our cabin."

After dinner we sat before the fire. For a supposedly quiet retreat that cabin was one of the noisiest places imaginable. Creaks and rattles and thuds sounded all about. I tried to be gay, but it was forced. My wife was enjoying herself to the fullest, for she had no fears whatsoever. Finally I heard a noise that sounded like a step on the porch. Then shuffling sounds, and another step. Cold chills ran up and down my spine. "Could it possibly be the fugitive murderer?" I thought with a chill. But I had to act like a man before my bride.

"Don't be afraid," I said blusteringly. "I'll handle this."

She looked at me questioningly. "Who's afraid? What's the matter with you?"

"There is someone outside," I explained, "and the only thing to do is to walk right out there and face him. So, here goes."

I walked over to the door, stood a moment pulling myself together, then jerked it open violently and there—sat a little chipmunk, looking at me with a twinkle in its eye.

I told this story one night when I sat with the late Wendell Willkie at a dinner of the Ohio Society of New York. His comment was, "All my life I have discovered that when

I stand up like a man to the things I am afraid of, like your chipmunk, they shrink into insignificance."

This is not to say that everything you fear in this life is chipmunk size. Some fears are substantial. But you can handle the real ones more efficiently when you are not afraid of them. Always remember that in fear your mind unnaturally increases the size of an obstacle. With boldness based on faith, even if there is a real difficulty, it will remain its own size and not be inflated; and you can handle it.

The deep unconscious fears which were, perhaps, planted in your mind in childhood can likewise be killed when you apply the cold light of reason and take a firm attitude toward them. Unconsciously, parents project their own fears, and children, like sensitive antennae, pick them up. Your present fears may have their roots in your childhood experience. When the original source of your fear is determined it is easier to eliminate it. Always remember, in dealing with fear, that it may owe its existence to some old, vague memory, and has no present substance.

I remember hearing of a strange fear developed by a farmer's horse. As a young colt it was driven past a dark stump. The horse shied at the stump rather violently. Every time, thereafter, that the farmer drove past this stump the fright was reenacted.

The farmer rooted out the stump and planted grass on the spot so that no vestige of the stump remained. But still, every time the horse passed the spot, he shied.

The farmer, a wise man, drove the horse around and around this spot, over it and past it and through it until the horse knew there was nothing there and was able finally to pass the place without fear.

We, too, shy in fear at shadowy remembrances, the meanings of which have long faded into the past.

As a child I often spent the summers at the home of my grandfather. He was a good and kindly man, but his fears unconsciously affected me. In closing up the house at night he would lock the door, shake the doorknob, walk away, then return and try it again. He would start up the stairs, then go back and shake the knob a third time. It was a ritual from which he never deviated. Doubtless it was a compulsive neurosis that if he did not try the doorknob three times "something" would happen. My grandfather was one of the finest human beings I ever knew, but this practice indicated a fear psychosis.

Years later I became aware of a curious tendency to retry doorknobs myself. But when I gained insight into the origin of this tendency I was cured of it. One night I was alone in my apartment in New York City. When I came home late that evening the doorman informed me that I was the only person sleeping in that huge fifteen-story apartment house that night. I turned on all the lights and was very conscious of the silence. I went around and locked all the doors. As I locked the main door I shook the doorknob, walked away, came back, shook it a second time and walked away. I started back to try the knob for the third time, impelled by an old childhood impulse buried in the subconscious.

But suddenly I realized that a long memory out of my early childhood was reaching out to control my present actions. Therefore, I stopped by the door and said, "Oh, no Grandpa, I love you, but I will not try this doorknob a third time. I've locked the door. It's locked. There is nothing to be afraid of. Everything is all right. I hereby break this long, shadowy, hitherto-unrealized hold of an ancient fear."

See your fears for what they are; then stand up to them and kill them. But in doing this you must have, not bravado, but faith. Nor is it a vague kind of faith; it is a strong, substantial faith in God. Only faith in God can kill your fear. The ultimate technique for ending worry is to bring God into every fear situation. No fear can live in the presence of

God. The deeper your faith in God becomes, the less power fear will have over you. The Bible outlines the process, "I sought the Lord, and he heard me, and delivered me from all my fears." (Psalm 34:4)

A demonstration of this truth is the experience of J. Edgar Hoover, Director of the Federal Bureau of Investigation. One would never think that a dynamic personality of proven courage would have had a struggle with fear; but all real men do.

Mr. Hoover told me, very sincerely, "I lost my fear in the power of my Lord." I liked the way he stated the matter. It is indeed a most powerful method for overcoming worry; lose your fear in the power of the Lord.

The power of faith is not intended, however, merely to free you from something, even from fear. The power of faith is a positive technique for developing your power to live efficiently. Worry has a stultifying effect upon mental aliveness. But when worry is cast out, then the mind, with fresh vigor and sharpened insight, can effectively function in developing creative ideas.

John M. Fox, President of the Minute Maid Corporation, movingly tells of his battle against worry and the tensions which affected him when he was starting his great new industry. He formed the first frozen juice concentrate company and directed it to its present dominant position in the concentrate field. But when he entered the business it was small indeed. In a public speech I heard Mr. Fox say:

"I should like to tell you of an experience I had during the early days of the company. Our problems had become seemingly insurmountable. Working capital had fallen to a zero level, sales were nonexistent, the frozen food industry, generally, was on the verge of going broke.

"At this juncture I decided to attend the Canners Convention in Atlantic City. This was a mistake. Misery loves company and I found a plethora of company that year on the Boardwalk.

"My stomach began to ache—I worried about the stock we had sold to the public—I worried about the employees we had wheedled away from secure, well-paying jobs. I went to sleep at night, eventually, worrying, I woke up early in the morning worrying, I even worried about the sleep I was losing.

"My family lived in Atlantic City so I was staying with them. Besides, it saved the hotel expense which we could ill afford. One day I was asked by my father to accompany him to a Rotary Club lunch. I had little stomach for this, but I knew Dad would feel hurt if I refused.

"My unhappiness with the decision to go to the Rotary lunch deepened when I saw that the speaker was to be a minister of the Gospel. My gloom was so abject that I was in no mood for a sermon. This minister was Dr. Norman Vincent Peale. Dr. Peale announced that his subject would be 'Tension—the Disease that is Destroying the American Businessman.'

"From the first words he uttered it was as though he were talking only to me. I knew I was the tensest man in the audience. The formula he gave for relaxing and putting aside worry I would like to repeat.

"First, you relax physically. This is done by stretching out in bed or in a comfortable chair. Then you methodically and carefully concentrate on relaxing each part of your body. Start with your scalp, then your face, your neck, your shoulders and so on down until you are as loose as a pan of ashes.

"Second step—you relax your mind. You recall a pleasant incident in your life: a vacation, your honeymoon, a play, a book, anything that brings into your mind's eye a pleasant scene.

"Then finally, you relax your soul. This for most of us businessmen is a little tougher. But it can be done by renewing your faith in the Lord. You get right with God. You check your fears and worries with Him. He can handle them much better than you can. You do this in prayer. If you know no other prayer, the age-old children's one will do quite well, 'Now I lay me down to sleep, I pray the Lord my soul to keep.'

"The first thing you know you'll be fast asleep. I know because, in desperation, I tried it out that very night I heard Dr. Peale tell about it. It not only worked, but I awoke the next morning refreshed and renewed and convinced we would work out of our jam some way. We did."

Scarcely have I seen an audience so deeply moved as were those five hundred businessmen at the New York luncheon who heard this dynamic industrial leader give sincere testimony to the power of faith to overcome worry in a practical situation.

Finally, may I remind you that victory over worry is not a complicated process. A long held fear pattern is not quickly or easily changed. But change is not impossible. I do not want to over-simplify the method but, actually, it is as simple as to take your worries to God, leave them with Him, and then go about your business with faith that His help is forthcoming.

George A. Straley tells about the sexton of a big city church who was puzzled, for every week he had been finding a sheet of blue lined note paper crumpled into a small wad lying in a corner of the same rear pew. He smoothed out one of the little wads of paper and it had several penciled words: "Clara-ill, Lester-job, rent."

After that the sexton began looking for the paper wads weekly and they were always there after every Sunday morning service. He opened them all and then began to watch for the person who sat in that particular corner of the pew.

It was a woman, he discovered, middle aged, plain but kind-faced, unassuming. She was always alone. The sexton told the pastor what he had observed and handed him the notes. The pastor read the cryptic words with furrowed brow.

The next Sunday he contrived to meet the woman at the church door as she was leaving and asked her kindly if she would wait for him a moment. He showed her the notes and inquired gently about their meaning.

Tears welled in the woman's eyes. She hesitated and then said softly, "You'll think it's silly, I guess, but I saw a sign among the advertising posters in a bus which said, 'Take your worries to church and leave them there.' My worries are written on those pieces of paper. I write them down during the week, bring them on Sunday morning, and leave them. I feel that God is taking care of them."

"God is taking care of them," the pastor said softly. "Please continue to bring your worries and troubles to church and leave them here."

On his way out of the church the pastor paused to pick up the freshly wadded note that had been left that particular morning. Smoothing it out he saw that it contained three words, "John—in Korea."

So, to be rid of your worries, simply take them to God and leave them there.

I once asked my readers to send me techniques for overcoming worry which they had tested and found helpful. One came from a distinguished professor of English Literature in one of our oldest Universities. She has used this simple but very sound method for many years with great effectiveness. She writes:

My dear Doctor Peale: You ask us to let you know how to control worry. Here is my method. At night before going to bed, I sit in a covered straightback chair, let my hands drop over the arms of the chair, and relax my whole body. Then I say the following, each three times:

> Tranquility, serenity, quietness
> Peace, Faith, Love, Joy.
>
> I have the habit of happiness.
> I have the habit of expecting the good.
> I have the habit of never giving up.
> I have the habit of patience.
> I have the habit of trusting the living God.
> I have the habit of helping others.

If I find myself getting stirred up about anything during the day, I say,

> The tendency to brood and fret
> Never solved any problem yet.
> Worry is a rocking chair
> That never takes me anywhere.

Sincerely use the methods outlined in this chapter and throughout this book and you can kill your worry and live longer—and better—and happier.

❖ ❖ ❖

How to Handle Worry

Worry may be described as a spasm of the emotions in which the mind takes hold of a thought or obsession, clutches it spasmodically, and will not let it go. To break its hold one must gently, but forcibly, insinuate a healthier and stronger idea into the mind's convulsive grasp. This stronger idea is that of faith in God. When faith, rather than fear, becomes your obsession, you will master worry.

Picture yourself as boldly attacking and overcoming your fears. Picturized concepts in the conscious mind will, if reiterated, impress themselves deeply within the subconscious.

CHAPTER V

YOU CAN HAVE POWER OVER YOUR DIFFICULTIES

"When you get into storm, use the panorama philosophy, the big view. Then you will know it will not last forever. With faith in your heart you can ride it out."

THE PRESIDENT of a small steel company made a curious comment: "Your business and mine aren't too different." Since I am a minister, the remark seemed incongruous. But his explanation made sense: "I make steel for people, but you put steel into people." It is indeed true that faith does put steel into you, enough to give you power over your difficulties.

This chapter is designed to show how, by the help of God, you can overcome your difficulties and live a vital and victorious life. Never settle for less. You do not need to. When the full strength potential within you is mustered you have sufficient power to deal successfully with any difficulty.

In Greece, I heard an interesting story about Alexander the Great who conquered much of the world. Unhappily, he did not conquer himself. According to the story, Alexander slept every night with the story of Ulysses under his pillow; his purpose no doubt being to drive deeply into his consciousness the unconquerable spirit of that immortal figure.

Of course it is not necessary, actually, to sleep with the Bible under your pillow. But if you fill your consciousness with the great words and tremendous faith of the Bible, you will become conqueror of all your difficulties. Indeed, the Bible states this truth in so many words, "Nay in all things we are more than conquerors through him that loved us." (Romans 8:37) This filling of your mind with big thoughts of faith, conditions you to look big at life, at yourself, at your problems. And as you develop big attitudes you can then look down upon your difficulties, seeing them in true perspective. Then they no longer seem overwhelmingly formidable and you can master them.

Through a recent experience I have become more than ever aware of the importance of thinking big. To complete this book I rented a chalet or cottage on a mountaintop in Switzerland and here I have been living for some weeks. Around the Lake of Lucerne, which lies before my house, are four noble eminences: the jagged heights of Pilatus, the towering cone of the Stanserhorn, the gentler slope of Rigi, and the brooding heights of the Burgenstock. It is atop the Burgenstock, one of the most beautiful places in Europe, that I am writing.

From my rear windows I see immense snow-capped mountains rising tier on tier, an incredible vista of peaks: the majestic Finsteraarhorn, the noble Jungfrau, the stately Eiger, and the towering Mönch, its precipitous face covered with fresh snow which fell last night to add to the eternal drifts already deep on its summit. From these white-clad mountains, scintillating waterfalls leap, and cold, blue-gray rivers race with incredible speed to the sea.

The view from my front terrace is a little gentler, dominated as it is by the Lake of Lucerne. But there are enormous mountains, a half dozen lakes, the picturesque villages of Küssnacht, Vitznau, Weggis, and one larger city, Lucerne. At night the lights of the famous city on the Vierwaldstättersee gleam like jewels.

Day after day this vast panorama calls out to one to think big. Perhaps that is why God makes panoramas. You cannot squint at a panorama. Your eyes, trying to accommodate to the vastness of the view, must open wide to take it all in. Instead of seeing life through a slit, you begin to look big at it. Unconsciously, the vast world makes you stretch in an effort to adjust to your tremendous environment. Thus you tend toward that bigness which potentially is within all of us, even as it is in nature.

Living with a panorama helps develop that big philosophy that overcomes difficulty. For one thing, it teaches you that the circumstances of life at a given moment are not necessarily permanent, they only seem that way. On our mountain top, when the weather is fair, you have no assurance that it will continue so, for often in the far distance storm clouds can be seen gathering over the enormous peaks. And you know that in all probability the storm will shortly hurl itself upon you. But, being able to see it from the vantage point of the panorama, you have time to make the necessary preparations to meet it.

Then the colossal storm breaks with heavy clouds, rolling fog, dashing rain, and thunder reverberating down the gorges of the Alps. But often, even in the midst of the storm's tumult, you may see, far away, through a break in the clouds, a green mountain side bathed in sunlight. And you are encouraged that soon there will be fair skies again.

Often people tell me, "I have nothing but trouble; everything goes wrong; I am surrounded by difficulties." But the philosophy of the panorama reminds you that all storms pass and, more important, that you are big enough to live with them while they last.

And you need not be discouraged, for storms or difficulties are limited in extent and they do pass. Fair weather always comes. This is a required philosophy for living courageously in this world. All men who deal with natural phenomena are aware of the ephemeral shifting of storm and sunshine.

I came home one time on a ship sailing from a Mediterranean port. Soon after Gibraltar the Captain invited us to the bridge. It was a glorious morning, sunlight shimmering on the water and blue skies overhead. We had just passed through the Gates of Hercules, with Africa on the left and Spain on the right. The surge of the Atlantic made you realize you were out of the Mediterranean and on the ocean, but the sea was calm and the day radiant.

"How is the weather ahead, Captain?" I asked.

He laid a chart before me. Pointing to it he said, "Over there is a hurricane called Flora. We are traveling at twenty-two knots in a westerly direction. Flora is traveling seven knots northerly. If the speed of the hurricane does not change I compute that we will meet it early Friday morning."

"You mean we will be on the outer edge of it?" I asked hopefully.

"No," he told me grimly. "We shall go right through it."

"Why do we need to meet it?" I asked. "You've got a fast ship. Why not go around it?"

"I would lose two days," was his answer. "It would throw me off schedule. But do not be concerned, the hurricane is only about a hundred and fifty miles in area, and on the other side there is beautiful weather. Besides, we have a ship that can ride it out."

Early on Friday I was practically knocked out of my bed. I rose and gazed at the black vastness of the ocean. Believe me, Flora was a tempestuous lady! The violence lasted until around two o'clock Friday afternoon when we began to run out of the storm. By midnight the moon was shining and the seas were calm.

Next day the Captain said, "I have always lived by the philosophy that if the sea is smooth, it will get rough; if it is rough, it will get smooth. But with a good ship you can always ride it out."

So it is with life, isn't it? When you get into storm, use the panorama philosophy, the big view. Then you will know it will not last forever. With faith in your heart you can ride it out. There is fair weather ahead. See life big. Don't let your thinking deteriorate into little thoughts. Live on a big scale. Look big at life.

These reflections remind me of a great personality whom I knew years ago and who left an unforgettable impression on me. He was Harlowe B. Andrews of Syracuse, New York, one of the most rugged and yet gentle characters I ever knew. He was one of those very different human beings whom God makes now and then.

As a young man, I often went to him for advice. One day he said something which I have used to good advantage ever since. "Norman, the way to handle difficulty is very simple: think big, believe big, pray big, act big." Then he added, "God can make you bigger than your difficulties."

That dynamic and utterly sound statement constitutes a sure method for getting power over your difficulties. Think big, and powerful forces are released. For example, the great United Nations building in New York City was built in what had been a slum and low-grade business district. It was one of the creative dreams of William Zeckendorf, whose projects are all immense ones. He operates on a huge scale of thinking. Recently I heard him say in a public address, "My experience has been that only the biggest plans are really easy." How true that is, for little plans have no lift or dynamism.

I was impressed with that philosophy, for I believe that when you plan something big you are actually thinking the way God intended men to think. And the reason you get big results is that a super-power potential is back of big concepts. When you project a big thought you must necessarily put big faith and big effort into it. Such faith and effort generate dynamic creative power. Moreover, to support a big idea you must give it all you've got. That, in itself, exerts extraordinary force. Those who plan little, uninspiring things have little faith, little enthusiasm, and it is not surprising that little comes of them. Little faith equals little results. And, conversely, big faith equals big results. Big dreams, plus big thinking, plus big faith, plus big effort, that is the formula by which big things are done; and, I might add, the formula by which big difficulties are overcome.

Select some big goal, some big objective, some big dream. Then hold it in your mind, dedicating yourself to it, no matter how many difficulties oppose you. By big thinking, which is really a form of God-thinking, you can surge past all difficulties.

In the office of a beautiful store in a western city I sat with the proprietor, an old friend of mine. He had come to that city many years before with his bride and only fifty dollars in capital. His first shop was so small he called it a "hole-in-the-wall." This later developed into a good-sized store. Then, due to circumstances largely traceable to a disloyal partner, he lost his business.

"I took stock," he said, "and decided I must not give in to discouragement. When I added up my assets they looked pretty good, in fact I was in a more advantageous position than when I started originally. I still had my wife and, this time, I had a thousand dollars instead of fifty. Also, I had a lot of experience and a deepened faith. So, I began again and built this new store. I have a simple formula," he concluded, "God, faith, big thinking, Helen, America, and work."

A mighty strong combination, isn't it? Believe, even though it may be hard to believe, that there are creative values in your difficulty. The usual, undisciplined tendency is to focus the mind only on negative factors. That is a decidedly wrong slant of thought. The wise method is to walk calmly around a dark situation, hopefully looking for any possible chink of light—and it is an unhappy situation indeed, where there isn't some faint flicker. Look at your problem in a creative and positive manner and you will find bright opportunities which you have not thought of. Never think negatively. Be realistic, face all the facts, but always look on the hopeful side.

A man telephoned to tell me of his "bad" situation. "I'm calling you for encouragement," he explained. "I thought you might pray with me over the telephone."

"What seems to be the trouble?" I asked.

"I run a furniture business," he said, "and selling is slow in our area. I've got to persuade more people to part with more money. Perhaps I bought a bigger inventory than I should carry."

While he was talking I was thinking and praying, too. If you pray when faced by a problem, really pray and believe, you will get an answer. So, out of my prayer came this thought: "Your attitude should not be to 'get people to part with their money.' Rather it should be to help them. The purpose of business isn't merely to get money from people, but to render services to people. Take Mrs. X.," I said. "Maybe Mrs. X. wants a chair and hasn't the money to buy it. So, she stands outside your store and looks in your window at the chair and wishes she might have it. You stand inside and look out at her and wish she would come in and buy it."

And the merchandise doesn't move and so both Mrs. X. and you are unhappy about it.

"That is just the way it is," he said.

"Think first of helping Mrs. X. And to do that you must get to know her and her family; study her needs. Do not think so much about putting her money in your pocket as about putting your chair, that she needs, into her home. Pray about a way to help her have the furniture she requires. Do this with all your customers. Think of them as people needing your goods instead of yourself needing their money. Find ways of helping them overcome their difficulties, and you will overcome your own in so doing. And," I added, "if you will go around your community spreading joy and faith and trying to help people, instead of merely thinking about yourself, the Lord will bless you and you will turn over that inventory and have a wonderful time living."

"Where did you get these ideas?" he asked curiously.

"From the greatest of all experts," I said.

"Who is he?"

"Just take it from me," I said. "I got it from Him."

"I get you," he replied. "You mean just practice Christianity."

Some weeks later he telephoned again. "I want to report," he said. "I have turned over enough of the inventory to be in the clear. I never went out among people before, but now I am getting to know them and I find some mighty nice folks. And I want to tell you about something wonderful that happened to me. I found one husband and wife who were on the outs with each other. At first we talked about furniture. Then their marriage problem came into the conversation, about whether they should get furniture, for maybe they would split up.

"So what do you think I did? Believe it or not I just sat down and prayed with them. First time I ever did such a thing in my life. That seemed to make them feel better. And before I left I sold them two chairs instead of one. They paid what they could and they now have the chairs, but best of all, I believe they have a new spirit; they wouldn't have bought the chairs if they weren't going to stick with each other. I'll keep close to them for I believe we can hold that couple together."

This man learned, indeed, to think big about his business. He found that the furniture business and human problems and religion are closely related. By thinking big he got the creative idea of forgetting himself and helping others. His own difficulties were overcome in the process.

You may regard your work as dull and unromantic, but actually it is made that way if the person who works at that job becomes dull. Try this experiment. For one day think no drab thoughts about your job. Look deeply into its possibilities. Think big and exciting thoughts about it. I believe that just one day of this will surprise you, and if you continue the experiment you will find that even the most seemingly common occupation is not without its thrill.

Charlie Franzen was one of the best carpenters I ever knew. Running his hand lovingly over a paneled room which he had just completed, he remarked, "I would rather work with wood than anything in the world." He thought big about carpentry and learned to meet his difficulties, and he had plenty, too.

Any useful type of work can be just as big as you want to make it. And you can make it big by thinking big about it. For example, there is my friend, Charlie Horan who operates a grocery store in Pawling, New York. For years Charlie worked for a grocery chain in that little village. Then, the company closed the store and Charlie had to make a big decision. He knew the grocery business thoroughly, but it was not without trepidation that he decided to venture in a store of his own. Accordingly, he opened the Horan Superette, and I went in to wish him well. "I hope I can make a go of it," he said. "I know there will be problems, but I'll give it all I've got."

We went into his back room and had a little prayer, asking that he would be granted success and that through his business he could render a service to people. Competition came in the form of a brand new, shiny, modern supermarket, but Charlie Horan thought big, wished the best prosperity to the supermarket, and went on filling his own little store full of faith, happiness, and big thoughts. And so, despite all difficulty, his business developed.

Difficulties make no difference, really, when you think big about them and, in effect, think above them. That is the way a combat pilot gets the advantage, by coming up and over his opponent. In the battle of life marshal your spirit to take a high position that will enable you to look down upon your difficulties. Then you see them in realistic size and know you are bigger than they are. You can overcome them because you get above them in your thinking. It is easy to think little, but avoid so doing for it can make you little. Always think big.

A Negro boy said to me glumly, "I can never amount to much in this country."

"Why not?" I asked.

"You ought to know," he answered.

"You are healthy, aren't you?" I asked. "And smart?"

He grinned and agreed.

"You have a good mother? A good father?"

He nodded.

"Let me feel your muscle."

He rolled up his sleeves and grinned again when I congratulated him on his well-developed muscles.

"And you have a wonderful smile." I added this item to his assets.

"But I am colored," he objected.

"So is Ralph Bunche, who used to be a janitor," I reminded

him. "So is Jackie Robinson. So is the President of the Borough of Manhattan, Hulan Jack." And I went on to mention others. "Your thinking is twenty-five years behind the times, son. Then it was more difficult for Negro men and women, but some of them did mighty well, all the same."

I told him about a small Negro boy at a county fair. A man was blowing up balloons and letting them float up into the sky to the delight of a crowd of children. The balloons were of all colors. "Do you suppose that black one will go as high as the rest?" the Negro boy asked.

"Watch," the man said, "and I'll show you." He blew up the black balloon and it went just as high as the others. "You see, sonny," he told the boy, "it isn't the color that determines how high they go, but the stuff inside them that counts."

I added for my young friend, "If you will get self-doubt out of your mind, and rid yourself of the inferiority complex you are nursing, and believe that God will help you, and then if you give everything you have to whatever you do, you will get along all right."

I fully realize that many people have very difficult problems. But when you stop thinking negatively about your problems and obstacles and start doing something constructive about them, you will come through. The help of God, positive thinking, a desire to serve others, and the willingness to work are all you need. If you believe you can do it, you can. Think big.

I heard of a boy who badly needed a job. There was a good job advertised and he started out early that morning to apply for it, but when he got to the address given he found twenty boys waiting in line ahead of him. Still that did not stump him.

He scribbled a hasty note, folded it, and handed it to the secretary of the man doing the hiring. He told her it was important for her boss to see it at once. She was convinced by his manner and took it to her employer.

It read, "I am the twenty-first kid in line. Don't do anything until you see me." Here, obviously, was a boy who was alert, eager, imaginative, and self-confident. Naturally, he got the job.

Henry Kaiser told me that when a new project is started in his organization they give it to a man who knows all the difficulties yet is enthusiastic about it. The man who says, "It's a great idea, but I doubt that it can be done," doesn't get the job. The assignment goes to the man who says, "It's a great idea; I will have the time of my life doing it."

Some people are vibrant with life and filled with energy and dynamism. They think big. Others, however, are dull, lethargic, and pessimistic. They have not learned how to think and live dynamically. If you belong in this second group, make up your mind, today, that you can live a full and abundant life. Start now by putting into practice the policy of thinking big about everything.

Praying big prayers is of tremendous importance in gaining power over your difficulties. God will grant big things if you ask for them and are big enough to receive them.

You must have faith if prayer is to do big things for you. And if you are not getting answers, it may be that your prayers are not big enough. Do not pray little prayers—pray big prayers. You are praying to a big God. Perhaps He knows that a small prayer is backed only by small faith, and the Bible tells us He rates our sincerity by our faith. Perhaps He also rates our capacity to receive by our faith. Ask for right things, and ask right. Ask with faith, and pray big.

You want health? Pray for it. You want financial security? Pray for it. You want happiness in your home? Pray for it. You want a life filled with abundant joy? Pray for it. You want to do something worthwhile in life? Pray for it. Pray big prayers and you will get big answers.

One of the suggestions given by my old friend Mr. Andrews was to act big. Thinking big about difficulty reminds us that it is not without value. Channing Pollock, the famous playwright once said an interesting thing to me, "Men and motor cars go forward by a series of explosions." Even as a motor car cannot fulfill its true function apart from a series of internal explosions, just so a human being cannot really go forward unless propelled by rightly directed and controlled difficulties. You can permit the explosions of difficulty to tear you to pieces and destroy you. Or they can become your motive force. The secret of successful living is to control and use the power which difficulty releases into your personality.

It has been demonstrated countless times that difficulty leads people to the greatest things in life, that is, if they have the inner strength to stand up to difficulty. Jack Fleck, 1955 United States Open Golf Champion said, "Before I could win I had to learn to lose. I had to weave my bad breaks into the pattern of my golf." This man, who had to learn to lose before he could win, was the man who defeated the great Ben Hogan to win the championship.

Perhaps even more dramatic is the story of another holder of the same championship, Ed Furgol, who, as a boy, suffered an accident which made one arm eleven inches shorter than the other. By sheer perseverence, courage, and faith he became champion. When asked who might succeed him as title holder, several names were mentioned, but he shook his head saying, "No, none of them will ever be champion, they haven't been hungry enough." That is to say, none of them had suffered enough difficulty and opposition and therefore had not developed the rugged vitality necessary to win through gruelling competition to attain the top honor. Difficulty is not at all a bad thing, unpleasant as it may be.

More than twenty years ago Hartly Laycock was a banker in the Midwest. Then came the great depression and at age sixty he was without money and without a job. He walked the streets of Chicago. His only training was banking and banks were closing every day. Anyway, no one wanted a man past forty.

He prayed for guidance. Then "something" strange happened. One day in the want ads "something" caught his eye. It was the advertisement of an old Florida Hotel for sale at a sacrifice.

"Something" said to him to write the owners and ask about it. But he couldn't imagine being in the hotel business, so he kept looking for a job. But he found that he was continually thinking about the hotel. He called and asked the price, a sum far beyond his slim resources. He hadn't even a hundred dollars left.

He prayed again and said, "Lord, You brought that advertisement to my attention. I know nothing about the hotel business, but am willing to try it, though I haven't the money it will take." He raised a small down payment and had the hotel. But the paint was peeling off, the floorboards were rotten, it was filled with cobwebs, there wasn't a stick of furniture or a piece of carpet in the place.

"Lord," he asked, "why did You ever get me into this?"

And the Lord seemed to say that things would work out all right. There were lots of headaches and years of work, but that hotel was booked solid last season.

My dynamic friend, now eighty-two, discovered that when you believe and pray and are willing to be guided you get amazing solutions to difficulty.

So, to overcome difficulty, pray big, believe big, and act big.

One of the greatest American singers is Marian Anderson, who says in *Guideposts* magazine, "Failure and frustration are in the unwritten pages of everyone's record. I have had my share of them. We were poor folk," she continues, "but many people were kind to me. A group of well-meaning friends hastily sponsored me for a concert in Town Hall in New York. But I wasn't ready, either in experience or maturity.

"On the exciting night of my first concert I was told that Town Hall was sold out. While waiting in dazed delight to go on, my sponsor said there would be a slight delay. I waited five, ten, fifteen minutes. Then I peeked through the curtain. The house was half empty. I died inside.

"I sang my heart out, but when the concert was over I knew I had failed. The critics next day agreed with me. I was shattered within.

" 'I had better forget all about singing and do something else,' " I told my mother.

" 'Why don't you think about it a little, and pray a lot, first?' she cautioned."

But Marian Anderson was so crushed in spirit that for a whole year she brooded in silence, refusing every invitation to sing. Her mother kept gently prodding her, saying, "Have you prayed, Marian? Have you prayed?"

"No, I hadn't prayed. I embraced my grief. Then, from my torment I prayed with the sure knowledge there was Someone to whom I could pour out the greatest need of my heart and soul. Slowly I came out of my despair. My mind began to clear. Self-pity left me.

"So, one day I came home unaware that I was humming. It was the first music I had uttered for a whole year. When my mother heard it she rushed to meet me and put her arms around me and kissed me. It was her way of saying, 'Your prayers have been answered.' For a brief moment we stood there silent. Then my mother said, 'Prayer begins where human capacity ends.' "

Marian Anderson stood up to difficulty, prayed and acted big, and the result was one of the most glorious voices that the American people have ever heard. But it was developed out of difficulty.

There is a curious yet certain law that if you expect difficulty and hold such expectation deeply in your mind, the expected difficulty may actually materialize. Perhaps it is because people who take a defeatist attitude never give themselves wholeheartedly.

But other people burst into life's problems with the irresistability of dynamism. With boundless enthusiasm and confidence they give all they have and difficulties seem to fade away. What you do with life depends upon the enthusiasm and vitality which you give to it.

Branch Rickey tells a marvelous story in *Guideposts* magazine about a baseball game that occurred many years ago when he was managing the St. Louis Browns: "There is nothing else like it in the record books anywhere. There was a player on my team by the name of Walker, a man who had all the physical qualities to be a great player. During the game Walker hit what should have been a home run and was thrown out at third.

"Walker's slow start to first base, as he watched his hard line drive fall between the left and center fielders, cost him twenty feet. Next, he lost another thirty feet making too wide a turn around first toward second base. Then, seeing the elusive ball still going, (the left field fence was down for repair) he slowed to a jog trot. This easily cost him still another fifty feet, and he was now one hundred feet behind schedule.

"Suddenly the ball struck some object, a board or stone, and bounced back into the hands of the surprised centerfielder, a boy by the name of Al Nixon. Nixon's quick turn and his strong arm brought the throw toward third. Walker, seeing that a play could now be made on him, put on a great burst of speed. He made a fall-away slide to the right and into the very hands of the third baseman. Walker actually tagged himself out.

"Exclamatory groans came from our bench. One chap in disgust kicked over the water bucket, and another threw a bunch of bats helter-skelter into the air. In discussing the play later, however, everyone agreed that if Walker had not made any one of four mistakes—the slow start from home plate, the wide turn at first, the walking trot around second, and the slide to the wrong side at third—there could have been no play upon him. And, if he had made all four correctly, he would have scored a home run standing up.

"The baseball records tell of another player, one dynamically alive. Detroit came to bat in the last half of the eleventh inning, score tied, two men out, nobody on base, and a player named Ty Cobb facing the pitcher.

"Cobb got a base on balls and then scored the winning run without another ball being pitched. By sheer adventure and skill he forced two wild throws by St. Louis infielders. His daring at first base, his boldness and skillful turn at second, his characteristic slide ten feet before he reached third, his quick co-ordination following his slide—all brought about four 'breaks' in his favor. He made what amounted to a home run out of a base on balls.

"What is the difference between Cobb and Walker? They were about the same age, weight, height, and running speed. Walker had a stronger arm than Cobb and more power at the bat. Only one rose to unparalleled fame. Cobb wanted to do something so much that nothing else mattered; Walker punched the clock," says Branch Rickey.

And I might add that Ty Cobb probably never even gave difficulty a thought. He loved the game, he gave it all he had, and he developed, thereby, an enormous power over difficulty. Walker, on the contrary, was psychologically ready for difficulties to interfere with him, and they accommodated him, as they always will if you are mentally conditioned to them.

I have been teaching positive thinking for years and, as a result, many people write telling me how they and others have overcome difficulty by applying principles of faith, big thinking, big praying, big acting. One particularly inspiring story is that of Ike Skelton.

Not too many years ago Ike Skelton was a normal, healthy

youngster. Then, suddenly, at twelve years of age he was stricken with infantile paralysis. The disease left his arms dangling helplessly by his sides. His legs recovered satisfactorily and he could function otherwise, except that he could not move his arms.

Yet this boy entered Wentworth Military Academy with one burning ambition—he wanted to make the track team. The coach told him kindly, "Why, son, you can't run without your arms. You need them as much as your legs."

Nevertheless, Ike Skelton kept at it. He trotted around the track all season, but he didn't make the team. He continued to run the following season, and each succeeding year but he couldn't make the grade competitively.

Finally came the last big track meet of his school career, the one with Wentworth's arch rival, Kemper. The boy begged the coach to give him a chance in the two-mile run, the most gruelling event in the meet. Finally the coach broke down and did. "Go out there and run," he said, "but promise me you won't be disappointed." Then the coach fastened his arms to his sides so they would not get in his way and started him in the race.

The crowd had eyes only for this strange runner. When the race was over, the students surged down from the stands and lifted him enthusiastically upon their shoulders. There wasn't a dry eye in the crowd.

Had he won the race? Not at all—he came in last. But he came in, and that is the important fact. While he didn't win that race, he is winning the most important race of life through his demonstration of an undefeatable spirit. At the University of Edinburgh as an exchange student, he became one of the popular men there. Later he made a brilliant record in law school and is now in a successful law career and getting a start in politics.

What enabled this boy to overcome his difficulties and live confidently and successfully? Karl Menninger, the psychiatrist, pointed out that men do not break down because they are defeated, but only because they think they are. So don't think you are. Think big, believe big, pray big, and act big. To this add work and struggle. That is the formula for gaining victory over your difficulties.

❖ ❖ ❖

Remember:

You are not defeated, though it may be you think you are.

By the help of God you can overcome your difficulties and live a vital and victorious life. Never settle for less. You do not need to. When the full strength potential within you is mustered you have sufficient power to deal with any difficulty.

Think big; and powerful forces are released.

Believe big; faith and effort generate dynamic creative power.

Pray big; God will grant big things if you ask for them and are big enough to receive them.

Act big; only the biggest plans are really easy.

CHAPTER VI

YOU CAN HAVE LIFE IF YOU WANT IT

"When your interest and appreciation are widened to include the whole great world, life becomes even more fascinating. Interest, projected outside yourself, has the power to force even hardship, suffering, and pain into the background. The more vital your interest, in others and in the world, the more certainly you can live triumphantly over your own difficulties."

WHAT DO YOU really want? What do I want? What does everybody want? Of course, the answer is we want life. And what is life? It is vitality, energy, freedom, growth, dynamism. It is a deep sense of well-being. It is the elimination of all feelings of deadness and desultoriness. It is to be fully vital and vigorous. It is a useful participation in worth while activities. It is the satisfaction of creating something, giving something, doing something.

Unfortunately, many people do not have a quality of life that squares with this definition. They are filled with gloom and apprehension. They suffer fear, discouragement, and frustration. Their spirits have been sapped of vitality; they are lethargic and apathetic. It is terribly tragic to die while you live. It is almost as terrible to be asleep when you should be wide awake. And it is quite unnecessary.

Your life is meant to be fully alive. You are designed to have vigor of body, mind, and spirit throughout your years. In studying life, as I observe it in many persons, I have been amazed by the infectious and magnetic quality it sometimes demonstrates.

I gave a talk on the same platform with a man who was advertised as "The Greatest Speaker in the United States. Such designation is perhaps extravagant, no matter to whom i is applied. But this man did, indeed, prove to be an excellent speaker. He exerted an astonishing magnetism. The temperature in Tennessee that day was nearly one hundred degrees. Yet, late in the afternoon after three other men had spoken, he held his crowd spellbound.

Although his speech was extraordinarily well delivered, what made him outstanding was his projection of an alive personality. He transmitted life to people who were hot and tired; he inspired them so that they forgot they were hot, and as they listened they were no longer tired. He was alive; and they, too, came alive.

Later, at dinner, I studied him. Then I understood. He had one of the brightest pair of eyes I have ever seen in a human being. "I know your secret," I said suddenly. "You are one of those alive-eyed people."

"What do you mean, alive-eyed?" he asked in surprise.

A personnel manager told me once, I explained, that he hires men by the kind of eyes they have. "I look over their application papers and their past record and experience. But those questionnaires are really a minor consideration with me," he said. "If a man's eyes are dull, I don't want him. And," he added, "all too few applicants have the alive-eyes which I am seeking and which, in my opinion, mark a dynamic personality." Ever since that conversation I have almost hesitated to look into a mirror.

Your spirit can stay alive through long years if you keep your mind and heart alive; and if your spirit is alive that very fact helps to keep the rest of you toned up. That is what we really want, isn't it, to be alive in every element of our being?

A person should be so eager about everything that, actually, he can hardly wait for morning to get started again. Life should be perpetually fascinating. We are designed to have enthusiasm, freshly renewed every day. The human spirit was never constructed to run down. It is we who allow that to happen. And it is a great pity.

In saying that you can have perpetual enthusiasm I certainly do not mean you should become a flippant or superficial person who falsely assumes that everything in this world is sweetness and light. We know that such is decidedly not the case. The world is full of sorrow and trouble. But it is also full of the overcoming of sorrow and trouble. And an effervescent spirit of joy and enthusiasm can help in making possible a better life for everyone.

One way to have that quality of life is to get outside yourself. People who live within themselves lose that vital something which stimulates verve and excitement. As a matter of fact, many are actually ill as a result of nothing but self-centeredness. When you lose yourself, letting your personality flow outward, your life takes on creative joy and even health. Half dead, listless, desultory people everywhere could find the vital life they really want by the very simple expedient of practicing self-forgetfulness.

A few years ago in Florida I met a man who haunted the doctor's office in a big resort hotel. He thought he was sick, and indeed, he acted so. His chauffeur brought him South in a big car and he had three nurses on round-the-clock duty. He asked to see me, when he heard I was in the hotel. The first thing he said when I entered his room was, "I feel terrible," and he kept repeating it at intervals throughout our short call. He showed many symptoms of despondency, depressiveness, and extreme listlessness.

The hotel doctor is a close friend, and when I spoke about this man he said, "He isn't well, but medicine alone won't cure him. If you could help him overcome self-preoccupation and give him a good dose of outgoing Christianity it might even make him well."

I decided to see what I could do toward applying the suggested therapy. As we were seated on the porch of the hotel I noticed an elderly woman trying to pull a chair into position. The chair was too cumbersome for her to handle and it became hooked under a railing. I suggested to the "sick" man that he help the old lady with the chair. I said, "I think it will actually make you feel better."

He groaned and put up a protest, but I insisted and, complainingly, he went over and helped her extricate the chair; then he put it into place for her. She gave him a nice smile in return. He came back, sank in his chair beside me and said, "Do you know, believe it or not, I got a kick out of that."

"When you do something helpful for another person you always feel better," I said and I reminded him of what Jesus Christ said: "He that findeth his life shall lose it: and he that loseth his life for my sake shall find it." (Matthew 10:39.)

"I have heard that all my life, but I never thought of it as a healing procedure," he said thoughtfully. I explained that we can become physically sick through a process of selfishness that poisons our thoughts and drains off our life force. "You see how good that simple little act made you feel? Imagine how you would feel if you become outgoing in bigger things."

About a year later I returned to the same hotel and happened to see a man striding down the corridor toward me. The thought crossed my mind that here was a vigorous person. I was engrossed, however, in other matters and was about to pass him when he grabbed my arm. Then I recognized him, but he was so different. Health and energy actually seemed to radiate from him.

"I am glad to see you so much better," I commented. "Where are your nurses?"

"Oh, I don't need nurses," he said. "I'm a well man."

When I asked him to explain the change, he said, "It was caused by a very simple act which you asked me to perform." And he reminded me of the experience on the hotel porch when he helped the elderly woman. "That little service made me feel so good that I began looking for other opportunities to do something for people, just little things. Then I found a few bigger services to render. One thing led to another until, strangely enough, I began to feel so much better that, finally, I came to the day when I saw myself. I got a clear view of how I was actually destroying my life by self-centeredness. But living in a more outgoing manner has made me a healthy man," he declared.

That case is an illustration of how, by self-centeredness and overpreoccupation, you may unconsciously retreat from dynamic living. But when you project yourself outside yourself, you may thereby regain a normal mental, emotional, spiritual, and even physical condition. The final result is often a sense of complete well-being.

You can allow the cares, troubles, and difficulties of this world not only to cloud your mind and depress your spirit, but actually to limit life within you. By an accumulation of anxiety thoughts and trouble thoughts the personality languishes inwardly and presently transmits its lethargic condition to the physical body, so that one gets to feeling tired and below par.

No doubt there are people everywhere who, while perhaps not physically sick, actually suffer real symptoms due primarily to ingrown thinking. They have actually depleted the life force within them. Like the man in Florida they need only to take stock of themselves and to see themselves as they are. The next step is to get insight into what they can become. Then, they need to do a reconstructive job on their thinking. By eliminating destructive thoughts they can really begin to live with dynamic force and very great joy.

It is a truism to say that all of us have problems, troubles, and hardships. That of course is the way life is. There is no such thing as easy living. Life can be difficult, even hard. But it does not need to be so difficult or so hard that you cannot live with a joyous sense of strength. I hope, therefore, you may believe that, by the help of God, you can have what you deeply want; namely, a life of vitality and joy.

In developing dynamic life another factor is to put animation into your daily work. Your life's vitality can be increased by taking an immense pleasure in all that you are doing. Practice liking it. By this attitude, tedium is eliminated and the distinction between labor and pleasure is erased. Being alive in the fullest sense you will get enjoyment out of your activity because aliveness stimulates the sense of excitement.

Take my good friend Branch Rickey, an extraordinarily inspiring personality. In baseball for over fifty years he has produced some of the greatest teams in the history of the sport. For many years with St. Louis, then with Brooklyn, and Pittsburgh, he may fittingly be called the great man of baseball. The Editor of our *Guideposts* magazine, Len LeSourd, visited spring training camp the year Mr. Rickey had been in baseball for half a century. He asked, "Mr. Rickey, tell me your greatest thrill in baseball in a half century."

Rickey lowered his big eyebrows and his eyes flashed. "My greatest thrill? I haven't had it yet."

There is a man vibrantly alive. In spite of all his great thrills, the greatest is always yet to be, perhaps tomorrow, perhaps next week, maybe even next year. Always ahead, always in anticipation.

One night I attended the circus with a good friend of mine, Beverly Kelley, who held an important position in that organization. He was so busy that he could spend only part of the evening with me in his box. I observed his keen delight in acts going on in the rings. "Beverly, how long have you been with the circus?" I asked.

"Twenty-seven years," he replied.

"Well," I asked, "do you like your job?"

I shall never forget his reply. "Norman," he said, "it's a hundred percent better than working."

That answer is a classic. Enthusiasm and eagerness can make any job thrilling. Love your job. If you do not like it now, learn to like it. Study it, analyze it, see its possibilities, believe in it. One way to do this is upon awakening every morning say to yourself, "I have a fine job and I am going to enjoy working at it today." Affirm in this manner day by day until, gradually, your mind accepts and makes permanent the attitude expressed. This practice will generate zest and dynamism. Your entire reaction to your life by this method can undergo revitalization. And when you revamp your attitude toward your work, in effect you revamp your life, for basically your work is your life.

Still another way to add to the dynamic quality of your life is to cultivate interest in everything. A famous philosopher once pointed out that aliveness is measured by the number of points at which we touch life. A person having one hundred interests, let us say, is twice as alive as one who has but fifty interests. Depth of interest, often referred to as a consuming interest, is also a measure of aliveness.

And you can make yourself interested when you try. To make a start simply begin thinking interesting thoughts. Also, practice being interested in people and events, even if it requires an act of will to do so. If you really work at this, your interest will become actual and you will then discover that you are developing an interesting life. To the degree to which you cultivate an interested attitude you will create a life full of zest and vibrancy.

I have a very satisfying hobby, that of collecting people. Some people collect china, others collect stamps. I once knew a man who collected clocks. But I collect people. This hobby adds greatly to the joy I get from life, which I assure you is considerable.

For example, there is my friend Nino. I collected him several years ago. He has a long Italian name, but his nickname is Nino. He drove us for three weeks, from Naples to Venice, to St. Moritz, to Geneva. Another summer we drove with him from Stresa to Venice to Rome to Sorrento, and a score of beautiful towns and cities in between.

At first I was a bit uneasy with Nino. His English was broken and my Italian practically non-existent. But by drawing upon some French and German as well as English we understood each other very well. I liked his sunny smile and glorious disposition and we got along famously. Once I said, thinking I was extending to him the highest possible compliment, "Nino, why don't you come to the United States to live?"

"Oh, Doctor," he said, "I know that is a very nice country, but why should I leave my beloved Italy?"

"I don't know," I said non-plussed, "it is just a suggestion."

Then he began describing Italy to me, the glories of its towering mountains and blue lakes, the warmth of its soft, golden sunlight. He had me almost dreaming of a villa in Florence or a house in Capri or a cottage under the eternal snows of Cortina d'Ampezzo.

When we separated at the end of the trip we vowed we would meet again and travel many hundreds of kilometers together in the years to come. I collected Nino and added him to my precious assortment of friendships.

Then, I collected a little girl in Damascus, a dirty little girl of about six. I met her outside the ancient walls of that famous city. She looked me over with a level gaze from deep, dark eyes; then gave me a fragile, wistful smile, the sweet and innocent smile of childhood. She did not ask me for anything. I said, "Hello," to her in English, and I am sure it was an "Hello," in Arabic with which she responded. She understood my smile and I understood hers. I have heard sociologists describe refugees of all races and nationalities and have listened to innumerable statistics about them. But they were only statistics to me. Now, every time I hear of a refugee I see that little girl outside the old walls of Damascus with her deep, dark eyes and wonderful smile. Perhaps I shall never see her again, but I collected her and her sweetness filled me with joy and added to the vibrancy of my life.

Because human relationships touch life in its deepest meaning is the reason we are taught to love people. When we truly learn to love them we are getting very close to satisfying life's deepest desires. To prove that, notice the warm glow in your heart when you take an outgoing interest in other persons.

Then, when your interest and appreciation are widened to include the whole great world, life becomes even more fascinating. Interest, projected outside yourself, has the power to force even hardship, suffering, and pain into the background. The more vital your interest, in others and in the world, the more certainly you can live triumphantly over your own difficulties.

Not long ago my father died. He was eighty-five years old according to the calendar, but measured by zest and interest and kindliness he was always young. I never knew anyone who loved life more than he did, or who got more out of living. Whenever I think of life at its vibrant best I think immediately of Dad. Shortly after his death I received a letter from Dr. Clarence W. Lieb, an old friend of the family, a retired physician now living in California, but who was a distinguished doctor in New York City. Twenty years ago I had taken my father to him because of his then critical physical condition.

"I am saddened," Doctor Lieb wrote, "by the news of your father's death. He lived much longer than his physical condition of twenty years ago promised. I am confident that it was his fine mind and superb spirit which added greatly to his longevity. It was my privilege to have served him professionally. I bless his memory."

Charles Clifford Peale was a minister for many years, but before that he was a physician. His intellectual curiosity and his mental vitality were tremendous. He read prodigiously and was able to master and explain books and other material which many people, including his son, had great difficulty in comprehending. The late Fulton Oursler once told me that he read Du Noüy's *Human Destiny* four times before he could condense it for the *Reader's Digest.* Of course, Fulton Oursler did a masterful piece of work with that book as he always did with any writing. But he said that my father helped him greatly, having mastered the difficult book so thoroughly that his explanations were amazingly clear and cogent.

My father was the type of man who would never give up and he did not permit his sons to give up, either. He always told us, "The Peales never quit." When I was writing my book *A Guide to Confident Living,* which later became a bestseller, I became discouraged with my work and literally threw it away. My wife rescued the manuscript, gave it to my father, who found a publisher for it.

He loved to speculate about the world and everything in it, the stars and man and God. He reveled in philosophy. He loved all of nature and, strangely enough, became one of the greatest amateur authorities on snakes. Even after arthritis crippled him so that he could hardly use his hands, and a series of strokes confined him to a wheel chair, he could always think, and think he did. He became interested in astronomy and studied the heavens from his wheel chair.

He was one of the finest conversationalists I ever knew and discussed the greatest questions with charming wit and inspiration. People loved to sit at his feet and listen. He put the touch of glory on everything he handled intellectually.

Finally, the day came when a new stroke took away his speech and he could no longer form words. The last thing he ever said to me was, "I am studying heaven. Scientists say, 'It's in the Milky Way . . .' Tonight, look at the Milky Way."

Following his death the doctor came from the room and said, "The light of reason was in his eyes until I closed them." How my father would like that statement. Charles Clifford Peale lifted himself above his physical difficulties by a mighty upthrust of courage and spirit and mental alertness and faith. And it was that which kept him alive for twenty years past his time, as the doctor of medicine declared.

Crippling limitations of pain could not dim the happiness that welled up in him. He lived alertly in the mind and in the spirit and in the soul, and so life never lost its fascination for him. He genuinely loved and was interested in every kind of person. Crippled though he was, he was alive to the very moment of his physical life's ending and I believe that he still lives, passing from life unto death, but to life again, because within his glorious personality he was always alive. He found the answer to the deepest desire of the human spirit which is life that triumphs over all difficulties.

To have dynamic life it is also necessary to make provision for adequate intake of inspiration. Inspiration is as necessary to your well-being as is food and drink. Without it life may of course be maintained, but it will lack the motivation that gives it meaning. Your aliveness may be determined by the degree to which inspiration is present in your mind.

The relation of inspiration to well-being is illustrated by a case in which a physician asked a pastor to see a patient of his. The doctor explained that this patient had been complaining of having no life or zest. His enthusiasm had vanished; he "just didn't feel good."

The doctor stated that he had made the usual tests, finding nothing physically wrong; yet the man continued to complain that he felt badly. It was at this point that the physician telephoned the pastor to enlist his aid.

"Really, I have no medicine to prescribe and surgery is not indicated. But you and I know that men get sick in spirit and depressed feelings can often manifest themselves in bodily ailments. I suggest that you give this man a good shot of inspiration. Give him an injection in the spirit. Get his soul toned up. Inspiration," concluded the doctor, "means to be in-spirited, or to have spirit put into you. And since spirit actually is life, without it this man cannot be well and vigorous."

Over a period of time the minister was able to get the man reinspired by teaching him to pray and to master creative faith. The doctor telephoned some weeks later saying, "The patient is much improved. It just shows what a good shot of inspiration will do."

Your supply of inspiration may indicate how healthy, how dynamic, how vital you are. Real inspiration is a widespread need of people today. So many have no lift or buoyancy of spirit. If this is true of you, possibly your lack of inspiration may very well explain your lack of satisfaction with life.

How do you get this re-creative inspiration? Of course travel, music, art, stimulating friends, and good books contribute to inspirational living. Perhaps nature, in all its varying moods, is second only to the spiritual as a source of life-stimulating inspiration. At least it affects me in that way and at this very moment I am receiving a good "shot" of inspiration.

I am writing these lines at midnight far above the Arctic Circle. Our ship is passing among the amazingly beautiful fjords of Norway. Though the hour is nearly one o'clock in the morning it is as bright as mid-afternoon. I have never seen anywhere such a dramatic demonstration of light and beauty. It is incredible, unbelievable. The nearby and far off mountain peaks are covered with snow and there rests upon them ethereal and unearthly light. Drifting clouds of soft blue-gray are rifted here and there by lighter pastel shades, soft colors made by the reflection of a midnight sun. As far as the eye can see, in a great encompassing circle, loom enormous giants of mountains, eternal bastions of rock, pushed up long ago from these vast seas here at the top of the world.

One wonders at such a time and place and in the presence of such beauty if, in a deep and inexpressible sense, this may not be a basic meaning of life itself. Perhaps the ultimate end of human existence is in being able to respond to the beauty, the everlasting peace, the glorious wonderment of the mystic world itself.

Nature provides inspiration, not only in such magnificent and tremendous demonstrations of beauty as I see this mid-June night in the Arctic, but as is also portrayed in some quiet meadow in New York State or in Ohio or in the deep South. But in whatever form we may find it, a purpose of inspiration is to stimulate us to greater living. Thus the objective of inspiration is to assist in overcoming your weakness, your sickness, and your inner conflicts.

The fundamental meaning of life, then, is to learn how to live. And that is possible only by finding God, for God alone can satisfy your deepest desire. As Augustine said, "Our souls are restless until at length they rest in Thee." And Tolstoy, who tried everything in his restless search for inner peace, at last found the answer which he expressed in these words, "To know God is to live."

Dr. Viktor Frankl, Professor of Psychiatry at the University of Vienna, told me that many in Europe today are ill simply because life has no deep meaning for them. That is no less true in our country, also. Dr. Frankl practices what he calls "logo-therapy," healing by God. He feels that many unhappy, dissatisfied people can be healed by finding life through God-centered thinking. God is the source of vital life, declares this famous psychiatrist.

We may not realize that God is our deepest desire. I have seen many men unhappily and restlessly, even blunderingly, search for their basic desire, looking for it in the wrong places and therefore missing it until, finally, they did find it in God. That is the reason God has become so popular now-a-days, and that is why churches are packed to capacity. That also explains why millions are reading religious and inspirational literature. This restless longing for God, this desire for life, has stimulated the great spiritual resurgence of modern times.

I was scheduled to speak before a convention of business men. The man who served as my host was one of the most extraverted, thoroughly outgoing, and likeable individuals I had met in many a day. Extremely popular with everybody, he radiated happiness, geniality, and a definitely dynamic quality.

Something I said in my speech got him to talking and he said, "I was a restless, dissatisfied, and very unhappy man. I haunted doctors' offices because it constantly seemed that something was wrong with me, or at least I was afraid it was. If an associate developed any kind of sickness I contracted the same thing, in my mind, at least, and would rush to the doctor.

"I guess I was sick psychologically as well as spiritually and I was really low in spirit. I got drunk a great deal and lived a pretty wild life, I must admit. I see now that, actually, I was trying to find a way out of my misery and I tried every angle. Of course, I was going at it in the wrong way so I felt no better and got no answers.

"Then, a young minister, a regular fellow, came to our community and I liked him immensely. He was an old college football star and a real athlete and a man's man in every respect. We played golf together and his game was every bit as good as mine, maybe better. After a game we would go to the clubhouse and I would start drinking again.

"The minister stuck with me, however, for I think he really liked me. Presently, I got so I could talk with him in plain language, and I poured out all my conflicts. And believe me, brother, there were plenty of them.

"One afternoon, coming back from the country club, the minister was driving and he turned out into the country. I asked where he was going.

" 'Oh, I want to drive out of town for a while,' " he replied vaguely.

"Presently he stopped beside the road and turned off the engine. He looked at me and said, 'Bill, I have listened to you for a long time and I have been studying you and I am going to give it to you straight. I can tell you how to find what you are looking for, how to get over your conflicts, how, really, to be something and somebody.'

" 'The trouble, Bill, is that you're fighting God. You are a smart man and you should know that what you want, down deep, is God. If you don't know it, I'm telling you now. I think you will find it out if you are honest about it. And I know you will be that, for I've always found you a square shooter. If you will quit fighting God and let Him come into your life, He will solve your conflicts, He will bring your divided personality together and give you peace and health and happiness. He will make you one of the greatest fellows who ever served Him.'

"I laughed when he said that, but I got to thinking about what he told me. I thought about it for several days and decided he was right. That minister helped me to find God."

I was deeply moved by the way that man looked at me when he said, "Everything that minister promised that God would do for me He has done. And now I am trying to do something for God. At last, I have what I really wanted all along."

He had, at last, discovered how to live.

❖ ❖ ❖

Eight Rules for Keeping Vital

1. Admit that you want to feel wholly alive. Everyone does.
2. Realize that life is full of the overcoming of sorrow and trouble.
3. Get outside of yourself.
4. Live in the present.
5. Put animation into your daily work.
6. Seek inspiration: in books, friends, music, art, travel.
7. Interest is a measure of aliveness.
8. "To know God is to live."

CHAPTER VII

STOP BEING TIRED—LIVE ENERGETICALLY

"A constant flow of energy develops when you hold such thoughts as hopefulness, confidence, positiveness, and good will. When your mind is dominated by thoughts of this character, a high level of vigor results."

An advertisement pictured a man of about fifty years, slumped in a chair, head in hands, face showing abject despondency. The caption read: "Have You That Gray Sickness—Half Awake, Half Asleep—Half Alive, Half Dead?"

A pathetic aspect of life today is the astonishing number of tired and weary people. Many give the impression of crawling through life on their hands and knees.

But you can live without tiredness or fatigue. You can maintain energy and vitality. Surely our Creator meant us to live with continuous vigor, for the entire universe is charged with renewable energy. Since energy maintains itself steadily in the natural world, we must believe it was also meant to do the same in your life and mine.

In my house are two clocks. One is an eight-day type which I wind every Saturday night. But there are some Saturdays when I forget, or am away, and on Monday or Tuesday it stops. The other clock is electric, and because it is attached to the continuing energy in the universe it never runs down.

You can attach yourself to the continuous flow of God-powered energy through definite techniques of faith, right thinking, and sensible living. By such practice you may possess an unbroken supply of energetic force and never suffer from the "Gray Sickness."

A prominent personality returned to his boyhood home to find relief from heavy burdens and there took his life, in a sad ending to a notable career. An editorial writer, in commenting, said, "He was a tired man. He went home to rest, but apparently had forgotten how to rest." Then the writer added, "Unhappily, many of us seem to be in the same pathetic situation. We do not know how to rest."

Indeed it seems that many have no snap, no verve, no vibrancy. The CDT's have them in their grip; Cares, Difficulties, Troubles. The conflicts and confusions of the world have seemingly invaded their minds. Such people are tired, weary, and even old before their time. They need to be connected to the illimitable energy-renewing power in God's universe.

A method for doing this is illustrated by an experience in a Midwestern city. In a shoe shining parlor I noticed that the chairs were more comfortable than such places usually offer their patrons. A man entered and, with a sigh, sank down beside me. "I don't particularly need a shine," he said, "but I get so tried that I come here now and then to rest in these easy chairs."

He was a friendly-looking man of early middle age, so I said, "You shouldn't be tired, a young man of your age."

"Oh, I'm not so young," he said. "I'm fifty-three." Then he added, "I sometimes wonder whether I know how to rest. Do you?"

We discussed the subject and presently left the place together. Standing outside, as we continued the conversation, I said, "May I give you a suggestion about resting? Please don't think I'm a busy-body or trying to preach to you, but really I do not think you are tired in your feet. Your weariness is probably centered in your mind. So the cure is to refresh and re-stimulate your thoughts. One simple technique is to repeat to yourself a half-dozen times every day, until it deeply penetrates your consciousness, the familiar Bible passage: 'But they that wait upon the Lord shall renew their strength; they shall mount up with wings as eagles; they shall run, and not be weary; they shall walk, and not faint.' (Isaiah 40:31) And there is another: 'My presence shall go with thee, and I will give thee rest.'" (Exodus 33:14)

"I know the first one," he commented, "but am unfamiliar with the second."

I repeated it. He thanked me and, watching him walk away, I felt that I could see him straighten up. He turned, smiled, waved to me, and disappeared into the crowd. I never saw him again. Perhaps I never shall. No doubt he wonders who gave him such curious medicine; but I was merely acting as an agent of the Great Physician, who teaches that we do not need to be weary or suffer fatigue, that we can have continuous energy of body, mind, and soul.

We are at last realizing that health and religion, scientifically used, are closely related. We are now learning the important truth that one's physical condition is determined to a considerable extent by his emotional and spiritual condition. The emotional life is very profoundly regulated by our thought pattern. Hitherto, people have rather generally accepted the notion, long current, that at middle age vital energies must begin to decline, and that one must thereafter carefully conserve himself in order to keep going until his older years. We have more or less passively accepted the inevitability of aches and pains and general deterioration which advancing years are expected to bring upon us. Sometimes, with a kind of pious attitude, we have ascribed these physical conditions to God's will, accepting a state of decline with resignation.

Personally, I do not believe this point of view is valid. It is my conviction that we can go on living with aliveness, and the secret of so doing lies in a dynamic religious philosophy. The outstanding concept of the Bible is "life." Jesus said, "I am come that they might have life, and that they might have it more abundantly." (John 10:10) If you fully practice the creative and recreative principles of Christianity you can live with vitality long past the period of life when energy is supposed to have gone by.

Have you not observed some people who live to a great age, but still have adequate energy and impressive vital force? How are they able to overcome deterioration? Their sustained vigor is simply because they have achieved harmony with the basic sources of vitality and energy, having adapted their thought patterns to dynamic faith and enthusiasm. They have demonstrated that by eliminating hate, worry, and tension, and by the application of simple rules of hygiene and mental health, they can avoid tiredness and have continuous energy.

The secret of a continuous power-flow is in adjusting yourself to God's controlled pace and tempo. Synchronize your thinking and living with God's unhurried timing; God is in you, and if you go at one rate and God at another, you will tear yourself apart. The maintenance of energy, the absence of tiredness, depends upon being in the natural rhythm of God.

This identification of the personality with that even tempo and rhythm basically inherent in life is one of the surest ways of eliminating destructive fatigue. Constant excitation of the emotions, plus over-stimulation by hurry and hecticness, draws more heavily upon the supply of energy than our naturally stored-up resources can resupply. But when you synchronize yourself with the harmonious flow of energy at the normal rate at which it moves when measured in God's natural world, you will then be living on the emotional level which God intended. And when you do that you are not likely to break down. On the contrary, you will have steady power.

A woman executive had over-driven herself without regard to her diminishing energy supply. Her reserves depleted, she was unable to fight off an infection. Due to lack of physical recuperative resources she was forced to leave her work for a lengthy period of convalescence.

She went to Daytona Beach, Florida, and it became her habit, every day, to go to a quiet spot on the beach and lie on the warm sands in the sunshine. After some days of this relaxation, she began to notice a curious phenomenon. From where she lay she idly watched the beach grass waving gracefully in the gentle breeze. One day her eyes chanced to single out one particular blade of grass and she was struck by the fact that it seemed to sway in a definitely rhythmic movement. She found herself beating this rhythm as one follows a musical score.

Presently, as she listened to the roaring of the surf upon the sand, she became aware that it, too, had a rhythm, and that, though on a different level, it was essentially at the same rate as the waving of the beach grass. This curious discovery fascinated her and she found herself looking and listening for rhythm in the natural world about her. As she lay with her ear close to the ground to pick up its low-keyed, harmonious sounds, she became aware of an easy but continuous flow of rhythmic energy throughout all life.

The climax of this recuperative experience came, however, the day she happened to detect her own heart beat. She became fascinated in feeling it throb as she lay with her ear in a certain position on the sand. In one illuminating moment the realization came to her that the rhythm of her heart beat was at one with the rhythm of the waving beach grass and the surging sea and the myriad sounds all about her. She experienced the electrifying consciousness that she was identified with the rhythmic and harmonious flow of nature itself. She sensed, as never before, her personal harmony with the energy of Almighty God, who is the source of all creative and re-creative power.

This was followed by the exhilarating and comforting realization that hereafter, if she kept herself steadily in harmony with the tempo and the time-beat of God, she could work and produce and carry heavy responsibilities without loss of energy. In this experience she discovered the priceless secret that when one lives at God's tempo he need not be tired and can have all the energy his responsibilities require.

If you inharmoniously build up stresses, you are bound to lose power and energy. But, by living in harmonious rhythm, you reduce stress and automatically renew energy and vitality. So, "They that wait upon the Lord"—that is, accommodate to the basic pace of life, shall indeed "renew their strength" and remain energetic. To know what this "basic pace" is, live with God in the mind awhile and you will find it.

And never forget that continuing energy is exceedingly important to your success in life. Emerson says, "The world belongs to the energetic." Keep that truth in mind as you study men, or read history. Achievement and usefulness do indeed belong to those who keep alert and vital through long years. And remember always the important fact that the truly energetic are those who have disciplined their minds to avoid conflict and stress. And they have also learned to keep their thinking zestful and enthusiastic.

We must realize that much, perhaps most, tiredness originates in the mind. We become tired when our thoughts tire. If you wish to maintain energy it is a dangerous practice to complain, using such statements as: "I am tired; I have too much to do; I am swamped; I am worn out." Such weariness-thinking and negative-affirming tends to transmit itself to the subconscious mind and actually reproduces itself in tired reactions.

The muscular organization of the body has much more potential resiliency than we realize. An experiment was made in which an arm muscle was blocked off from the brain impulse. That muscle was then stimulated for several consecutive hours and continued to react without any evidence of tiredness, demonstrating that muscles can continue functioning almost indefinitely. The nerve block was presently removed and the patient was then told that the arm was tired. This suggestion rather quickly took affect. The muscle itself began to feel tired and presently ceased to function with the same tone.

An authority on the heart is reported to have said that "the toughest muscle we have is the heart muscle. During a normal lifetime it produces enough energy to lift a battleship fourteen feet out of water." But even the heart muscle can lose its resiliency and suffer loss of effectiveness through the destructive power of wrong thinking. Fear, resentment, fretting, frustration, tension—all such unhealthy thoughts, if long held, have repeatedly demonstrated their ability to undermine the vast strength of this most powerful muscle, with disastrous results.

We must emphasize, as previously stated, that much tiredness, perhaps the major part, originates in the thoughts. But a constant flow of energy develops when you hold the type of thoughts which feed and supply vitality; such thoughts as hopefulness, confidence, positiveness, and good will. When your mind is dominated by thoughts of this character, then re-creative forces are stimulated by the spiritual harmony they develop. A high level of vigor results.

Generally speaking, fatigue is not caused by work, even by what we think of as overwork. When men break down from what they call "overwork," the real cause is likely to be the result of extra heavy weight on the emotional-spiritual mechanism; burdens such as anxiety, grudges, or tension. Such fatigue is more often the result of a let-down or sagging of the thought-tone. If your mind holds a picture of yourself as tired it will not be long before your muscles and nerves will accept the thought. They, too, will become tired. The mind will have effectively transmitted a concept of fatigue to the muscles.

You can demonstrate this to yourself by observing how an infusion of some new and overwhelming interest into your thoughts can suddenly dissipate weariness and give you new feelings of energy and aliveness. A friend who has a sixteen-year-old boy wanted to raise his son in the traditional American fashion of making him get out and work. So, at the father's insistence, the boy unenthusiastically got a job in an industrial plant for the summer vacation, his working hours being from eight o'clock in the morning until four in the afternoon.

One evening, when the boy came dragging wearily home from a job which did not interest him and against which he was mentally resisting, his father said, "Bill, the grass needs mowing, and will you please do it right away."

"Oh, gee, Dad," the boy protested, "I worked hard in the plant all day long. I'm just about ready to drop. I'm all in."

"I'm sorry, son," said the father. "But if you don't mow the grass I'll have to, and I'm sure you don't want to see your poor, old father struggling around that lawn, do you?" So the boy plodded wearily along at the grassmowing job, building up the thought that it was an overwhelming task. His tiredness deepened as a result.

Presently a vision of loveliness, also age sixteen, appeared, carrying a golf bag. "Come on, Bill," she said, "let's have a game."

Suddenly Bill was galvanized into energy. "Just wait until I finish mowing this grass," he replied; and he did that lawn in nothing flat. He played golf until dark, missed his supper, and then danced until midnight. Obviously Bill's muscles were not really tired. It was only in his thinking that he was fatigued. When an interest seized his mind that was stronger than the tired ideas, his body responded, since it was filled with potential energy that was not being used.

A mother who had worked hard all day sank into bed, groaning, "I'm so tired my bones ache." She fell into a deep sleep. But in the night her youngest child cried piteously. She rushed to the crib, found its face burning with fever, and called the doctor. She sat by the child throughout that entire night, showing no evidence of tiredness, until finally the crisis passed. Her muscles had been tired, but even more tired had been her mind. When consuming interest seized her mind, her body became alive and alert.

Of course, there is such a condition as healthy, physical tiredness. After working hard all day to fall into bed and sleep gives a delicious sense of rest. That is plain, normal, healthy tiredness from physical effort. A night's rest will restore energy in such cases. There is also a tiredness that may arise from physical illness. To cure this is the function of the doctor of medicine. But there is also a deep fatigue that is mental or emotional in origin, and for this there is another form of "medicine."

Manifestly, this refers to no concoction in a bottle or in the form of a pill. It is rather a medicine in the form of right thinking and right living. It is the freeing of the mind from unhealthy attitudes. Of course it stresses the giving of healthy treatment to the physical body, but primarily this medicine is the constant intake of creative energy through prayer, faith, good will, and selflessness. It is the positive affirmation of God's activity in the re-creative process.

Practice daily the dynamic principle described in the words, "For in Him we live, and move, and have our being." (Acts 17:28) Hold the belief that, since God created you, He is continually re-creating you as well. The identification of yourself with God, pictured in the Scripture statement, means that you may actually live in His vast energy. This explains why the most genuine and wholesome Christians are so vibrantly alive.

This is a practical and powerful law of vitality. Use it and you will be surprised by the manner in which your vigor and energy are stimulated. The use of spiritual techniques will also help you to eliminate overdrive, overworry, overpressure. And, of course, you cannot have real energy unless they are eliminated.

In this process it is important to practice thinking *alive* thoughts. By conditioning your mind with thoughts of aliveness you tend, actually, to be alive. The more you do this the more alive you will feel.

Think tiredness, affirm tiredness, and presently you will become tired. Think energy, affirm energy, and gradually you will come alive. Alive thinking reproduces itself in aliveness. And the more you demonstrate aliveness, the more energy and vitality you will have.

When your mind shifts into a vitalized pattern of thinking, it starts at once casting off debilitating thoughts such as fear, hate, and other conflicted attitudes. As they empty out, thoughts of zest and enthusiasm surge in to take their place. In this way tiredness is arrested and a definite re-energizing takes place.

The eager, zestful mind does not become tired in the sense of becoming fatigued. Therefore avoid growing tired in your thoughts and attitudes. Keep your interest and eagerness in every aspect of life at a high level. The tonic effect of so doing will be felt in definitely increased vitality, both of mind and body.

I cannot stress too strongly the importance of a daily emptying out of all tired thoughts and a deliberate day-to-day filling of the mind with fresh, dynamic concepts. A specific time should be set aside every twenty-four hours for this mind-drainage or mind-emptying process. Personally, I use a fifteen-minute period at retiring time. My own method is to empty the mind, even as I empty my pockets before hanging up my suit of clothes. Another way of expressing it is to undress your mind even as you undress your body. You would not jump into bed with your clothes on. But many people go to bed with their minds full of unhappy stuff, and wonder why their sleep is restless and why they are tired the next day.

A tailor once suggested that clothes will look better and last longer if all articles are removed from the pockets at night. Therefore, before retiring I empty my pockets of items such as knife, pencils, money, memoranda, and arrange all of them neatly on the dresser. I drop into a wastebasket as many as possible of the slips of paper, memos, and various accumulated items. This act gives a sense of things finished and their disposal removes the burden of them from my mind.

It occurred to me one night, while in the process of pocket-emptying, that it might be beneficial to "empty" the mind as I empty my pockets. Throughout the day we tend to pick up a miscellaneous collection of irritations, regrets, resentments, and anxieties. If permitted to accumulate, these clutter the mind and become a disturbing factor in consciousness. I developed an imaginative process whereby I visualized "dropping" these mental impedimenta into an imaginary wastebasket. This gives a sense of relief from mental burdens, and makes it easier to go to sleep. The mind, being thus relieved of energy-depleting factors, is able to relax and enjoy restful renewal.

This procedure helps me to awaken refreshed and with energy replenished. This technique has also worked in similar fashion for many to whom I have suggested its use. Since it tends to remove strain and stress from the mind, it has proved generally effective in reducing tiredness. It has proved to be an efficient method for draining off the poisons of fatigue and for maintaining a high level of vitality.

As to the filling of the mind with dynamic concepts, the practical program for maintaining continuous energy suggested by my friend the late Lawrence Townsend is extraordinarily effective. Lawrence Townsend was one of the healthiest, happiest, least-old, old men I ever knew. At ninety-one he stood lithe and straight and was quite muscular. He never required glasses. He was vigorous, witty, and alert until almost the day of his triumphant departure to the other side, where surely he is having a wonderful time, even as he did here.

He had a distinguished career in the United States foreign service, at one time serving as Minister to Austria. He and his wife were intimate friends of leading figures in many countries. They were frequent guests of Their Majesties, the late King George V and Queen Mary.

Lawrence Townsend stands out in my memory as one of the greatest demonstrations of continuing energy I have ever known. He ate heartily, yet made it a policy to leave the table with an "unstuffed" feeling. He took a balanced diet with minor emphasis on sweets and starches, and extra stress on fruit and vegetables.

He retired early at night but made no fetish of this any more than of diet. If he wanted to stay up later, he did so, but he believed in the old truism, "Early to bed, early to rise, makes a man healthy, (perhaps) wealthy, and (certainly) wise." He arose early and took setting-up exercises, followed by a stimulating bath and brisk rubdown, administered with a rough towel. He then spent fifteen minutes reading the Bible together with selections from inspirational writings. Having washed his body, he declared it an equally important health principle to "wash" the mind and soul.

He spent some part of each day working with his hands. He was a rather expert carpenter and cabinet maker. He believed in "the therapy of handwork," holding to the view that such activity, employing as it does brain centers and muscles other than those commonly used in sedentary work, relieves strain and pressure. Also, he found that preoccupation with such occupational therapy tends to reduce anxiety, which he regarded as a most insidious, tiring factor.

At some time during the day, weather permitting, it was Mr. Townsend's habit to retire to a sun house, which he had personally constructed. In this roofless structure he would disrobe and take a series of physical exercises, followed by a sun bath and a period of relaxation. Then he practiced "emptying" his mind of all "thought poisons," following which he "poured" into his mind the healthiest, happiest, and most dynamic thoughts he could assemble.

Standing tall in the sunlight, he voiced aloud the following creative affirmation, and conceived of that which he affirmed as happening, even as he spoke: "I breathe in pure, beautiful, positive thoughts of God and Jesus Christ, which entirely fill my conscious and superconscious mind, to the total elimination of all negative, impure, enviable, uncharitable thoughts of hatred and malice, which, with God's help, I dismiss completely from my conscious, unconscious, and superconscious mind."

While Mr. Townsend's program and method may seem a bit extraordinary, yet his conquest of the aging process, and his amazing energy at ninety-one years of age, demonstrated conclusively the validity of his method. I have suggested his technique in many speeches and radio talks and not a few persons have practiced it with excellent results. I have myself made use of Mr. Townsend's re-creative technique and feel certain that, if you will practice it, and persevere, you, too, can develop energy and vitality greater than you have ever previously experienced. If you are willing to pay the disciplinary cost required, you can, I believe, master tiredness.

Another treatment is to utilize fractional moments of busy days to prevent "fatigue pockets" from forming in the mind. A good method is to vocalize energy-insinuating Scripture passages while driving your car, waiting for a bus, or in any interim period. While doing this, hold a mental image of those creatively spiritual truths as activating an unhindered energy flow. This plan, followed over a period of time, will tend to prevent old, worn, tired attitudes from forming unhealthy mental deposits in the personality. Some physicians have suggested that such unhealthy thought accumulations may cause actual physiological changes which can adversely affect your general health condition.

Of course, a final technique for eliminating tiredness and living with continuous energy is to learn how to throw off responsibility and enjoy untroubled sleep. This is a skill which can be learned. One man who complained of being a poor sleeper came to our clinic for counseling. His daily and nightly habits were analyzed and it was discovered that, after he retired, it was his custom to take pad and pencil and make a series of notes about what he was going to do the next day.

He planned out tomorrow, making an outline of each matter he expected to handle, and prided himself on this "efficiency" method, regarding it as a unique procedure. He kept a pad and pencil on his night table and would often reach for them in the darkness, adding additional memos that his restless mind supplied. He related with pride how he had mastered the skill of writing legibly in the darkness.

Oftentimes, upon awakening in the morning, he would find numerous memos which he had made during the night.

Why couldn't he sleep? Why was he tired all day? Simply because he was taking tomorrow to bed with him. We, too, believe in efficiency. We respect the principle of "Plan your work and work your plan," but there is a time and place for all things; and in bed, ready to go to sleep, is certainly not the time to plan the next day. In fact, if you are going to bed at eleven o'clock it is not efficient to do any tomorrow-planning later than nine o'clock. Do no planning later than eight P.M. if you are going to retire at ten o'clock. This interval of two hours will give the plans time to pass from the surface of the mind, where they agitate, to the deeper levels, where they become creative.

If, in your sleeplessness, apprehensions of the next day disturb you, simply remind yourself that God has helped you through every day you have lived heretofore, and that tomorrow will be no exception. Slowly repeat aloud the following lines of an old and familiar hymn, "So long Thy power hath blest me, sure, it still will lead me on." This will convince your unconscious of God's continuing care, and a comforting, relaxed feeling will come. Go to sleep using the conscious thought and affirmation that whatever you may be called upon to handle the next day God and you will be able to do together.

The secret, then, of continuous energy is, through whatever techniques serve you best, to "empty" the mind of thoughts and attitudes which cause tiredness. Then go on to complete the renewal process by "filling" the mind with such thoughts as will channel in to you the re-creative energy of God's dynamic universe.

❖ ❖ ❖

Following are some suggestions for overcoming tired feelings and maintaining energy:

1. Through your thought and faith, keep attached to God, the source of all energy.
2. Avoid the gray sickness: half awake, half asleep; half alive, half dead.
3. Realize that energy sags when your thoughts sag, so vigilantly keep your thinking alert.
4. Think of yourself as a child of God, a constant recipient of His gifts of boundless health, energy, and vitality.
5. Avoid the concepts of "growing old and feeble." Picture the youthfulness of your spirit as resisting the aging process.
6. Empty your mind every night as you empty your pockets. Before going to bed forgive everybody, naming those forgiven. Leave the past in the past, and believe that God watches over you as you sleep.
7. Slow down and keep the even rhythm of God.
8. Train your mind to block off worry and frustration, two attitudes which siphon off energy.
9. Affirm that God's constantly renewing energy flows through your being giving you sufficient vitality to live effectively.

CHAPTER VIII

LEARN FROM MISTAKES—AND MAKE FEWER

"It has been said that history turns on small hinges. So do peoples' lives. Over a period of time you make a series of decisions, each seemingly of little consequence. Yet, the total of these decisions finally determines the outcome of your life. A successful life depends upon developing a higher percentage of wisdom than error."

THE YOUNG MAN slumped in my office chair. "What's the use?" he said dejectedly. "I'm a flop. Once I had lots of hopes and plans, but that's a laugh now. Everything has gone haywire for me. I've flubbed everything by my stupid mistakes. Nobody will ever believe in me now." So ran his slangy defeatism. He fell silent, then sighed, "And that isn't the worst of it, I guess I've lost faith in myself."

At twenty-nine he had been dropped from a good firm for making a serious mistake in a responsibility assigned him.

"Why did I do it?" he cried in miserable futility. "I had the chance of a lifetime with that firm. I've blown the best opportunity I will ever have. Why did I do such a stupid thing? What's the matter with me?"

"Better fall back on the old philosophy," I reminded him, "and, 'Don't cry over spilt milk.'"

Who doesn't make mistakes! But the greatest error of all is to let any mistake destroy your faith in yourself. The only sensible course is to study and analyze why you made the mistake. Learn all you can from it, then forget it and go ahead. Figure on doing better next time.

It is very important, in life, to learn how to make fewer mistakes. For example, I told this young man about that day, years ago, when a rookie batter just up from the Minor Leagues, made three extra-base hits off the great pitcher, Christy Mathewson. The young player was elated; he had all but knocked the old master from the box. As he strode triumphantly to the club house after the game, a veteran player fell into step alongside him. "Did you carefully notice what balls Christy threw you?" he asked.

"Oh, no," flippantly replied the youngster. "I paid no attention. I just hit 'em."

"Well," replied the other, "you can be sure Christy will remember. He made a mistake in the pitches he gave you today, but he won't make that same mistake again. He'll remember, and he won't let today's bad time get him down, either."

According to the story that batter never again got an extra-base hit off Mathewson. The famed pitcher carefully analyzed his mistakes and learned profitable lessons from them. Perhaps his technique for dealing with mistakes helped build his amazing career.

I made another suggestion to this young man who, because he had made a mistake and lost a good opportunity, was so deeply discouraged. I told him that years ago I was a newspaper reporter for an outstanding editor, my old friend, the late Grove Patterson of the *Toledo Blade*. Mr.

Patterson's editorials were human and kindly and wise. I happened to have one of them on my desk and read it to this dejected young man.

The editorial is called "Water Under the Bridge," and here are a few lines from it. "A boy, a long time ago, leaned against the railing of a bridge and watched the current of the river below. A log, a bit of driftwood, a chip floated past. Again the surface of the river was smooth. But always, as it had for a hundred, perhaps a thousand, perhaps a million years, the water slipped by, under the bridge. Sometimes the current went more swiftly, and again quite slowly. But always the river flowed on, under the bridge.

"Watching the river that day the boy made a discovery. It was not the discovery of a material thing, something he might put his hand upon. He could not even see it. He had discovered an idea. Quite suddenly, and yet quietly, he knew that everything in his life would some day pass under the bridge and be gone, like water. And the boy came to like those words, 'under the bridge.'

"All his life, thereafter, the idea served him well and carried him through, although there were days and ways that were dark and not easy. Always, when he had made a mistake that couldn't be helped, or lost something that could never come again, the boy, now a man, said: 'It's water under the bridge.'

"And he didn't worry, unduly, about the mistakes after that, and he certainly didn't let them get him down—because it was water under the bridge."

When I finished reading that sensible piece the young man sat silently, lost in deep thought. Finally, he pulled himself erect. "O. K." he said, and there was a new tone in his voice. "I get the idea—one mistake or a dozen mistakes can't lick me. I'll get it back—my faith in myself." I am glad to report that he successfully wove that mistake into the pattern of his very useful life.

In dealing with a mistake tendency which can plague you and get you into a lot of trouble, it helps to develop the psychology of rightness. Much error content can build up in the mind; but it is also possible to build up a rightness content. Two powerful forces are truth and error. These are constantly at war with each other, both in society and in the individual. If your mind is filled with error, then error tends to become assertive. If permitted to dominate, naturally, it will cause you to perform error. You will think incorrectly, will get the wrong slant, arrive at wrong conclusions, and make wrong decisions. Your net result will be a general, over-all mistake pattern.

If, on the contrary, your mind is filled with truth, you will be conditioned by rightness. You will have correct slants, will reduce the mistake average, and things will tend to come out right. It is as simple as that. The matter seems well expressed in a passage from the Scriptures: "And ye shall know the truth, and the truth shall make you free." (John 8:32) And, indeed, the truth will set you free from many things, including the psychology of error.

The error tendency occasionally erupts in seemingly abnormal ways into the orderly, conscious mind. Sometimes we are driven by deep impulses which we do not understand and which, actually, are shrewd attempts of our own unconscious to hurt us. One of these impulses may be the will to fail, the strange desire to inflict punishment on oneself for perhaps a guilt feeling or some other inner conflict. It is difficult for the rational, conscious mind to accept such "queer" doings as a plausible explanation of the mistakes we make, but we must realize that the unconscious mind often acts in a seemingly irrational manner, though actually it is not irrational.

A factory manager consulted our counseling clinic about a girl employee who had started making mistakes in operating a rather complicated machine. No other worker on a similar machine had such accidents, and previously this girl had been a precise and accurate operator. In studying the problem we made an investigation of the home situation and discovered that the young woman lived with her elderly father, a querulous, whining, demanding old man. He allowed his daughter no social activity, apparently wanting her entirely at his service. He was filled with the acids of self-pity and constantly reminded her of "all I did for you as a child," insisting that "it is your turn to do something for me."

She served his breakfast and prepared his lunch before going to work. Upon returning from the plant she did the breakfast and lunch dishes in addition to getting dinner. The father indolently sat around all day, never turning a hand. Throughout the evening he complained and criticized. The girl became very resentful and increasingly had the thought of escape. Then, the fact that she entertained such thoughts which she construed as disloyal, gave her a feeling of guilt. The guilt feeling created a conflict.

Finally, her subconscious transmitted to her conscious mind, in effect, the message, "I will come to your aid. I will get you out of this." The mistakes her fingers performed, as she worked at her machine, actually resulted from the effort of the subconscious to injure her and thus free her from an intolerable situation. The mistakes made by this young woman came from inner conflict, a mixture of guilt, resentment, and frustration.

Our psychiatrists explained this psychological mechanism to her. She was shown how to take an objective and dispassionate attitude toward her father. Insight was given into her own reactions and her father's as well. She was encouraged to be firm and kindly, yet to be master of her own life.

She had become rather dowdy in appearance. Our counselor suggested such obvious improvements as neater dress, a hair-do, and a facial. Then she was urged to join an active young adult group in the church.

Some weeks passed and, as she became a happier person, the mistakes ceased, and her former efficiency returned. She got on better with her fellow workers. In fact, within a year she met a young man at the church and they were married. Now they have a baby boy and the grandfather, who dotes on the child, has lost much of his self-pity. A more constructive life has come both to this father and daughter as they corrected the disturbed psychological status of their lives.

One of the best correctives of destructive error tendencies is simply to increase your spiritual understanding. This builds up truth and reduces the error content in your mind. Daily saturate your thoughts with the power-packed faith of the Bible. Develop effectiveness in prayer. Learn the art of spiritual meditation. Subject every question to spiritual testing and make no decisions that do not jibe with the best ethical insight.

One specific method for eliminating error and bringing truth into a practical situation was taught me by a hotel manager. When I registered at his hotel I was told by the clerk, "Our manager wishes to see you and has asked me to bring you to his office when you arrive." So, he sent my bags up to my room and I went into the manager's office.

"I have been waiting for you," he said. "I have a difficult problem to handle and want you with me while I decide it."

When he told me the nature of the problem, I said, "I'm sorry, that is entirely out of my field. And I don't believe in giving advice about something of which I know nothing."

"I don't want advice," he protested. "I want you to join me in bringing truth to bear on my problem. My technique for doing this is to empty my mind completely and let spiritual truth 'pour' into me." And he added, "I have discovered that this is always more effectively done when two persons whose minds are attuned pray together. Two empty minds," he explained, "furnish a better intake channel for truth." I let the "empty mind" reference pass and joined with interest.

At his direction we sat quietly and he prayed aloud, somewhat after this fashion. "Lord, we now empty our minds of all error, all preconceived notions, all misconceptions, all stupidity, all ineptness." He paused and we sat in silence for fully two or three minutes, conceiving of the mind-emptying process as taking place. Presently he continued. "We now fill our minds with truth. It is coming into our thoughts and taking possession of our minds. We are now receiving the right answer to our problem. Since we are being filled with truth we will get a true result." So went his very original affirmation.

Then he gave thanks for the help he felt he was then receiving. Concluding his prayer he declared, with absolute confidence, "The right answer will come."

I was astonished at this extraordinary technique, and awaited the result with interest. And the answer he got was a good one as subsequent results proved.

Upon concluding the error-emptying and the truth-filling process we again sat in silence for a minute or more. Finally he asked, "What answer did you get?"

I was a bit doubtful of whether I had "gotten" anything, but I did have the clear impression that I should ask this question, "Is the matter you have under consideration a right thing? Are you sure you are ethically sound in the proposition?"

It was a random shot, or at least I felt that it was, but I was later certain I did "get it." He gave me a queer look, a combination of embarrassment, and relief. "I was afraid you would say that, and yet I am glad for, frankly, I will have to admit that I have been trying to do a wrong thing. I have been attempting to tell myself it's O. K., but I see clearly that my mistake lies in always trying to do what I want to do rather than to discover what I ought to do, and then do that. That is the reason I have gone off the beam so many times. Now I clearly see the right course and will follow it."

I was so interested in the wisdom and practical value of this method of receiving guidance that I have practiced it myself. And the method holds up under testing.

"I have always had to deal with a tendency in myself to make mistakes," the hotel manager later explained. "I fumbled several excellent opportunities until, finally, I came to realize that these mistakes were coming from within my basic mental structure. In an effort to correct myself it occurred to me that the surest way to eliminate error would be to displace it with its contrary quality, truth. Then I began to seek for truth in an effort to change my mistake patterns. By experimentation I found that as I deepened my understanding of spiritual truth, I could actually reduce my mistake tendency. Now I am doing much better in my decisions, though, of course, I have much to learn. At any rate, my home-made method has proved a valuable formula," he concluded.

If you constantly fill your mind with rightness, seeking always to know God's guidance, your mistakes will decrease in number and importance, since your basic wrongness will be proportionally reduced. The following daily affirmation has proved helpful: "I am a medium for God's truth. God's rightness is now flowing into my mind. I am now developing perception and insight." Such affirmations stimulate a mental clean-up and help eliminate wrong thought patterns.

To perform with efficiency one must develop wisdom and skill in right thinking. The wisdom of God is perfect. Therefore, if you become a "medium" through which God's wisdom flows, you will receive guidance and direction that will amaze you. I believe we can actually bring the wisdom of God to bear upon our personal decisions and, in so doing, greatly reduce our mistakes.

Of course, there is a right and wrong way to do everything. There is a right and a wrong way to sing, a right and a wrong way to swing a golf club, a right and a wrong way to bake a pie. There is also a right and a wrong way to live. Living is a science, based on definite laws. If you do not cooperate with its laws life can go very badly. When you learn those laws and live within them your life will be wonderful.

A concrete suggestion for living in harmony with those laws is to spend not less than fifteen minutes every day applying selected spiritual thoughts to everything in your life that is not going well. By selected thoughts I mean the application of everything you know about prayer, about faith, and about God. In a spirit of prayerful sincerity bring these selected spiritual thoughts to bear upon your faults and errors. Repeat this process until you are thinking spiritually about the particular matter that needs improvement. This practice will modify your attitudes, making them increasingly right, which will tend to result in right outcomes.

People who habitually think about their daily problems according to God's laws will, in time, develop something of God's skill in solving those problems. Your former mistake tendency will then shift to an efficiency pattern of thinking and doing.

Thoughtful people today are definitely applying Christianity to personal, business, and social problems as the method best designed to develop the highest degree of effectiveness. And the motivation for this widespread spiritual practice is not a desire to get ahead or make money. Indeed, such a debased use of spiritual principles would surely defeat its purpose, being in itself the application of error. The vast number of people today who live by spiritual techniques are sincerely motivated by the urge to use their lives and abilities to the fullest extent in creative activity. God put into you the desire to amount to something and to be a vital factor in the world. Those who minimize the importance of making something of themselves actually do violence to the creative objectives of Almighty God.

A business man who has greatly reduced his mistakes always applies one simple test in arriving at a decision. "I simply ask myself, is it ethically right; is it absolutely fair to all concerned; is the decision based, not upon who is right, but upon what is right; and finally, will it do the most for the most?" This gentleman says, "Whether the problem relates to ten thousand dollars or ten dollars, unless what you do is honest, unselfish, and right it will not, in the long run, turn out right. And," he added, "more often than not, if it is wrong, it will not even be a long run."

Many people fail simply because they make too many wrong decisions. It has been said that history turns on small hinges. So do people's lives. Over a period of time you make a series of decisions, each seemingly of little consequence. Yet, the total of these decisions finally determines the outcome of your life. A successful life depends upon developing a higher percentage of wisdom than error. Then you will do fewer things wrong and more things right. In improving your right-decision percentage the knowledge of how to make a decision is very important. And more and more people are learning that the highest percentage of right decisions is attained when spiritual methods are employed.

There was a time when so-called practical people did not realize the importance of prayer, guidance, and insight in solving daily problems. But they have learned that there are subtleties and imponderables in every issue that may well be determinative in making decisions, and these can best be dealt with through spiritual procedures.

While vacationing at the beautiful Mountain View House at Whitefield, New Hampshire, a favorite retreat of mine, a man telephoned me long distance about a personal problem.

"I have a very important decision to make and cannot afford to make a mistake. Will you help me?" he asked.

When I inquired why he thought I could help he explained that he had read in a newspaper column of mine about a man who telephoned asking for help in making a decision, and that the decision turned out to be a good one.

"Evidently you told that other man the right thing to do. Now, I want you to tell me," he said.

"I cannot tell you what to do," I said. "I have no such wisdom. Every human being must make his own decisions. But what is the problem?"

"I am plant superintendent in a steel mill," he explained, "and have been offered the superintendency of a larger plant. Where I am now employed I have charge of personnel and that is my chief interest. In the plant which is offered me I would not be in charge of personnel, although there would be other advantages. But," he added, "I do not like the vice-president to whom I would have to report in that other organization. So, I am in a quandary."

"It seems," I said, "that a very important negative must be eliminated. You are holding a spirit of ill will toward the vice-president. To be sure of a right decision I suggest, first of all, that you definitely pray out this destructive negative. You can never get a positive answer when your mind is emphasizing a negative; so, you will need to pray it out. Also, never try to think with your emotions. The brain is for thinking, and only a cool and utterly rational thought and prayer process will bring about a right decision."

"That is a new angle to me, Doctor," he said. "I am not much of a religious person."

"Religion," I answered, "is a scientific methodology for thinking your way through problems. So let us apply to this decision the key to successful problem solving. First, pray and ask God definitely to reveal to you your own abilities and how best they can be used. Then, pray that all hate shall be taken from you. You must pray with an attitude of good will for that vice-president. Third, pray that you may receive God's guidance and believe that you will."

"But," he said, "I must make this decision by nine o'clock Monday morning."

"Today is only Thursday," I said. "That gives you four days to pray and get mentally conditioned to receive the truth. You must keep all nervous hecticness out of this matter."

"But the deadline for decision is coming fast," he reiterated, "it crowds me."

"Keep your thoughts off deadlines and practice being calm and relaxed. Pray for mental peace. Place your problem confidently in God's hands. Leave it there, with faith, and you will have your right decision Monday morning at nine o'clock."

I could hear him sigh. "It will give me high blood pressure to let it go that long," he complained.

"Don't worry," I counseled. "Practice the spiritual process of developing rightness and you will have your answer in time."

On Sunday I telephoned him, just to be sure he was doing all right.

"Yes," he said, "I am following your suggestions. But the answer has not yet come. How will I know when I have God's guidance?"

I told him of my friend, the late J. L. Kraft, famous cheese manufacturer, who said that he prayed about a matter until he felt that he had prayed enough. Then he believed that whatever came up in his mind and held there like a steady light was the answer to the problem prayed about.

Some days later a letter arrived from this man who had telephoned. "The answer came just as you said," he wrote. "Clear as a bell, I got it. I have accepted the other job. I talked with the vice-president in an open-minded attitude and I think we can get along O. K."

There was a sequel to this incident which suggests a subtle point in avoiding mistakes and making right decisions, and which underscores the importance of deciding things spiritually. There may be hidden in any decision the real end to which your life is being directed by higher wisdom. The alternatives which we face in any given decision may seem to be the whole question at issue, but frequently there is something else which does not show. And this something else can be the most important matter. If you could ascend to some great height which would afford a view of the whole future landscape of your life you could recognize and know the best things, and choose them. But since we cannot see very far ahead, we must take each step with all the wisdom we can muster, and have faith that we will do that which is right for us.

For example, the man who asked for advice over the telephone, and who received guidance through a practical spiritual formula, was more accurately directed than he realized. A later letter from him describes an unforeseen development that probably would not have materialized had he not followed the spiritual method for avoiding mistakes. I quote his letter in full.

> "Dear Dr. Peale: Perhaps you will recall my distressed phone call to you during the latter part of June when you were in Whitefield, New Hampshire. My company had offered me a change of job, which would have put me under the supervision of a man in whom I had no confidence. The new opportunities offered by this change were overshadowed by distinct disadvantages, and the decision was far from being clear-cut.
>
> "Your prayer with me over the phone did calm my anxiety considerably, but it was your return call on Sunday afternoon that gave me the help I needed. At that time I had

not yet reached a decision, but was feeling more composed than when we first talked. You stated that I should not become alarmed, but have complete faith that God would provide the right answer at the required time.

"Well, sir, it worked just that way. I called my boss on Monday morning and spoke quite freely. I accepted the new job, but told him I thought I should have my head examined because I liked the personnel work I had been doing, the people with whom I was working, the location, and the man I was reporting to. However, I felt that the new job had greater opportunities, and therefore I would accept it. His reply was 'That's interesting.'

"That was Monday. On Friday he called back and said that the remark I had made about liking personnel work came to mind when they were reviewing the problem of selecting someone to head a development group which would operate on the West Coast. Because this work would closely parallel that which I had been doing, they thought I would prefer it.

"I made a hurried trip to the West Coast for an interview, was accepted, and moved out here last month. It is a big job, but with God's help I know I can do it successfully. It is true that if you have complete faith in the Lord He will provide a way."

You see? This man thought he merely had two jobs to decide between, but there was a third alternative hidden in the situation which had not yet materialized. Through his right thinking, that job moved into focus as the actual answer to his problem. God has greater things in store for you than you think. So, think God's way and let Him give you His greater blessings.

This is a dynamic and mysterious universe and human life is, no doubt, conditioned by imponderables of which we are only dimly aware. People sometimes say, "the strangest coincidence happened." Coincidences may seem strange, but they are never a result of caprice. They are orderly laws in the spiritual life of man. They affect and influence our lives profoundly. These so-called imponderables are so important that you should become spiritually sensitized to them. Indeed, the more spiritually minded you become the more acute your contact will be with these behind-the-scenes forces. By being alive to them through insight, instruction, and illumination, you can make your way past errors and mistakes on which, were you less spiritually sensitive, you might often stumble.

It is true that a spiritual conditioning of your mind to the Divine purposes which underlie your life will help you to make fewer mistakes. It is helpful to go into a church and sit quietly in meditation and spiritual concentration for fifteen minutes every day. If going to a church is inconvenient, the same quiet period may be observed in your own home or office. During this period talk your problem out as in actual conversation with God. Conceive of your mind as open to receive impressions and insights. Believe that you are receiving guidance. Indicate your willingness to follow faithfully whatever insight impresses itself forcibly upon your mind. At first you may not get clear direction. You will need to adjust to a spiritual type of thinking which will presently make you keenly sensitive to guidance. Not only from personal experience, but from results obtained by the many who have tried this method with success, I assure you that it is one of the most effective of all procedures for reducing mistakes.

Several years ago I struggled with a problem for days. I asked advice and went over the matter again and again, but the solution evaded me. I was about to force a decision prematurely, which is a mistaken thing to do, when I was invited to a Quaker meeting.

This meeting was held in the living room of a home and not more than ten persons were present. Except for some simple directive thoughts on the technique of meditation we sat in complete silence for forty-five minutes. During the first half of the period I was physically uncomfortable, being unused to sitting without some kind of activity or speaking.

Then I tried yielding myself to quietness. I consciously held my problem up to God and "dropped" it into the creative and dynamic spiritual fellowship which existed in that room. Presently my mind slipped into a quiescent state. It felt rested, but fully alert and alive. A strong feeling of peace, such as I had not felt in days, pervaded my consciousness. And then, like a flash, came a clear, fully-formed answer to my problem. It was not exactly as I expected it to be, but instinctively I knew it was right. And it did indeed prove to be so.

Another, and somewhat similar experience demonstrated again the effectiveness of meditation in obtaining guidance and in avoiding mistakes. For some weeks I had been struggling with another problem to which I had given not a little thought, discussion, and prayer. I had received an answer and was satisfied that it was correct, but shortly thereafter it was confirmed in a little wayside chapel, high on the Burgenstock, one of the alpine heights on the shores of the Vierwaldstättersee in Switzerland.

My wife, our son John, and I went into this picturesque little chapel for prayer and meditation. We found there a rather plain Swiss mother and her two boys. Rucksacks strapped to their backs, they were obviously out for a hike, but had stopped for a prayer before the day's outing. One of the boys was noisy and proceeded to take snapshots, completely indifferent to our desire for quiet. Soon, a couple, talking loudly, entered, carelessly banging the door. Then they departed, as did also the mother and boys.

We sat in a welcome silence. Sunshine flooded the little church, lighting up the altar decorated with geraniums, the inevitable Swiss floral piece. Sunlight fell softly on the heavy wooden pews and well-worn stone floor. In the distance, tinkling cowbells could be heard from the charming little valley of Obburgen, lying cupped between the Burgenstock and the Stanserhorn.

Then an old man entered. I knew him to be a rich old man, but was aware that he was poor, too, since he was ill and lonely and unhappy. He bowed in prayer, breathing heavily because of his bad heart and obviously in pain from his arthritic limbs. He hobbled out pathetically.

Suddenly it occurred to me to stop praying for myself and instead to pray for the mother and her two boys, for the noisy and thoughtless couple, and for the poor, old, rich man, suffering and miserable. As I did this an astonishing thing happened. No sooner had I finished those prayers than a wave of peace and joy swept over me. With it came a profound feeling of certainty about the answer to my problem. I knew that the decision I had made was not a mistake, that it was the right thing, and that I had been spiritually guided. The shift of prayer emphasis from myself to the other people very definitely had a releasing effect upon my thought processes.

Many men whom I might name, some well known, all effective in living, utilize this method of a daily short period in a church for clearing their minds, stimulating their thoughts, and keeping themselves in contact with basic truth.

Another suggestion for developing practical rightness is to cast out the mental picture of past mistakes. Holding such failure pictures, or dwelling upon memories of mistakes may cause the error pattern to repeat itself. The mind seems to learn a mistake habit quickly and easily. Do something the wrong way a few times and the mind tends to accept that as the proper method. Therefore, when an error has been made, the procedure is first to learn all that you possibly can from that mistake, particularly how to avoid making it again. Even a mistake may have value in teaching how not to repeat it. Second, learn specifically what the right way is. Third, practice mentally visualizing that right way until your consciousness accepts a picture of yourself as performing correctly.

The late Mrs. Charles P. Knox, head of the gelatin business bearing her name, had a thought-provoking motto on her office wall: "He who stumbles twice on the same stone deserves to break his own neck." A childhood truism advised: "Turn your stumbling blocks into stepping stones." Certainly it is the part of wisdom to mark safe routes past old mistakes. A good rule is, don't make them twice and turn every mistake to good use.

A friend of mine, a small town merchant, opened a haberdashery shop in a building where three others, in the same business, had previously failed. He was warned to avoid that particular site, "because nobody could succeed there."

But my friend refused to accept this pessimistic appraisal. He adopted the scientific, spiritual method. First he made a careful analysis of the failure of each previous merchant. And, second, he prayed for guidance. By studying previous mistakes he was able to avoid them. By prayer he developed new approaches. Now, it is said, that his business site is the best in town. That result was gained by studying the mistake experience of the others and by tapping God's wisdom to guide his decisions.

One of the mistakes of his failing predecessors was that they did not do a primary thing important to any business, namely, to cultivate a friendly spirit in their shops. So, this man employs only clerks who have what he calls, "the gift of friendliness," or are willing to cultivate it. He holds a meeting of his entire staff every morning and opens that meeting with a brief prayer. He urges his employees to "fill the store with the spirit of friendliness." In addition, he stocks only top quality merchandise, using the most attractive modern display techniques. He makes a constant study of salesmanship and teaches this important skill to his employees. In short, he drained every mistake of the previous owners of all the know-how it had to offer. First he discovered how not to do a thing, then how to do it well; first the negative, then the positive procedure.

Finally, may I emphasize that to think right and to do things right with assured certainty it is necessary to be a right person. Error in thought and action always results directly from error within the self. And it is of little use to attempt correction of specific mistakes without first correcting the central core of error. Get yourself right. Then things will go right.

❖ ❖ ❖

Following is a list of principles which are important in learning to make fewer mistakes. They have been formulated from real life experiences.

1. Do not pessimistically assume that having made a mistake there is no hope, that a mistake means ruin.
2. Calmly and objectively examine your mistake. Learn all you can from it. Then move away from it with a new know-how.
3. Get psychological insight into the underlying causes of your mistake-tendency.
4. Increase your spiritual understanding. This will displace error from your mind by an intake of truth through prayer and faith.
5. Do not continue to hold mental images of past mistakes for that may stimulate repetition of the error.
6. Get your personality organized and your thoughts tightened up. Effective thinking and action will result.

7. Keep your efficiency high by stopping the leakages of power caused by fear, inferiority, etc.
8. Recondition your mental equipment by a daily reading program designed to fill your mind with the constructive thoughts of men who teach truth, not error.
9. Keep studying, keep trying. Always believe you can learn to do better. Constantly seek for self-improvement. Never believe you have arrived.
10. Apply the supreme personal test at all times, "Am I a right person?" If you are "right" things tend to go right.

CHAPTER IX

WHY BE TENSE? HOW TO ADJUST TO STRESS

"If you are to maintain power to meet your responsibilities and to continue effectively over the long pull, you must give as much consideration to that delicate, yet powerful, mechanism known as your human personality as engineers give to their engines. You can purchase another engine, but that 'engine' known as yourself cannot be reproduced if it fails, and stress is a major cause of that failure."

TENSION IS a number one problem today. We have never had a national patron saint, officially, in America, but apparently we do have one in a practical sense. The patron saint of the British is St. George; of the Irish, St. Patrick. The patron saint of Americans must be St. Vitus. We are a nervous, high-strung, tense generation of people.

Yes, America is full of tension and yet, actually, it isn't America that is tense, for the land is just the same as it has always been: wide, sweeping prairies; huge mountains, lifting their peaks against the sky; broad rivers, lazily moving toward the sea; mountain streams, splashed with sunlight, singing over rocks. The land is still the same and the land is peaceful. It is the American himself who is filled with tension and who, deep within, longs for quietness and relaxed strength.

Apparently the prevailing tension even affects the dogs, for an Associated Press dispatch from Los Angeles (a city that is not without tension) tells of a sixty pound Airedale dropping dead of a heart attack when two smaller dogs barked at him.

Also, all tension is not in the United States, though with our national tendency to depreciate our own country we talk as though it is. The Paris edition of the New York *Herald Tribune* recently carried a story headed, "Paris Traffic Said to Affect Policemen's Nerves, Heart." The story reads: "Many of Paris' 18,500 policemen have developed cardiac conditions as a result of the French capital's nerve-wracking traffic situation. Some 2,500 of them are absent from duty every day because of nervous exhaustion after a day's work whistling, yelling, and pointing their white sticks in Paris streets."

I noticed in the paper recently an advertisement offering "peace of mind" tires for sale. The reference was to non-blowout tires. This brought to mind a statement by a rubber manufacturer who says that his industry did not learn to make efficient tires until they were designed to absorb road shock rather than merely to resist it. The time has come for all of us to learn to relax and absorb tension rather than rigidly battle it.

Many have learned to develop inner peacefulness and live without tension. On a plane I sat with a prominent business man, a dynamo of driving energy. His daily schedule is packed to the time limit. He has many responsibilities and directs innumerable activities, but handles himself with quiet and impressive power. Asked his secret, he replied, "I simply begin and end each day calmly."

As to his method for doing this he explained, "I say to myself four statements each morning and evening; and I repeat them slowly, meditating on each. One is from Confucius: 'the way of a superior man is three-fold: virtuous, he is free from anxieties; wise, he is free from perplexities; bold, he is free from fear.' The second is Robert Louis Stevenson's advice: 'Sit loosely in the saddle of life.' The third is from the Sixteenth Century mystic, St. Theresa: 'Let nothing disturb you, let nothing frighten you. Everything passes away except God. God alone is sufficient.' The fourth statement is that familiar quotation from Isaiah: 'In quietness and in confidence shall be your strength.'" (Isaiah 30:15)

"Apparently you believe that tension can be overcome by filling the mind with philosophical and religious thoughts at the beginning and the end of the day," I observed.

"That is entirely correct," he said. "And you can underscore the word religious."

Another excellent technique for overcoming tension, as I mentioned in the preceding chapter, is the practice of silence. At sometime during every day it is a good thing to observe a period of absolute quietness, for there is a healing power in silence. Go into a quiet place. Do not talk; do not do anything; throw the mind into neutral as far as possible; keep the body still; maintain complete silence. William James said, "It is as important to cultivate your silence power as it is your word power," and Carlyle declares, "Silence is the element in which great things fashion themselves together."

Beneath the tension-agitated surface of our minds is the profound peace of the deeper mental levels. As the waves beneath the surface of the ocean are deep and quiet, no matter how stormy the surface, so the mind is peaceful in its depths. Silence, practiced until you grow expert in its use has the power to penetrate to that inner center of mind and soul where God's healing quietness may actually be experienced.

A friend of mine once had a problem that had been agitating his mind for days and could not get an answer. He decided to practice creative spiritual quietness. He went alone into a church and sat for an extended period in absolute silence. Presently, he began to be conditioned to quietness. He dropped his problem into a deep pool of mental and spiritual silence and meditated upon God's peace rather than upon the specific details of the problem. This seemed to clarify his thinking and before leaving that quiet place an answer began to emerge which proved to be the right one.

Having observed the beneficial effect of creative silence in the lives of so many I felt it could be used as effectively by groups as by the individual. I became convinced that the use of spiritual silence in services of public worship might help people, not only to overcome their tensions, but to find better solutions to their problems as well.

Accordingly, in the Marble Collegiate Church moments of directed, creative quietness are observed during services. Suggestions are offered by the minister of the most effective manner in which to relax the body and induce a state of quiet receptivity in the mind. It is pointed out that spiritual silence is not desultory and apathetic, but creative and dynamic.

Verses, such as the following, are spoken to create an awareness of the spiritually creative possibilities of silence: "Be still, and know that I am God." (Psalm 46:10) And again, "In quietness and in confidence shall be your strength." (Isaiah 30:15) An amazing silence falls upon a huge congregation of twenty-five hundred people. The only sounds are faint street noises, muffled by the marble walls of the church edifice. Sunlight, sifting through the great stained glass windows, falls softly upon the multitude and enhances the deep impressiveness of the moment.

Many testify to the profound effect of this corporate and cooperative practice of silence. One business man declared that in the silent period he received an answer to a perplexing production problem of his company. It seems that he and his officers had come to New York for a conference involving this problem. Their meetings had lasted all day Friday and Saturday, and they had met for breakfast on Sunday morning. But there had been no solution. The problem was a baffling one, and men were tired and tense. At this point our friend announced he was going to church.

The customary quiet period was held and the congregation was directed as follows: "Put your problem in the hands of God. Hold it in the conscious mind for a moment, just long enough to formulate it clearly. Then think of the problem as being solved in God's way, which is the right way. Relax, and believe that the healing peace of God is touching your mind, that the blocks which have prevented guidance from flowing through are being removed. Rest your mind and body and soul in the Lord, and let your answer float to the top of your conscious mind."

This tired and tense man followed the suggestions given. In his mind, of course, were all the facts necessary to a proper understanding and solution in connection with his business problem, but these facts had not been properly assembled and organized. Because of the tension within him the component factors of the problem did not fall into the right order. Even though his answer was potentially present all the time in his unconscious, not until he came under the influence of creative silence did the solution rise from the deeper level of consciousness and become clarified. In speaking of the experience afterward he said, "The right answer, fully formed, suddenly came up into my mind. Stress had overlaid it with a rigid barrier, and it could not get through. But spiritual silence revealed it."

Mental stress always causes the mind to be heated, and when the mind is hot it cannot deliver properly. To be fully effective the mind must be coolly rational. You must think with your mind, not with your emotions. Creative answers to all your problems are in your subconscious. You can revolutionize your life if you learn to draw on this deep inner source of power. The practice of creative silence is a method for doing so. It will stimulate into activity basic insights which God has laid up within you and which you may use for greater efficiency.

Many people are learning to overcome their tensions and achieve calm control by such spiritual silence techniques. An example is the young man who was assigned the job of dealing with the most difficult customers of his business firm. He was given this responsibility because of his skillful handling of a particularly ticklish personality situation.

His method is interesting. When preparing for a difficult interview he uses the principle of spiritual meditation. One day the firm's most difficult customer was coming in, and it was the first time he had dealt with this individual. So he went into a store room for a period of meditation and prayer. As he came out he bumped squarely into his boss. "What were you doing in there?" asked the boss, a suspicious employer who severely keeps track of the actual working time of each employee. This young man was very much on the job, but in a manner the boss, at that time, did not understand.

"I was praying and meditating in quietness," said the young man.

"Business is good," snapped the boss. "Why should we pray?"

"I have a difficult customer coming in shortly," explained the young man, naming the individual, "and I wanted to find composure and deeper understanding. I need special insight and control to handle this problem."

Naturally, the boss watched him deal with the customer, whom he knew to be a very difficult person. He observed his employee's honesty, sincerity, understanding, and firmness. Afterward he said with a grin that did not belie his sincerity, "Perhaps I had better join you in that silent prayer technique." Little wonder the young man was assigned such a responsible job. His success was in no small part due to the relaxed control he had achieved by creative spiritual quietness.

Until you learn this skill you may work under that stress which is a cause of many nervous breakdowns. If you are to maintain power to meet your responsibilities and to continue effectively over the long pull, you must give as much consideration to that delicate, yet powerful, mechanism known as your human personality as engineers give to their engines. You can purchase another engine, but that "engine" known as yourself cannot be reproduced if it fails, and stress is a major cause of that failure.

The Captain of a Pan American DC-6B airplane told me that, at take off, the full twenty-five hundred horsepower of each engine is used to lift the tremendous aircraft off the ground. But immediately upon being airborn the pilot cuts back to eighteen hundred horsepower per engine for the long climb. When cruising altitude is reached power is still further reduced to twelve hundred and, for long-range flights, to as low as one thousand horsepower. The pilot explained that it is important to use full power for not more than two minutes. Its continued use beyond that maximum is likely to harm the motors.

Obviously, moments come in life when a crisis demands full use of all our emotional powers and energy, but we must learn to reduce for the steady climb and for long-distance cruising. And certainly our energies cannot be conserved if, through tension, we constantly run our "motors" at full power.

As I have indicated, effective emotional control is best achieved through spiritual means. I had a number of conversations a few years ago with a man whom I never met personally, but who kept calling me by long distance telephone, complaining of tension and exhaustion. Each time I tried to say something helpful to him, and apparently gave him temporary relief.

But he telephoned more and more frequently, and I soon realized that he was leaning on me, that I had become a kind of psychological father to him, simply because he felt my desire to help him. Since everyone must stand on his own feet and conquer his own difficulties, I knew I must effect a transference of this tense person to God, if he was to achieve permanent healing of his tension.

"Say something to me that will help me to stop being tense," he kept repeating in a kind of desperation. "The only way I can get any relief is to pick up the telephone and dial your number," he explained, miserably.

One day when he called I said, "Instead of dialing me why not 'dial a Book' which you have in your possession. It will do you much more good and save you money as well." The suggestion mystified him, and I explained that I meant for him to go to the Bible for Scripture references designed to help reduce his tension. "Whenever you cannot sleep and are filled with tension and anxiety, just 'dial the Book' and read the words of the Bible. Say them aloud, conceiving of them as penetrating to the source of your nervousness and bringing you peace." I was able, also, to arrange with a local pastor and physician to work with this man in a more personal way.

One of the passages I particularly suggested that he "dial" is the fourth chapter of St. Mark which describes the disciples and Jesus in a violent storm at sea. It will benefit every tense person to read it at regular intervals.

This storm arose while the disciples were in the ship with Jesus. They were filled with fear and made their way to the stern of the pitching vessel, only to find Jesus sound asleep, His head pillowed on His arm. Such complete relaxation was surely a demonstration of perfect physical and emotional health. They cried excitedly, "Master, carest thou not that we perish?"

He opened His eyes and looked at the frightened men. He arose and studied the lowering sky and the tumultuous waters. A slow smile of understanding and kindliness came over His face. He crossed the deck, awash with the waves, and grasped the mast. Swaying there in the tossing craft, what a tremendous figure He was, His magnificent physique adding to the impression of power. He raised His right arm, and in a voice that rang out over the waters said, "Peace, be still." Then states the writer of the Gospel with the genius of simplicity, "And there was a great calm."

One wonders whether that calm was in the waves of the sea or, perhaps more significantly, in the minds of those men. Certainly it was manifested in their restored composure. Now the waves did not look at all terrifying. Little wonder that they said among themselves, "What manner of man is this, that even the wind and the sea obey Him." He can speak peace to your tension and bring calmness into your mind. It is indeed an excellent technique and a workable one, to "dial a Book."

Tension has curious sources and manifests itself in many seemingly strange ways. But it is curable when all the facts and causes are systematically assembled and analyzed, and when proper spiritual treatment is given by adequately trained counselors.

In not a few instances over the years, I have observed the close relationship of guilt to tension. A person will insist that he has lived a good life apart from "a few episodes" and, "surely it would seem that the emotional system should have long since absorbed earlier indiscretions."

But strangely, the personality seems to hold them in suspension. They fester in consciousness and pockets of spiritual poison develop. The fine balance of nerve and emotion is disturbed and a state of tension is created.

Lowell Thomas told me an interesting story about a man who visited a dentist in a New England city. A small drill broke in the patient's mouth. The dentist thought he had removed all the broken parts, but some fifteen years later the patient complained of a pain in the shoulder. An X-ray revealed a dark object in the upper arm which proved to be a piece of the drill broken years before.

In similar fashion a "splinter of guilt" may lodge in the subconscious. Later, the individual may be completely unaware of the cause of his emotional and psychological pain until a spiritual operation is performed. Then tension declines and emotional, spiritual, and even physical health returns. But pockets of poison or splinters in the subconscious cannot be cleansed or removed except by spiritual curetting.

I do not imply that tension is caused only by guilt. That is but one of a number of causes. The combination of life's pressures, its burdens and accumulated difficulties, can rest so heavily upon the mind that tension develops. One becomes nervous, high strung, and even disorganized. Here again, the cure is a spiritual therapy which, by penetrating deeply into attitudes, can substitute inner peacefulness.

Of the many illustrations of this fact one stands out particularly. I was scheduled to give a talk in a Western city and, in the hotel lobby, met a man whom I knew slightly. He was about forty years of age, a fine looking specimen of manhood, and the picture of physical health. He introduced me to his wife, a nice-looking woman, perhaps a couple of years his junior.

I asked the man the usual question as to how he was, which was an unnecessary inquiry, for obviously he was in the pink of condition. Then I asked his wife how she was, which was a mistake, as she took me seriously and proceeded to tell me in detail how badly she felt. Her husband, who presumably had listened to this unhappy recital on many previous occasions, excused himself, asking if I would talk to her for a few minutes until he returned.

She outlined a number of ways in which she felt badly and told of her fears and tensions. One phobia was that her husband, contrary to his healthy appearance, was in imminent danger of a heart attack, as she had been told that men of his age and responsibility were "dying like flies," to quote her graphic expression. She actually told me that in the night, she would put her ear close to him to see if he was still breathing.

I had a curious feeling, as I listened, that a sort of gray veil covered her face. Actually, of course, there was no such veil, the impression probably being an emanation of her unhappy spirit. She then told me that her face constantly twitched. She further declared that her eyes burned like fire. I could see no outward indication of either twitching facial muscles, or redness of the eyes, but both seemed a real source of suffering to her. She finally concluded her unhappy recital by saying, "It is impossible to describe how tense I feel."

Then occurred an amazing happening. Since her husband had not yet returned, I suggested that we sit in the lobby. It occurred to me to ask if she believed in the actual presence of Christ. She replied that she did. I then asked if she believed, since the doctor said her trouble was largely in her thought pattern, that through faith in Christ she might be healed by the creative force of the transformed mind.

She agreed to this possibility, provided she could believe strongly enough, which was, incidentally, a considerable insight on her part.

I then explained that her tension had become an obsessive, fixed idea and pointed out that the mind will hold spasmodically to such an obsession, refusing to let it go unless and until a stronger thought or good obsession is substituted. The powerful idea that we desired her mind to take hold of was that of the healing presence of Christ. So I asked her to affirm aloud, using the following affirmation, "Jesus Christ is by my side. He is touching my body, my mind, my soul with His healing Grace." While affirming this she was to visualize the healing process as actually taking place then and there.

She was hesitant about this suggestion at first, but under my urging affirmed as directed. Presently I noticed that her emphasis became more positive. She continued to voice the affirmation, but each time with a heightened fervency and it was obvious that the healing thought was gripping her mind.

As I listened I had a curious consciousness of a Presence and she must have felt it too, for she stopped and, with a look of wonder, exclaimed, "He is actually here." And then I saw a strange phenomenon. The "gray veil" seemed to drop, as if by magic, from before her face and her countenance lighted up. Her face, at that moment, was beautiful, the strained look having passed. With deep feeling she said, "This is the most marvelous experience I ever had. I feel a strange sense of peace and, " she hesitated, "I feel so much better."

"What about the twitching cheeks and the burning eyes?" I asked.

With a surprised look she replied, "Why, I feel none of that at all, I am so relieved." The tension had obviously broken.

I knew that this could very well be but a temporary manifestation and cautioned her against overconfidence, but said, "Continue to use that same affirmation, practice your faith seriously, and I believe you can be a well person."

Some months later I met the husband at a convention where I was giving a talk. He said, "The spiritual treatment you gave my wife produced a most remarkable effect. As a girl she was gay and happy and had lots of faith. Everyone loved her for her wonderful spirit. Then we experienced some disappointments and difficulties. Life got a bit hard. We drifted from our spiritual moorings, and finally she got into the condition in which you met her that day. But now she has almost overcome the tension which made her miserable for many months. She is getting along fine."

This woman's change came by inserting into her mind a stronger force than her tension, namely faith, and healing resulted. It is very important to realize that tension can and often does have deeper causes than pressure and hard work. I have described how guilt causes tension and how anxiety produces a like result, as in the case of the woman just mentioned. Tension may arise from old and seemingly buried feelings that originally caused hurt and may have deepened into resentment. We seldom put two and two together to see the connection between our present tension and old antagonistic attitudes. But in any effort to eliminate tense feelings you should explore the possibility that resentment may play a part.

A young man consulted me who complained of acute tension. He was, he said, "Like a rubber band drawn taut." The tension was so strong that he felt he might snap at any time. His medical check-up, while not too good, revealed nothing serious physically. It was this high inner pressure that was troubling him most.

Both in this conversation and in previous ones, as we analyzed his background, I noted repeated references to a man with whom he had gone through school. It seemed that this boy had outdistanced him in athletics, extracurricular activities, and in scholarship. That boy was now in a rather humble position whereas our friend was head of sales for a fair-sized concern. He had forged ahead of his old rival at last, yet he still showed decided inferior feelings and resentment toward the other.

When I faced him with my belief that his tension stemmed from deep antagonistic reactions to the other man he spat out vehemently, "I have never said so before, but I hate that guy with all the strength I've got." It was a violent outburst and I encouraged him to keep on talking. He poured out long pent-up antagonisms which revealed that his whole life was actually based upon competition with the other. It was a clear-cut case of a build-up of hate and inferiority into an obsession. But hate had turned back on the hater and here he was "taut like a rubber band."

I was interested in the figure and picked up a rubber band from my desk and stretched it to its limit, holding it there. "That's me all over," he said. "How can I get over being that way?"

"I think the answer is as simple as letting go your ill will and competition. Then your personality will normalize itself like this," I said, letting go the rubber band which immediately became limp.

"That's easier said than done, that letting go," he commented.

"Yes," I agreed. "The only way is to pray the hate out and pray Him in. You will have to learn to pray for that fellow and mean it."

He sat silently, then said, "That's why I came to you. I knew you would tell me to do that. I have made myself ready to do what you suggest and I'll go at it sincerely, too. I can get it out of my system, I believe."

I asked him to offer that kind of prayer right then and

there, which he did. He stated that he felt better. "It will take a good many prayers to get where I want to go with this, but I'll pray them."

He shook hands and started to leave, but turned and came back to my desk. "May I have that rubber band?" he asked. "I'm going to frame it limp so as to remind myself to be that way. Why be tense when you don't have to?"

Why, indeed . . . ?

❖ ❖ ❖

Let These Thoughts Relieve Your Tensions

1. In quietness and in confidence shall be your strength. (Isaiah 30:15)
2. Be still, and know that I am God. (Psalm 46:10)
3. Thou wilt keep him in perfect peace, whose mind is stayed on thee. (Isaiah 26:3)
4. Come unto me all ye that labor and are heavy laden, and I will give you rest. (Matthew 11:28)

CHAPTER X

YOUR LIFE CAN BE FULL OF JOY

"In exact proportion as you give joy you will receive joy. It is a law of exact reciprocity. Joy increases as you give it, and diminishes as you try to keep it for yourself. Actually, unless you give it you will ultimately lose it. In giving it you will accumulate a deposit of joy greater than you ever believed possible."

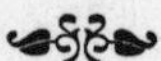

THE PRACTICE of joy will release your personality and set free your powers. It can even give you better health and stimulate your enthusiasm.

Dr. John A. Schindler, a physician, and Dr. Robert J. Havighurst, a Professor of Education at the University of Chicago, joint authors of a booklet having the intriguing title, *How to Live One Hundred Years Happily,* make the point that between thirty-five and fifty percent of ill people are sick, principally, because they are unhappy. Dr. Schindler, in his excellent book, *How to Live 365 Days a Year,* tells of the importance of happy thinking to sound well-being. He stresses the curative value of getting patients to lift their minds daily, if only for a few minutes, into the area of pure joy.

There is an even profounder relationship of joy to health in the opinion of a noted scientist, Dr. Clarence Cook Little, Director of the Roscoe B. Jackson Memorial Laboratory of Bar Harbor, Maine. Dr. Little is reported to have said, "Internal balance is health and internal unbalance is sickness. These bodily functions are controlled by glands that are influenced by mental health."

In the light of these statements it is not surprising that the Great Physician advises us to be joyful. "Rejoice in the Lord alway," He says, "And again I say, Rejoice." (Phil. 4:4) Of course we must not interpret His message to mean that joy is the ultimate end and aim of life. Such would certainly not be a worthy motive for living. Joy is urged upon us only for the purpose of teaching us how to be alive, how to make the most of all of the faculties with which we have been endowed, how to be released, how to be free from conflicts, how to enter into a state of harmony so necessary to being a well-ordered human being.

Joy and harmony are synonymous concepts. When you are in harmony, all elements of your life function cooperatively; you are in a rhythmic relationship with God, the world, and with other human beings. When you are in harmony your whole being, mind, body, and soul, operates as one unity. Then you are at a high level of efficiency as a person. Joy and harmony are fundamental factors in effectiveness.

On a DC-6 airplane I sat with an engineer who had helped to build the engines used in those planes. It was a beautiful day and we fell to talking about the joy of swift flight. I began to develop the theory that harmony is an aspect of joyful efficiency and could scarcely get the words out before he said, "How right you are. I am an engineer, and we know that the secret of making an effective engine is the degree to which we can get harmony into that engine. Efficiency depends upon reducing stresses and resistances to the lowest ratio. The parts of an engine, when working together in harmony, actually seem to sing for joy." He paused a moment and then said, "Listen to the roar of those mighty airplane engines, each delivering twenty-five hundred horsepower. There is harmony and joy in full operation."

Prior to that time the sound of an airplane engine had been only noise to me. Now I like to listen for their harmonious functioning and, indeed, it is not difficult to conceive of those engines as alive and actually singing with joy.

But this is as nothing when compared with a human being when he becomes harmonious. Then the whole personality seems to flow in unity and with rhythmic power. The stresses and conflicts having been eliminated, or at least greatly reduced, energy and vitality are increased proportionately.

Athletic coaches are aware of the importance of joy and harmony in developing effective sports contenders. Joy is a lubricant of the mind and therefore, of nerves, muscles, heart. It flows from the thoughts to the entire being, toning one up, and making for quick and responsive coordination. Joy causes a rhythmic flow of body, mind, and soul, creating that perfect timing and attunement which results in superior skills. It also supports stamina and puts heart into one. It is pretty hard to down a joyful and harmonious person.

An oldtime baseball man traced this quality of joy and harmony in some great ball players he had known over a period of many years. "An outstanding example," he said, "was Hans Wagner, one of the greatest of all shortstops. Wagner covered the area between second and third base like a tent. It seemed that he was everywhere at every minute, his great hands scooping up the ball from unbelievable angles. It was a joy to watch him because joy seemed to flow through him. He was a happy man; he played one of the happiest games of baseball I have seen in all my experience." So declared this expert.

"No man can play a really top game of golf unless he is basically happy," said a golf professional. When I expressed surprise, he explained, "Golf demands rhythm and timing which you cannot have in your muscles unless first you have it in your thoughts. An harmonious mind will send harmonious messages through the nerves to the members of the body which function in the execution of a golf stroke. The first demand I make of my students for mastering golf is to get inner harmony through right thinking."

The golf teacher told me an interesting story about a man, whom he called Joe, who was trying to perfect his drive. But he was not doing too well. He was tense and rigid, and he overpressed. Studying him, the instructor decided that Joe, essentially, was not a happy personality, that lack of inner harmony was tightening him up just enough so that his nerve and muscular responses were ill timed and, therefore, he was not delivering effectively. He outlined to Joe his theory of joy as a lubricant and told him that his game would not improve until he became lubricated with joy. To Joe's surprised question as to how that could be done the coach asked him if he knew any songs and he replied that he knew only one, "Let Me Call You Sweetheart."

"That will do as well as any," said the coach. "I want you to walk around the tee singing, at full voice and with all of the enthusiasm you can muster, 'Let Me Call You Sweetheart.' Keep singing until the hills give the song back to you in reverberating echo. Then, when I raise my finger, still singing, go into the stroke, giving no thought to the technique, for your muscles, as Ben Hogan would say, have already 'memorized' it."

It had been Joe's custom, painfully and meticulously, to

address the ball. He made very certain that his feet were in the proper position, he gave great attention to the precise manner in which his fingers held the club, he kept the arm stiff, deliberately and precisely pivoted, rolled on his feet, kept his eye on the ball, followed through; he did everything exactly according to the book—except that he didn't hit the ball right.

"Now," said the coach, "your mind has memorized the technical details of a proper golf stroke. I want you to release yourself and find abandon and freedom and delight in the game itself. Your muscles will know what to do. So, when I hold up my finger, keep singing and go into the stroke with a lot of joy."

Though somewhat abashed by this type of direction Joe began singing, at first hesitantly and with embarrassment. Soon, however, he got into the spirit of the procedure and sang wholeheartedly, walking around the tee, filling himself full of joy and harmony. Finally, up went the coach's finger and, still singing, his body flowing in beautiful rhythm, Joe went into the stroke and drove the ball two hundred yards plus, straight down the fairway. No doubt all over the country readers of this book, on many a golf course, will hereafter be singing "Let Me Call You Sweetheart." And that is all to the good, for did not the great Thomas Carlyle say, "Give me a man who sings at his work." To be efficient you must be harmonious, and to be harmonious you must be a practicer of deep and vibrant joy.

And how do you become a practicer of joy? How do you train yourself to live according to the joy technique? A first step is, simply, learn to think joy. There is a psychological law, and it is a spiritual law, too, that if you wish to live a particular way, think that way over a long period of time. If you are fearful and want to be courageous, you can do so by thinking courageously. You can become a calm person by the same method. Think persistently along the line you desire, and then begin to act on the supposition that you are just that. Act as though you felt the way which you want to feel. Do this long and sincerely enough and you will tend to become precisely that which you desire.

Therefore, every morning upon awakening, start the daily practice of joyful thinking. This may be accomplished by passing a series of joyful thoughts through your mind. Explicitly, upon awakening, say something like this: "This is going to be a fine day. I had a splendid night's sleep. I am glad that I am alive. First, I shall enjoy a good breakfast. Then I will have some happy fellowship with my loved ones before the day's work begins. And all day long I shall have the satisfying experience of being with people, of doing some good, and performing some worthwhile services."

Look out the window and note the freshness of the morning. If there is no sunshine, perhaps you will see rain; so remind yourself how fresh and rejuvenating rain is. In other words, talk yourself into being joyful. By thinking and by talking you can react a joyful state. You can become what you think and affirm. Think joyfully, talk joyfully, act joyfully and presently you will become, through your thinking, talking, and acting, a joyful person.

Your mind may try to block you in your desire to become a joyful and harmonious individual by telling you that such effort is falsely conceived, and will seek to impress you by that old saying, "thinking doesn't make it so." But thinking can make it so and often does, if at the same time thinking is implemented by diligent effort and by scientific and persistent practice. If you are determined to improve yourself, your mind must be controlled by you instead of controlling you. Presently it will adjust and accommodate itself to the changed pattern of your thinking and acting. Thus, by believing, thinking, and acting you can, in time, make of yourself a joyful person in harmony and in tune with the creative forces of life.

The person whose mind has long been packed with gloomy thoughts and with negative attitudes may find this procedure difficult at first. It may require strict discipline to train the mind to think in this new and creative pattern, but remember that nothing worthwhile comes easily. You have to work at this persistently and diligently, using great effort, finally to achieve skill.

It will help to take pencil and paper and list the joyful experiences that occur to you every day. You will be quite surprised at their number and extent, and as you continue listing them they will grow in number and in meaning. Every day, systematically, pass the memory of your joyful experiences through your thoughts. Dwell upon them, relive them, immerse your entire thought process in the most moving and uplifting experiences you ever had. Your mind will presently begin to experience pleasure in this reliving of joy, and having whetted its taste, will want to create more such enjoyable experiences. As your joyful stimuli increase in number, they will penetrate to your deep consciousness, creating in you a permanently joyful state of mind.

The power of thought-conditioning in developing joy and changing your mental state is illustrated by the experience of a man whom I met on a train going to Chicago. This man, whom I knew slightly, was, at that time, an extraordinarily gloomy and negative personality. To him everything from the condition of his health, to the state of the country was very bad.

"Isn't this a terrible train?" he growled. "And did you have dinner in the dining car? Wasn't it awful? You never get any good service anymore. I couldn't eat a thing." (Later, a man who dined with him said he "ate everything in sight.")

Then he spent a little time criticizing several people whom we both knew. "By the way," he said, "I read one of your articles in the newspaper about being vital and joyful. Now I ask you honestly, do you really mean that, and can you imagine anybody in this world being joyful as you indicated?"

"Sure I can," I said. "I am."

"But how?" he inquired, perplexed. Then he added dubiously, "You do seem to get a big kick out of living."

"The way to be joyful," I said, "is to think joy, affirm joy, believe in joy, practice joy, and give joy. For example, instead of saying, as you did, 'This is a terrible train,' say enthusiastically, 'This is a wonderful train.' As a matter of fact it is. Actually, it is a work of art, the product of scientific genius. And besides, there is a great deal of romance to it. It is a city on wheels, streaking through the night. And, as to the meals in the dining car, they are not bad at all. Get in the habit of taking an urbane, positive, and happy attitude toward conditions, situations, and circumstances as you meet them daily. Instead of thinking in terms of dissatisfaction, discontent, and gloom, as you are now doing, practice slanting your thoughts toward joy. Make a sharp mental shift in your view point."

I realized that this man had practiced negativism and gloom for so long that he had become, you might say, an expert in such attitudes. However, I outlined to him the joy-producing principles and techniques described in this chapter. Apparently I became quite enthusiastic, since I felt that way, and painted for him a picture of what he could be. It came over me that I was stating exactly what, unconsciously, he wanted to be.

Oftentimes, people who talk glumly and negatively are, in a reverse manner, indicating what they would like to be; namely, the exact opposite of their expressions. At any rate, he seemed genuinely interested and promised that he would try the simple techniques outlined. Evidently these new ideas began to register almost immediately, for when we arrived the next morning in the La Salle Street Station in Chicago, the weather was hazy and overcast. I happened to leave the train just as the porter was saying to him, "I hope you had a good night."

"Oh, not so good," he replied, "but then, not as bad as sometimes." He looked around at the weather and remarked, "It looks pretty gloomy today, doesn't it?" Then he saw me. His face changed, a grin crossing his countenance. "Oh, good morning, Doctor," he said, a bit chagrined. But he spoke with a new cheerfulness. Then, with a wider grin, "Wonderful day, isn't it?" Already he was beginning to realize the power of optimistic thinking, plus optimistic affirmation.

And I know he continued to work at it, for his wife told me of his sincere efforts to change himself. His new thinking was presently reflected in his much improved attitudes and in the fact that he felt better. "It is amusing to watch my husband," the wife said. "Actually he stands before a mirror and affirms that he is standing tall, thinking tall, and believing tall. It all seems sort of queer, but it must work, for life is certainly much better for him than it used to be. And," she added significantly, "for his family as well. What does he mean by that statement, 'standing tall, thinking tall, and believing tall'?" she asked, a bit perplexed.

I explained that in my conversation with her husband on the train I had referred to my friend, William H. Danforth, for many years head of a large St. Louis industry. He wrote a wonderful little book called, "I Dare You." It was based on a boyhood experience when he was suffering from ill health. A teacher said to him, "I dare you to be healthy," and gave him a method that helped him to become so. It was simply this, "stand tall, think tall, smile tall, and live tall." Mr. Danforth pulled himself up to dynamic health by daring to believe that he could become a strong, healthy individual.

I suggest that you, too, for a moment before the day begins, take a deep breath and say, "I am standing tall, I am thinking tall, I am believing tall." This is a slight variation from Mr. Danforth, but the affirmation will pull you up straight and bring the organs of your body into natural position. It will tend to slough off unhealthy thoughts from your mind and it will pull your faith up to a new level.

I was impressed by the common sense expressed by Dr. John C. Button, Jr. in an address to the American Osteopathic Association. "We sit at breakfast, we sit on the train on the way to work, we sit at work, we sit at lunch, we sit all afternoon. Sloppy sitting is turning too many Americans into a hodgepodge of sagging livers and squashed pelvic organs. Try, frequently, standing erect to avoid indigestion, neurasthenia, chronic grouch, and a thousand and one similar ailments."

Perform that technique and you are bound to feel better and be better. The disciplinary uplifting of the body, the mind, and the soul, practiced repeatedly, definitely rejuvenates and re-energizes. It takes the sag out of the body, dullness from the mind, and strengthens the spirit to better handle the burdens that usually depress.

As I have pointed out, the development of inner joy and dynamic harmony, as in all spiritual improvement, requires practice and more practice. You can never become proficient in any skill without practice. Based on the actual experience of the many who have demonstrated the beneficial effect of these techniques, I assure you that the practicing of new joy-attitudes will, in time, bring about substantial improvement within you.

At an airport a young woman approached me, asking pardon for the intrusion but saying she wanted to ask a question.

"Do you think," she said—and there were tears in her eyes —"that a person who has messed up her life horribly can ever know joy again?"

Obviously her question called for analysis and at that moment my plane was being called. So I scribbled a sentence on a card and handed it to her. "Try that prescription," I said. "And let me know how you come out." The sentence I wrote on the card was from the Bible: "If ye know these things, happy are ye if ye do them." (John 13:17.)

A good many months later a woman came up to me following a talk I had made. "Do you remember," she asked me, "giving a card with a Biblical prescription on it to a woman at an airport? Well, I am that person and I was fascinated by the words and read them over and over. 'If ye know these things' and I asked myself 'What things?' I read through quite a bit of the New Testament trying to find that verse and finally I did find it and in the reading I came to realize what it meant. I knew then why I was unhappy. I wasn't living right and I wasn't thinking right. I was filled with fear and hate. I had done things of which I was ashamed. That one sentence," she ended simply, "changed my whole life."

This lack of joy is a problem for many people today, young and old. I was interviewed not too long ago by the young editor of a high school newspaper. She said, "I want to ask you a question that all of us are interested in; how can you really be happy?"

"Let me get this straight," I said. "Are you telling me that one of the great questions to which high school students are seeking an answer is how really to be happy?"

"That's right," she said. "Dr. Peale, so many of us are all mixed up. We just want to know how to be happy."

So I gave her that same sentence: "If ye know these things, happy are ye if ye do them."

Everybody really knows what to do to have his life filled with joy. What is it? Quit hating people; start loving them. Quit being mad at people; start liking them. Quit doing wrong; quit being filled with fear. Quit thinking about yourself and go out and do something for other people. Everybody knows what you have to do to be happy. But the wisdom of the text lies in the final words: "If ye know these things, *happy are ye if ye do them.*"

It is amazing and pathetic, too, how many people go

through life victims of inward disharmony. They struggle along having no gladness in them at all. Imagine not being glad you are alive! Do you wake up in the morning eager to be up and at the job? Do you have a good time all day long? If not, do you want to know how to become glad you are alive? One answer is to use the simple and completely practical spiritual and psychological principles outlined in this book and in other writings of similar nature.

Still another good technique is this: in exact proportion as you give joy you will receive joy. It is a law of exact reciprocity. Joy increases as you give it, and diminishes as you try to keep it for yourself. Actually, unless you give it you will ultimately lose it. In giving it you will accumulate a deposit of joy greater than you ever believed possible.

Recently, in a magazine, I noticed an interesting story about a television star whom I have known for some years. I remember her in the early days of her career. Then she was very negative and unhappy. Of course she was not doing very well either, for her gloomy thinking dulled the basic charm in her personality. Then she began attending church where she met some vital people whose lives had been dynamically changed. She felt this alive something that they had and she wanted it. Through their help she became a vitally spiritual person. This experience was so complete, so thorough-going that she was eager to share it with everyone. She had achieved for herself a deep personal joy and it meant so much to her that she just had to give it out to everybody.

She took every opportunity to share her joy with others, especially with the people who viewed her programs. She filled her work so full of exuberance that it transmitted itself with dynamism and charm. Strangely enough, and yet not so strangely, her advancing success kept pace with her development in joy attitudes. She became a genuine dispenser of real happiness. There was now a magnetism about her that drew people to her and, of course, to her program, and therefore increased its value. She found joy; then she kept and deepened it by generously giving it away.

To succeed in any activity, or simply to succeed as a person, become joyful and dynamic. Get filled with power, the power of joy. What I have said does not imply that the purpose of learning the techniques of joy is to attain success. But surely, every normal person wants to do the most that he can with his life, and it has been repeatedly demonstrated that joy releases personality which then becomes outgoing. New creative capacity is stimulated. Negativism and dark thoughts tend to freeze personality. By self emphasis one actually shrinks into himself and, in so doing, loses personality force. He becomes so fearful and self-consciously tied up that he becomes clumsy and inept. As a matter of fact, such a person is disorganized and therefore is bound to be inefficient.

The best and surest of all cures for this condition is to pray for help; study the Bible to learn how to live victoriously; go to church for instruction and for fellowship that is spiritually alive; ask the Lord to become your organizing influence. Then your personality will take on new tone. It will become strong and well-directed. Christ puts people together on the inside and He is the only one who can really do it. The slang phrase "get organized" is your answer, but let God do the organizing.

I was in the washroom of an airplane. Those cubicals, as you know, are quite small. A fellow passenger kept pushing at the door, trying to get in. I said, "If you will just wait one moment . . ."

"I don't want to wash up," he interrupted, "I want to talk with you. I saw you come back here and I thought it would be a good time to have a word with you."

I leaned against one wall and he against the other in that small room. "What's on your mind?" I asked.

"I'm absolutely miserable," he said, "and I'm disgusted. I have a terribly hard time with myself. I can hardly stand living with myself. And besides, they load responsibilities onto me that are too big for me and that adds to my unhappiness."

"What is your business?" I asked.

"Oh," he said with disgust, "I'm just a peddler, a sort of salesman. But now my company is sending me out around the country to give inspirational talks to our salesmen. Isn't that a laugh? Do I impress you as an inspiring personality or able to inspire other people?" and he laughed mirthlessly. "I haven't got the ability to do this job. I've got to talk to college graduates and I never had more than a high school education myself. Why did the head office pick on me and make me miserable this way?"

Obviously he was abnormally depressed to so completely belittle himself. I looked at his dejected figure. "Would you mind standing up straight?" I suggested. He looked surprised. "Yes, I mean it," I said. "The way you stand or sit has a good deal to do with how you feel. If you stand straight you are likely to start thinking straight."

He straightened up, pulling himself erect against the wall. "That does make me feel a bit better," he commented.

"Of course it does, and I hope you will keep practicing it." I told him about the stand tall, think tall, believe tall technique. "Another thing, never depreciate your job. You said, 'I am only a peddler.' What you should say, and I hope you will say it, proudly, every day of your life is, 'I belong to one of the greatest occupations. I am a salesman. It is my privilege to deliver to people from an honest manufacturer an honest and needed product or service.' Say also, 'I am a descendant of a great breed of men. I am a trustee of the American economy and American free civilization.' Never go around saying in a minimizing fashion, 'I'm only a peddler.' Never think yourself or your job down."

Then I added, "I am sorry you work for a concern headed by such stupid men."

"Who said they are stupid?" he demanded.

"Well, they must be," I insisted, "to send you out to give sales talks."

He bridled. "My bosses never make a mistake. They are the smartest men in the business," he asserted proudly.

"Well, then, that means they believe in you and if they are as smart as you say it must be because you are worth believing in. Even though you are deficient in education they know that you use your brain, that you give all of yourself to your job, that you love your work, and that you believe in their product. They know that you have qualities that can help other people. As practical men they do not make mistakes. They know they can trust you to do a good job. This should make you very happy and you need happiness in the work you are doing, for one of the best contributions you can make to your salesmen is to transmit a dynamic spirit to them. When are you making your first sales talk?"

"This afternoon," he replied.

"All right," I said, "let's have a word of prayer about it now. And let us thank God that He has made you a salesman and such a good one that you can help other people have the joy of being salesmen. Let us thank God that you can show them how to be more effective human beings."

So, in that washroom, sixteen thousand feet in the air, we prayed and dedicated this man and his job to God and to human service. When he returned from his trip he telephoned me. "I had a wonderful meeting that afternoon and have had good going ever since. Do you know what happened to me on that airplane?" he asked. "God put me back inside of myself." He was reorganized, inwardly, by a new thought process based on faith and joy.

The practice of the principle of sharing joy has helped to develop some of the most remarkable people I have ever known. One, for example, is a good friend whom I encountered when I arrived at Grand Central station in New York one morning. All around me on that train were business executives and expensively dressed women, all prosperous in appearance, but most looking gloomy and nervous. As we emerged from the train I saw this friend of mine and noted the genuine happiness written all over his face. This man wasn't one of the big executives, but he is a big man, perhaps more so than many of the so-called bigs. He was piling up bags, putting them on trucks, for that is his daily work. He is Ralston Young, a Red Cap.

We exchanged happiness with each other. As I left him, stimulated as I always am by his great personality, I fell to wondering why Ralston still carries bags, for I am sure he would have no trouble at all in securing a better paying job. I spoke of this to another friend who also knows Ralston. "He thinks Grand Central station is the best place to spread joy and to share his spiritual convictions," explained this man. Then he told me about a man who was quite drunk who came into the station one night and asked Ralston, "Where can I get a present for my little girl? She is eleven years old and I want to take her something."

"Why do you want to give her a present?" Ralston asked.

"Why, to make her happy, why do you suppose?" growled the man.

"Mister, may I suggest a present to make her really happy?" Ralston asked softly.

"Sure, what is it?" the man grunted.

"Just give her a sober Daddy. That will make her very happy because she loves her Daddy and would think it wonderful to have a sober Daddy."

"What do you mean, preaching to me?" blustered the other.

"I'm not preaching," answered Ralston. "I'm just thinking about your little girl. Why not take her home a sober Daddy?"

The man cursed, grunted, and swayed slightly as he followed this interesting Red Cap to his train after they had, together, purchased a little gift. That man came back several days later and hunted Ralston up. "What you said sticks with me," he said, "but I want to know why you went to work on me."

"Because I could see you are not a happy man, but want to be," said the Red Cap. Then Ralston really did go to work on him and in due course transmitted his own spiritual joy to the man. Is it any wonder that Ralston Young is a joy-filled human being? He has spread so much joy to so many people in the great station where he works, and outside of it as well, that waves of joy wash back to him from everybody, everywhere. So, for your job's sake, for your health's sake, for your mind's sake, for your family's sake, get joy. And you get joy by thinking joy, acting joy, and sharing joy.

Another technique of happiness is to saturate your mind with joy. Jesus Christ says, "The words that I speak unto you, they are spirit, and they are life." (John 6:63) This means that if you study the words of Jesus, meditate on them and saturate your conscious and subconscious mind with them until them become your dominating thought pattern, you will attain real enthusiasm, dynamism, and joy. Your spirit will no longer sag. By a process of spirit transfusion you will actually incorporate some of the vital dynamism of God into your own personality. That is bound to have a profoundly rejuvenating effect on your entire life.

There is a marked increase today in the number of joy-filled people. This is a result of the spiritual resurgence of our time. And it is also traceable to the new knowledge of spiritual techniques which so many are studying and mastering. I have been making a "collection" of people who are living joy-filled lives, and believe me they are everywhere. I have personally drawn joy from them and now, in this book, I am pleased to pass some of their joy along to you and to tell you, as they told me, how they got it.

While spending a few days in Florida, I received the following letter from a young college student up North. He had heard that I was in his home town and wrote to me as follows:

Dear Dr. Peale,

My grandmother lives in the same town in Florida where you are now staying. For years I have been saving to buy her a round trip ticket to New York because she says if she could only worship in the Marble Collegiate Church it would be the happiest day of her life.

She has inspired me for so many years and taught me that nothing is impossible with God. She had seven children and educated them all by herself. She reared two grandchildren and educated them. She sent my sister and me through school. I have seen her go to bed hungry, saying she wanted nothing so that the family could be fed.

She purchased the house where she now lives with a down payment of one dollar and fifty cents. A book should be written about her life and it is my prayer that I may be inspired by God to write it. She is an angel on two feet and has a laugh like music.

By the way, we are Negroes.

Thank you and God bless you.

Sincerely yours.

Of course I went to call on the boy's grandmother and, as he said, she proved indeed a wonderful person. Written unmistakably on her face was the reflection of that inner light which marks a truly joy-filled personality.

When I arrived at her house, a humble little place on a dirt road, no one was at home. Just as I was about to leave I noticed an old lady coming down the road with a basket on her arm. She had a rolling gait, somewhat like that of a sailor. She was singing softly. I knew she was the woman I had come to see and waited until she reached the house. "Are you Mrs. ——?" I asked.

"Land sakes, yes, honey," she said. "What do you want?"

"Oh, I just came over to see you," I said.

"Now isn't that nice of you, but why did you come to see me?" she persisted.

"Your grandson wrote me about you," I explained. "He told me you are an angel on two feet. And I just wanted to see an angel on two feet."

She chuckled and laughed in the most infectious manner. "Land sakes, honey, I ain't no angel," she said.

"And he told me your laugh was like music," I continued. At that she did laugh. And he was right, it was like music.

"That boy shouldn't be saying things like that," she said, but obviously she was pleased.

I went into the house with her and she showed me pictures of all those children that I had been told she had educated. I congratulated her and told her what a highly successful human being she was. "Oh, I ain't successful," she said. "I just love 'em, that's all." And I couldn't help but love her when she said it.

Just then her telephone bell rang. I overheard her end of the conversation. "Now, honey, don't you worry," she said to someone on the line. "I'll be over this afternoon and prop you up."

As she hung up the receiver she said, "That poor rich white woman. She's having a terrible time and I've got to go over and see her this afternoon. She does take an awful lot of proppingup."

I rather liked that phrase, "proppingup." She explained that people who need proppingup do not have any faith to sustain them. "You say that white woman is rich," I questioned, "and still needs proppingup?"

"Honey," she replied, "she ain't rich, she's poor. Folks ain't rich unless their riches are inside." She gave me one of those radiant smiles, the smile of a human being who is really rich and wise, too!

She was one of the most stimulating human beings I ever

met. I could not help asking, "Where and how did you get this joy?"

She chuckled. "Oh, I just love everybody," she said. "I didn't go out hunting for joy. I just love everybody and when you love people you are happy." And I could see that she meant that, too. Then she added, "But the real reason I'm happy is I have Jesus in my heart. When you have Jesus in your heart nothing bothers you, nothing discourages you. You are just happy, that is all."

Think joy, talk joy, practice joy, share joy, saturate your mind with joy, and you will have the time of your life all your life. And what's more, you will stay alive as long as you live.

❖ ❖ ❖

So convinced am I of the importance of joyful thinking in improving life that I deliberately practice it and have worked out a simple formula to aid me:

1. I searched through the New Testament for all references to joy, and there are many. Actually, the New Testament is a joyful book and Christianity is a joyful faith.

2. I committed many of these passages to memory. By this method your mind can be reconditioned. By a process of absorption joyful thoughts tend to displace unhappy ones.

3. I repeat quite a few of these passages daily. The constant saying of a thought will change you to harmonize with it. In time you tend to become what you think and say.

4. I listed all the joyful facts of my life. This list I read frequently to remind myself of the reasons for my joy.

5. I try to bring joy to as many others as possible. It is a curious fact that you get joy out of giving it; you lose joy by selfishly trying to keep it.

6. I try to see the joyful side of life. One must see the pain of life with clear eyes, and help all he can; but there is also lots of joy, and one should see that, too.

7. I got in the habit of acting joyful in a normal and reasonable manner.

CHAPTER XI

LIFT YOUR DEPRESSION AND LIVE VITALLY

"Any person can change from depression to power if: first, he wants the change to take place with all of the concentrated desire of which he is capable; second, if he will go all out to get it; third, if he will practice belief with all of the mental ability that he possesses; and fourth, if he will put himself in the way of having a deep and profound spiritual experience."

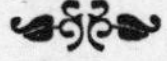

BRITISH WEATHER FORECASTS are interesting. A typical one read: "Cloudy, rain, fog, with occasional bright intervals." That seems also a rather accurate description of "weather" conditions in many lives. It is generally agreed that we can do little about the weather. But we can control the climate of the spirit. We can increase the number of bright intervals, we can conquer depression.

Depression may be serious or mild. The marks of serious depression are a perpetual sadness, slow reaction of mind and body, morbid and bitter self-criticism. A person suffering from these would seem to need profound therapy. In this chapter, however, we refer to mild depression, which is rather widely prevalent. Some authorities say that perhaps one out of every three persons has some degree of mild depression.

Symptoms of mild depression are discouragement, loneliness, disconsolateness, feelings of inferiority, and just getting no fun out of life. Mildly depressive people are always saying, "What's the use? Things are never going to be any better. I'm a flop."

I should like this chapter to be an effective effort to "Punch holes in the darkness" of your depressive attitudes, to borrow a graphic phrase from Robert Louis Stevenson.

An effective cure of depression is the practice of hope. The more hope you build up within your mind the more quickly your depressed feelings will lift. And as hopefulness becomes a habit you can achieve a permanently happy spirit. It is best to start very simply, as simply as saying hopeful words to yourself when you awaken in the morning. Tell yourself, for example, "This is going to be a great day. I am going to feel fine all day long. I am going to do constructive things today." Then keep on talking hopefully all day long.

By saying the words, you start the process which leads to the actual fact. Through repetition the idea of hopefulness will imbed itself in your thought pattern and, if continued, will force out depression and make hopefulness your prevailing cast of mind.

"But," you may object, "you cannot actually talk yourself into something!" Of course you can. Your mental attitude is very much affected by the words you say. If all day long you say gloomy, pessimistic, and negative words, you will be gloomy, pessimistic, and negative. Saying the words tends to develop the thought. Of course, the reverse is true also; hold the thought and you will then say the words. Either way, words and thoughts have a very definite tendency to reproduce themselves in fact. Think and speak gloom and you will create gloomy results.

If, on the contrary, you speak and think hope, you will tend to bring about a hopeful outcome. You can talk yourself into any desired state of mind. Much miserable feeling is self-manufactured by how we think and speak, or speak and think. Practice hopefulness, talk hopefulness, and you will begin to feel better. Then you will begin to do better.

This does not, of course, ignore the cold, hard, realistic facts of daily existence. But hope is a powerful method for overcoming cold, hard realities. Talk hope, think hope, and you will burn out depression. Then, with clear thinking and resolute spirit you can meet difficulty and overcome it. It is amazing how a hopeful person can make things go well, whereas others are defeated by obstacles.

Life is tough, no doubt about that, but no toughness can be as tough as genuine hope. One of the toughest things in the world is a mind filled with hope. The so-called toughness of difficulty cannot stand against it. Get your mind filled, therefore, with hope and it is bound to lift your spirit.

The cure of depression also involves improved personality-tone. A spiritual tuning up is essential. The human engine must be tuned up like any other engine, if it is to function efficiently. When an airplane is about to take off the pilots tune up and test the motors to get the engines ready to lift the great weight of the ship off the runway. When our human motors are sluggish and out of tune, we lack the lifting force necessary for powerful and vital living.

We then need complete body, mind, and soul revitalization. Right eating, right exercising, right thinking, right praying, right living, these are all part of the process of tuning life up to vitality. When piano strings have lost resiliency, the piano tuner brings them back to vital tone. Renewed life tone is important to dynamic living.

My long-time friend and personal physician, Dr. Z. Taylor Bercovitz, of New York City says, "To get in tone one must get in tune." His prescription is, "Every day spend five minutes on a rowing machine and five minutes on your knees."

Tune up the body and tune up the soul. Religion and medicine harmonize to give resiliency and vitality.

In this tuning process or development of personality-tone, the motivating force will come by deepening your spiritual experience. Fill your mind full of faith. Then you will have astonishing power over defeat and depression.

In Pensacola, Florida, I addressed the student naval pilots. I was given a ride in a jet airplane. What a process to be dressed for a jet ride; Mae West vest, and flares in case of disaster; then meticulous instructions about how to inflate the vest in case of a crash in the water.

They placed a shoulder harness over me and safety belt around me. They put a helmet on my head and down over my ears. My feet were placed in position, and I was told that it was very important to keep the heels on a certain catch and my finger on a release button for, if we should crash, I would merely have to press the button to be ejected from the plane. By this time a certain amount of tension had begun to rise in my mind. Then they put on the oxygen mask, pulled down the plane top and there we were, hermetically sealed in. For the first time in my life I had a bit of a tussle with claustrophobia.

"Isn't it wonderful?" the captain called back to me through the inter-communicating system.

"I never felt like this in my life," I called back, working away at my claustrophobia.

"You are in for the time of your life," he informed me, enthusiastically, "because we are going into another world."

I hoped that he meant another world in this world.

We roared down the runway at an incredible speed, then zoomed into the sky, in such a take-off as I had never experienced. "As soon as I can find a hole we will go into that other world," the Captain said.

He found it and zoom—I never knew a plane to climb so fast—five thousand, ten thousand, fifteen thousand, twenty thousand, twenty-five thousand feet. Then I saw what he meant. We were indeed in that other world. I had a sense of being suspended, motionless, in a vast and illimitable canopy of blue. There was practically no sound, only a faint hum, for we were traveling at a rate of speed that was running away from sound, running away from the world, running away from every defeat. Wordsworth's lines kept going through my mind and I said them aloud, "I Wandered Lonely as a Cloud."

Then I, too, became enthusiastic, and called to Captain "Smoke" Strean, one of the best pilots in the Navy, and my good friend, "This is wonderful! I wouldn't have missed it for the world. I feel a sense of freedom and release and uplift. Why," I said, "it's (searching for the best description of all) it's like a spiritual experience."

"That is exactly what it is," he called back, "a spiritual experience." Then he continued, "This is the experience for which we train our students." And he described it in this glorious phrase, "We lead a student step by step until at last he realizes that he is no longer earthbound."

One of the greatest facts in this life is that we, too, can be led step by step, until at last we discover that we are no longer earthbound. What experience can be greater than to have contact with a lifting force that can take us up above every depression in life. This process is very well described in a phrase given me by a good friend, Mrs. Winifred Pond, who herself has the lifted spirit. I asked her secret, "It's something I learned from a dear old Negro woman years ago in my home down South. She used to say, 'Live over the top of things.' "

This is indeed a wise suggestion. Condition your thoughts to live over the top of things and you will constantly have that lift of spirit which will deliver you from depression.

But the elimination of depression also involves a patient, persistent, perhaps long-term, clearing away of gloomy thoughts. And this you cannot do alone. You need God to help you. A doctor in Alabama wrote me saying, "Seventy-five percent of my patients do not need the surgeon's knife, or medicine; they need God." This physician is saying that much of the illness with which he deals is due to unhealthy thoughts which habitually occupy the mind. Of course, the sick often need medicine, and sometimes need the surgeon's knife. But they also need the help of God in clearing away unhealthy thoughts. You can make yourself sick by wrong thinking and, similarly, you can make yourself well by right thinking.

Dr. John A. Schindler tells of a grocer who came to his clinic complaining of severe stomach pains. No physical ill was found, the trouble being psychosomatic. His sickness developed because a big super-market had opened in the community where he had his independent grocery and was taking much of his business. He also had a son who was always getting into trouble. The poor man was so unhappy that his stomach pains were constant. He was sick of depression.

Twice every year it was his custom to go fishing and hunting in Wisconsin. Five miles out in the country he would stop his car and look back at his town and would still have stomach pains. But when he started his car down from the hill crest where he had paused to survey his town, the pains left him, not to return until he reached that same spot on his homeward journey.

Because he couldn't go hunting and fishing all the time to find relief, the doctors had to teach him to rid himself of his unhealthy thoughts. They lifted him to a higher level of thinking, they helped him find a new philosophy of life. As Dr. Schindler puts it, "We treated the man for gloomy thoughts and he became well."

The doctor suggests how you can prove for yourself the power of thoughts over your sense of well-being. "Go home and sit in the easiest chair you have in the house," he says, "so that you cannot blame what happens on the chair. Then worry, and think depressing thoughts for just one hour. Either you will have a crick in your neck or a pain will hit you somewhere else. Some people are susceptible in the neck; others may be more susceptible in the nose. You can even develop the sniffles by doing this," the doctor declared.

That emotion can produce bodily symptoms and actually affect you physically is brought out in William James' famous definition of an emotion as "a state of mind manifesting itself by a sensible change in the body." To refer again to Dr. Schindler, to cure psychosomatic illness he recommends substitution for the unpleasant emotions, such as anxiety, fear, apprehension, depression, and disappointment, of the pleasant emotions such as confidence, assurance, pleasant expectancy, joy, and hope. "The 'pleasant' emotions produce changes that make us feel *good*; that is to say, they are optimal changes."

A man came down from upstate to New York City one Sunday to attend Marble Collegiate Church and something really happened to him that day to relieve him of a depression under which he had lived for months.

This man received three devastating blows in quick succession: first, his business failed, largely due to a disloyal associate; second, his son was killed in the war; and third, his wife suddenly died. All of this together was more than he could take. He was stunned, and groped blindly in an unreal world. It seemed impossible that these terrible things could have happened to him.

Despite all that his friends attempted to do, still he walked the streets in a daze. He had no energy, no interest, no hope. He was utterly depressed. Months went by. Then, finally, he decided to spend a few days in New York City in the hope that a change of scene might give relief.

In telling of it afterward, he recalled that on Saturday night he went to a show, one of the most popular in town. But it left him cold. It seemed dull and uninteresting. He went to a well-known night club with no better results. Sunday morning he came to church. You can never foretell what great things may happen when you go to church. The very place is filled with mysterious powers which, if properly contacted, have the potential of revolutionizing your life. Actually, one should always enter the electric atmosphere of a church with a sense of excitement and expectancy. And the more you expect, the more you will receive.

This man told me afterward that he remembered nothing said or done in church that morning. So profound was his depression that apparently he could not concentrate sufficiently to listen with the conscious mind, but his subconscious, which is ever alert, picked up something that proved profoundly recreative. The healing atmosphere surrounding him penetrated deeply into his consciousness. All of a sudden, and without warning, the dazed condition which had affected him for months, passed, and he experienced an exhilarating sense of illumination.

"It was," he said, "as if a high powered light suddenly flashed on all around me. I had a feeling of lightness, as though I was being lifted into another realm of existence. I seemed to feel new waves of life passing over me, around me, and through my very being."

He struggled for words to give expression to an experience which, perhaps, is inexpressible. "Heavy weights," he said, "seemed to be lifted, and a feeling of immense relief overcame me. I became wondrously peaceful."

He says that he walked out of that church into a real world again. But more than that, he felt surging back into his reawakened personality a sense of mental and physical vigor. He returned to his home, well on the way to becoming a rehabilitated person, and thereafter worked with zest and efficiency. Gradually he rebuilt his life.

The powers which this man demonstrated after his spiritual reconditioning were, of course, within him all the time. They had merely been buried under a heavy mass of grief, disappointment, self-pity, and depression. The dynamic mood and atmosphere in the church created a state of mind in which it was possible for spiritual power to penetrate to the control center of his personality and release him. The log jam of negative, depressive thoughts broke up and a powerful stream of new thoughts swept his mind free of depression.

This type of release does not always occur in quite so dramatic or immediate a manner and is just as valid if its occurence is over a period of time, or even comes hard.

Any person can change from depression to power if: first, he wants the change to take place with all of the concentrated desire of which he is capable; second, if he will go all out to get it; third, if he will practice belief with all of the mental ability that he possesses; and fourth, if he will put himself in the way of having a deep and profound spiritual experience in the manner indicated. The tremendous powers of the mind are released only when the above positive conditions are present. But the most astonishing change does take place when these steps are sincerely followed.

Another illustration of the powerful spiritual process which burns off depression is that of a man who was an alcoholic for years. He had all but wrecked himself physically and financially. Formerly he had been an executive in a large commercial organization, but was now touching bottom. In a hospital he was told of a man in Brooklyn who had demonstrated unusual ability in helping people with the problem of alcoholism. This turned out to be "Bill," founder of Alcoholics Anonymous, but in those days Bill had not yet accomplished his great work.

"I went to see him," said this man whom I shall call Mr. X., "because I wanted to get well. I desired this with all the force that was within me, but I was utterly depressed. I hoped that Bill would not talk to me about God, because I had no use for God and I was sick of hearing about this God business. So I resolved that if he mentioned God I was simply going to walk out on him."

"Bill assured me that I could overcome my trouble, 'but,' he said, 'you will have to put your trust in the Higher Power.'

" 'By that do you mean God?' I asked.

" 'Yes, I mean God,' Bill answered.

" 'I knew you would bring up this God stuff, so I am walking out. I don't want anything to do with God and if that is all you have to offer, good-bye.' "

So, Mr. X. stomped out and down the street toward the subway station at the corner. As he walked, utterly despondent, he was muttering to himself, "God, that's all they talk about. God! I'm sick of hearing about God—God—God," he muttered.

Suddenly he stopped short, blinded by an overwhelmingly bright light. It seemed to be surging up from the street. The sidewalk undulated, and all around him swirled light. This strange light shown on the faces of people passing by. It was on the buildings; it was everywhere. In a daze, he stumbled down into the subway, only to discover that this same light also suffused the usually drab transportation system in its effulgence. He felt himself caught up in it. He rubbed his face with his hands, asking fearfully, "What is the matter with me? Am I going blind? Am I going crazy?" He bolted off the train and took another train back to Brooklyn and to Bill.

Shaken, he related his experience and then asked, "Bill, tell me, what in the name of God has happened to me?"

" 'You have named it yourself,' said Bill, echoing his own words. 'In the name of God, something has happened to you. Perhaps you should get a New Testament and read about a man named Paul,' Bill suggested. 'He, too, was quite down on God. In fact, he was persecuting the followers of Christ. While on his way to further persecution there came a great light and struck Paul to the earth. That is one way God comes to people, in a burst of light.' "

From that day Mr. X. was never again defeated by his old problem. Depression lifted from his mind as the returning sun drives the fog out of the valley. He filled all of the requirements set forth in the above formula. Actually, it was only with his lips that he said he did not want God. Deep within him, he was longing for God. His lips framed the fiction that he did not want God, but his heart was saying all the time, "With all my heart I truly seek him." Mr. X. got what, in his unconscious self, he really wanted, which was God.

As for that bright light which came up all around him, obviously this brilliance was not in the streets of Brooklyn, or in the subway. The light which dawned upon Mr. X. flowed from his own mind. It was a mystic, inner light and its brilliance was by way of contrast with the shadows and dark depression which had previously inhabited his mind. A profound and revolutionary re-emergence of spiritual power, stimulated by intense mental and emotional heat, cauterized that area of his personality where defeat and depression had formerly been generated. However it may be explained, the change through which Mr. X. passed amounted to a spiritual rebirth and drove off his depression, making life altogether new.

Another effective technique for eliminating depression and getting your spirits lifted is the practice of thought replacement. Our spirits sag because our thoughts sag. We become tired and depressed in our minds. The practice of thought replacement can bring about spirit transfusion. We can pump new life-giving concepts and ideas into our minds by the use of the words of faith, which are life-giving, life-changing words. Weariness leaves and depression vanishes.

One successful practicer of the technique of thought replacement, a prominent scientist, says that his method is to replace every weak thought with a strong one, each negative thought with a positive one, a hate thought with a loving one, a gloomy thought with a lifted one. Dr. Max Morrison, who tells of this man's experience, says that by this method the scientist also stopped persistent headaches, for they too can be caused by unhealthy and depressive thinking. Study your thoughts, write them down on paper, and analyze them, whether they are creative or destructive. Then, simply go about replacing the destructive ones with positive thoughts. You will find this literally a magical formula.

I receive a very large mail from people everywhere who give testimony to the marvelous way in which the replacement of depressive thoughts with faith thoughts has brought about remarkable improvement in their lives. Following are two letters out of the daily mail bag.

"My letter will be a bit different from the ones you usually receive. I have everything to make life wonderful, good, and beautiful. God and I are very personal friends. I can do all things I love to do for others because of His blessed help. I have a fine, kind husband, a beautiful daughter, and I also enjoy a host of wonderful friends. I sing, play the piano, and give talks of a devotional nature. I pray that I am a blessing to those who need a blessing. What more could anyone ask of life than this?

"Incidentally, I am without sight . . ."

A very different letter indeed! "Incidentally, I am without sight!" Here is a woman who knows how to handle a handicap that could be profoundly depressive. She seems actually to disregard it. She fixes her thoughts on God and the welfare of others, overcomes her handicap, and so lives joyously.

Fortunately, very few of us are born sightless or become blind. But all of us do grow older—and age and its problems seem a depressant to many. The other letter from my friend, Joe Mezo, shows how a man handles the age and retirement problem, which become such a difficult experience for some.

"I reached the retirement age of sixty-five and, against my wishes, was compelled to retire by the bank I had been with for twenty-four years. I won't go into detail as to how I felt. This happened on a dismal and rainy night—I was walking through Rector Street, and I never felt more depressed or useless in all my life.

"Suddenly, it happened! I felt I was not alone. A voice within me said over and over again, 'God is good; God is good.' I immediately felt uplifted. Every drop of rain broke the puddles into tinseled lights. It was beautiful. I went home, greatly comforted, and have had the feeling ever since that I am looked after.

"About two weeks later I had a call from another bank asking me to organize a credit department.

"I am now sixty-nine and in good health. I feel the best is still ahead. The good Lord is giving me the opportunity, the strength, and the courage to keep on."

Here is expressed that same dauntless, positive spirit. "I feel the best is still ahead!" This man is not depressed by his sixty-nine years. He has fixed his mind on the Source of eternal youth.

Depression, of course, is an attitude of mind. You become depressed because your thoughts are depressed. How change the depressive thought? By passing through your mind thoughts of faith. This must be done consistently and with great perseverance until the faith concept takes hold. Faith is always stronger than depression and if held and practiced will ultimately displace your mind's dark thoughts. One of the most effective thoughts for counteracting depression is the simple concept that God cares for you and will see you through.

Many years ago, I had my own struggles with depression. At that time I lived on lower Fifth Avenue, in New York. It was my habit to walk home from church Sunday nights and, on my way, occasionally, I stopped in at a little drugstore. It was run by A. E. Russ, a fine man, kindly and wise. Now and then, when I had done poorly, I would pour my woes into his ears: What a poor sermon I had preached that night; nobody would be in church next Sunday. So ran my dismal depression.

He would listen patiently and tell me to go back next Sunday and try again. Sometimes he would come to hear me. Then, one Sunday night, when I thought my sermon had been particularly poor, I stepped into his store and said, "Mr. Russ, I am looking for a job."

"What is the trouble?" he asked.

"I guess I had better give up preaching," I told him. "I can't do it. There is no use trying. I guess I will get another job."

"What kind of job are you looking for?"

I watched him making sodas and replied with a question: "Do you need a soda jerk here?"

"Well," he said, "as a matter of fact, I am looking for someone."

"I'll apply for the job. I can start right now."

"All right, put on an apron," he directed, "and come around the counter and see what you can do." I followed instructions and, taking a seat at the counter, he ordered, "Give me a chocolate soda."

"Yes, sir," I said. I hunted around and found the right ingredients and mixed them in a glass. When I squirted in the carbonated water, I didn't get quite the head on the soda a professional does, but it looked pretty good to me. I set it down before Mr. Russ. He inserted a straw and took a long draw.

Then he looked up at me and shook his head, "Better stick to preaching."

We went behind his prescription counter and sat down. "Son," he said, "everyone in every job has his moments of despair. You are going through the same thing everyone else does." He reached into his pocket for his billfold and brought out a picture of a lovely young woman. "Take me, for example. I lost her after we had been married only three years. The light of my life went out. There was nothing but darkness and despair. Then I turned to the Bible and one day, I found a message that was like a burst of light: 'He careth for you' (I Peter 5:7) Suddenly I knew in my heart that God did care for me and that He would see me through."

That experience gave him faith which helped him to overcome his depression. And from it he learned three things which are sure cures for discouragement: first, think right; second, believe right; and third, act right.

Another friend, the famous merchant, J. C. Penney, found that the simple act of turning to God will cure depression. When I use the phrase "turn to God" I do not use it glibly or piously as an old hackneyed phrase. By it I mean, wholeheartedly, to put your faith in God. Admit that you cannot help yourself. Then believe that only God can help and that such assistance will be forthcoming. I have found it of value to say over and over this affirmation, "God is the only presence and power in my life." When God takes hold as you let go, great things will happen. Remember, the word "believe" means to lean your whole weight on.

Mr. Penney made a tremendous fortune, and then he lost much of it. He went through a tragic time. He contracted heavy debts. Finally he suffered nervous breakdown with shingles, and other distressing maladies. He was in a sanatorium, very low physically, spiritually, and mentally. One night he became certain it was to be his last on earth. He wrote farewell letters to his family. It seemed to him in his depression that everybody had deserted him. He felt totally alone, in abysmal darkness, a beaten and defeated human being.

But, to his surprise, when morning came, he was still alive. As he lay in bed, weak and depressed, he heard the sound of voices singing a hymn. He got out of bed and shuffled down the hall where a religious meeting was being held. The people were singing, "Be not dismayed whate'er betide, God will take care of you." He leaned against the door and thought, "I was reared a Christian. Will God take care of me?"

He returned to his room and in a moment of complete surrender, gave his life to God. He began to feel as if a great blanket of fog was lifted and light was coming through. In the days that followed, a deep joy welled up within him. Life and zest returned. For years now Mr. Penney has been going up and down the country, telling what God can do for human beings. He has become one of the most constructive men in the United States.

Finally, a very simple method for overcoming depression is to learn to care for people as God cares, and help to lift their depression. A basic law of human nature is that you lose your own depression by taking on that of others. Love is well termed the greatest of all virtues, because of its remarkably curative properties. Love is always a symptom of self-forgetfulness and when you love people enough to forget your own miseries and take their troubles to heart, then you lose your misery and your depression is dissipated. This is why the Bible is constantly urging us to love one another.

One of the greatest and happiest human beings I ever knew was the late Hugh M. Tilroe, for many years Director of the Department of Public Speaking at Syracuse University. He was a huge man and frequently frightened his students by his rugged manner, but he had a kind and great heart of love. A minister who passed through a tragic experience told me the sad story of how his wife, a beautiful woman but lacking in character, became involved in a cheap scandal. He came home late one night to find her note telling of her infidelity and that she had decided to leave with a man, naming a person of low reputation in a nearby city. To that moment the minister had thought of his wife as a virtuous woman. He sat shocked and numbed. In his depression he called Dr. Tilroe. "Stay right where you are until I come" Professor Tilroe commanded in his brusque voice.

He drove the seventy-five miles to the little town where this minister lived and found him still sitting at the table, his wife's note crushed in his hands. It read something like this: "I have never been any good. You are as good as gold, but I am a bad woman and everyone knows it but you. I have tried, but I'm just no good. It is better that I leave you. I only hope that God, whom you so faithfully serve, will comfort you."

Professor Tilroe roughly, but kindly, threw his arm around the shoulder of the broken man. "Pack your bag," he said, "and get into my car."

They drove through that stormy night, mile after mile, without exchanging a word. "I could see the Professor's face reflected in the windshield," the minister told me. "I felt like a little boy with his father. He was a strong, good man. His very presence comforted me." They went to a fishing cabin which Professor Tilroe owned on Oneida Lake. Opening the cabin, he built a fire, cooked some food and said to his friend, "Eat what you can, then go to bed."

"Aren't you going to bed?" asked the minister.

"No, I'll sit up for a while," said Tilroe.

The minister tossed in restless sleep, but whenever he awakened during that long night he saw Professor Tilroe in a rocking chair beside his bed. He moved only to put wood on the fire. But not until morning did they discuss the problem.

"All night long," the preacher told me, "he sat up and watched over me. He was like my mother, my father—he was like God."

You can understand why, when Professor Tilroe's time came to die, the church overflowed with a great congregation at his funeral. It was composed almost entirely of men. Their wives wanted to come, but would not take the places in the church from their menfolk. He was a man's man and men loved him. Many in that church had found new life through the huge, kindly man who, in lifting depression from so many, became one of the happiest men I ever knew. Throughout all his years in Syracuse University he had loved people and had given of himself to them. He said to me one time when I was low in spirit, "Think of this text: 'If ye know these things, happy are ye if ye do them.' (John 13:17) One of those things is just love people. Love and help them and you will be happy all your life, even when life is painful and hard." How right he was. It is as simple as that. The real answer to depression is love of God and love of people.

❖ ❖ ❖

To Cast Off Depression

1. Identify the symptoms of depression.

   Serious depression: perpetual sadness, slow reaction of mind and body, morbid and bitter self-criticism.

   Mild depression: discouragement, loneliness, disconsolateness, feelings of inferiority, getting no fun out of life.

2. Practice hope. As hopefulness becomes a habit, you can achieve a permanently happy spirit.

3. Right eating, right exercising, right thinking, right praying, right living—these tone up vitality.

4. Practice of thought replacement can bring about spirit transfusion.

Replace each weak thought with a strong one.
Replace each negative thought with a positive one.
Replace each hate thought with a loving one.
Replace each gloomy thought with a lifted one.

CHAPTER XII

PEACE OF MIND—YOUR SOURCE OF POWER AND ENERGY

"We do not fully comprehend what we can do with our emotions. When we control them we have power. When they control us the results are often disastrous."

BELIEVE IT OR NOT, a New York professor is opposed to anyone having peace of mind. He says all this talk about peace of mind irritates him because it means being soothed into an easy and pallid existence.

But the professor misunderstands. Peace of mind does not mean soothing; quite the contrary. It is the source of great energy. It does not mean escape into a dream world, but more effective participation in a real world. It does not mean innocuous lulling, but a dynamic stimulation of creative activity.

A great value of peace of mind is that it increases intellectual power. The mind is efficient only when it is cool—not hot. The nervously excited mind cannot produce rational concepts or orderly thought processes. In a heated state of mind, emotions control judgment, which may prove costly. Power comes from quietness. Marcus Aurelius said, "By a tranquil mind I mean nothing less than a mind well ordered." Carlyle wrote, "Silence is the element in which great things fashion themselves together." Perhaps an even more graphic statement is Edwin Markham's picturesque line, "At the heart of the cyclone tearing the sky . . . is a place of central calm." The cyclone derives its power from a calm center. So does a man.

I knew another professor, a wise man to whom I went, greatly perturbed, years ago. "You cannot think your problem through," he told me, "with an overheated mind such as you have at this moment. You must achieve at least a measure of mental peace before we can get your thoughts to deliver a rational answer. Never trust your emotional reactions unless they are under full control."

Then he had me sit quietly in a chair. He read some lines of poetry, concluding with a few Scripture passages. Finally, after a long silence, he prayed, "Lord, touch this young man's mind with Thy healing Grace and give him peace of mind." Only then did he permit me to outline my problem. To this day I recall with admiration how he guided my thinking to a sound solution.

"Never try to think without a peaceful mind," he advised. I have since urged this procedure on others who have used it with excellent results.

Seneca, the philosopher, says, "The mind is never right, but when it is at peace within itself."

The headmistress of a preparatory school for girls tells her students, "Be still at the center of your being." She explains to the girls that "real power to meet life is developed in those deep centers of inner quietness where the soul and the mind meet God."

God evidently attaches great value to silence for He filled the world with silent places. Apparently He believes it wise for us to fill our lives with silence, too. Consider the fact that seventy-one percent of the globe's surface is water and only twenty-nine percent is land. The sea is a silent place, although not without sound; but the sound has no stridency; it is the voice of the great deep—God's silence.

Think how many cities we could have if all this water had been dry land. But, perhaps, God did not want more cities. He wanted silence more.

Great insight is stated in the Bible: "Be still, and know that I am God." (Psalm 46:10) This is to say, make room for silence in your life. It is an aid to peace of mind.

The power of silence in developing peace of mind and with it, depth of life, is inestimable. Silence fertilizes the deep place where personality grows. A life with a peaceful center can weather all storms and develop great strength. Take Lincoln for example. How may we best explain his strength, his poise, his amazing understanding, his keen insight? Lincoln matured amidst the silence of the primeval forests which whispered deep secrets to him. Perhaps we have wasted sympathy on Lincoln because of his lack of schooling. He went to school to silence, and thus grew a depth of soul and quality of mind of enduring superiority.

In this mechanical era the circumstances of our lives do not easily afford solitude and silence of this type. But we can cultivate inner peacefulness and, unless we do, we may suffer devastating stress and strain. Thoreau said, "Most men live lives of quiet desperation." If that was so in his time, how much more is it true today.

Why, then, do we write about peace of mind? Simply because all of us need it. Dante when asked what he sought in life replied, "I am searching for that which every man seeks—peace and rest." Perhaps never has modern man craved peace of mind as today. Since religion is not always presented in a manner designed to guide men to sound techniques of inner peace, millions are turning to materialistic methods for satisfying this longing. The sale of peace-of-mind drugs, for example, is assuming gigantic proportions.

I happen to be writing this chapter in Europe and have before me a copy of the *London News Chronicle* carrying a headline reading, "Are Drugs the Answer to Sick Souls." The newspaper article asks of the British people, "Are we becoming a nation of drug addicts? Have we reached the point forecast by Aldous Huxley twenty-five years ago in his *Brave New World* where all we need to do if we feel worried, anxious, or upset is to take a pill?

"Huxley called his wonder drug 'Soma.' It had all the advantages of alcohol with none of its defects: 'Take a holiday from reality whenever you like, and come back without so much as a headache. Euphoric, narcotic, pleasantly halluciant; that was Soma.'

"Now listen to our own drug manufacturers of today, extolling the virtues of their new tranquillising drugs, in their advertising to doctors: 'a tranquillising agent which places a barrier between the patient's emotions and his external problems.' . . . 'harassment and worry are replaced by an unfluctuating mood of untroubled composure.' . . . 'daytime sedation without hypnosis.' '. . . Calms the quaking inner self.'

"Man is entering the atomic age, with his thoughts and the control of his emotions at Stone Age level. Panic keeps breaking through. Anxiety is the malady of our time. But, instead of trying to show patients how to cope intelligently with their fears, doctors are prescribing more and more dope, aided and abetted by the drug companies." So concludes the newspaper story.

In my judgment this article is excessively severe regarding doctors and drug manufacturers. Most of the physicians whom I know are suggesting either spiritual or psychological solutions. Moreover, the elements out of which drugs are compounded were created by God and it is not unreasonable to assume that their proper use is within His purposes.

Where tension has a definite physical cause the use of a drug seems not improper. But most tension is, perhaps, related not to soma but to psyche, not to body but to soul.

The profound question is, shall people get peace of mind from drugs or from the Gospel of Jesus Christ? Shall they turn to that which will satisfy no longer than the effect of a pill, or shall they put their faith in that which never passes away? How can any thoughtful person, unless he is totally unconcerned with the misery of men's lives, flippantly cast aside peace of mind?

I attended a Rotary Club luncheon at Interlaken, Switzerland. At my table was a physician. I asked him whether there is as wide prevalence of psychosomatic troubles and diseases of hypertension in Europe as in our own country. "Oh, you mean the manager's disease?" he responded. He felt that anyone who must carry responsibility is susceptible to the anxiety-tension complex.

The "manager's disease" is apparently an American problem, also, according to *Time* magazine which says, "After checking the health of more than twenty-five thousand executives averaging forty-five years old, New York's Life Extension examiners found that only twenty percent were in normal health. In Chicago three doctors examined fifty-five executives under fifty years of age and found that only three were entirely free from organic disorders. Of three hundred and forty Standard Oil of New Jersey executives reporting for a medical check-up, two hundred thirty-five had something wrong and one hundred and ninety-two had ills that would materially effect their working lives. The American Fidelity and Casualty Company found that the average businessman dies six years before his time."

Perhaps this condition is one reason, among others, why so many business people today are evidencing a new interest in the teachings of Jesus Christ. And that interest is well placed, for through it they can, indeed, find peace of mind and new power to live.

In a radio talk I told about a West Coast druggist who sent me a prescription blank made out by a Los Angeles physician for a patient. It carried the usual RX insignia, meaning "take thou," and the prescription read, simply, "Be Imperturbable." The pharmacist said it was the most difficult prescription to fill that ever came to his shop. "Despite all the claims made for them," he declared, "we haven't a pill on our shelves that can guarantee the treatment prescribed by the doctor. I told the patient that he had better go to church, read the Bible, learn to pray, and live a clean life. In effect," he declared, "I told him to fill the doctor's prescription at church."

Since relating that incident I have heard from a number of bookstores that customers have presented prescriptions from doctors for books designed to help the patient find inner quietness.

In the current stress on heart trouble, peace of mind is an important healing factor. Dr. John P. S. Cathcart of Ottawa told the Canadian Psychiatric Association that his studies have convinced him that heart attacks nearly always occur at times of high emotional tension. In general, job and family stresses are the most important factors in attacks of this kind. Avoidance of emotional stress is most important. And concludes Dr. Cathcart, "A useful anti-coagulant is peace of mind."

Our trouble is that we push too hard. We are an overtense, high-strung people. We need to learn the great art of being still. Several years ago my friend, Augustus L. Bering, after watching business men passing through the lobby of Hotel Sherman in Chicago where he is the manager said, "It seems, that if a person misses just one section of a revolving door the day is practically ruined for him." I questioned if he did not mean one complete revolution rather than one section and he replied, "It used to be one complete revolution, but has now been stepped up to one section."

Recently Mr. Bering wrote me that the situation is even becoming worse, for he saw a man actually run for an escalator, brushing him aside to make one particular landing step. After landing, he did not walk on up, but stood triumphant with an air that implied, "Well, I made it!" And wisely asks Mr. Bering, "So what?"

The wisdom of Pascal applies today no less than in his own time: "Most of man's trouble comes from his inability to be still."

In gaining peace of mind an important step is to learn emotional self-management. This quality, like everything of value, comes only to those who use their own strength to get it. Emerson says, "Nothing can bring you peace but yourself." This means you will need to muster your will to eliminate all disorganizing thoughts, such as hate or fear or superstress. In so doing, you may require a spiritual operation to eliminate diseased thinking. And such unhealthy thought patterns can be very serious, often having definite physical results.

I delivered a sermon one Sunday in an Eastern community and discussed mental peace. A woman was present who had been attending that church regularly for some years. While a good person, apparently her religion had never penetrated to her emotional control center. She had quarreled violently with a number of people, particularly with an old friend. Her mind was filled with resentment and accompanying agitation.

For some time a rash had been on her body. The doctor finally diagnosed the skin irritation as "an outward manifestation of an inward emotional irritant"; in other words, her hate had broken out.

In the sermon I mentioned that unpeaceful thoughts can make us sick, and said that those who humbly desired it could find peace of mind. I then allowed a period of silence to ensue, during which the suggestion was made that all might experience a healing of thought and emotion. I stated that in achieving this result it was essential to empty out all unhealthy thoughts and sins. This woman humbly prayed for healing, asking forgiveness for her hates and other wrong attitudes. She really meant it, too. And when you are truly sincere, prayers become effective.

She reports that suddenly she felt "a warm feeling throughout her being." Then she became inwardly peaceful and "a sort of fresh clean happiness" began to surge through her mind.

A few days later she noticed that the rash was definitely reduced. Her physician encouraged her in the belief that she had experienced a cure. Within weeks the rash was gone altogether.

This incident was checked with the physician who said, "The facts are precisely as reported," and added, "this woman had allowed annoyance, irritation, and hate to accumulate in her mind to such an extent that it actually broke out into a physical rash. I believe the curative factor was the peace of mind which she developed."

It is not often that a lack of inner peace breaks out in actual physical irritation. But it is true that your emotional and mental system, and your physical being also, may be vitally effected by unquiet conditions in your inner life. Peace of mind heals.

My brother, Dr. Robert Clifford Peale, physician and surgeon, has had remarkable success in teaching his patients the healing qualities of urbanity. Not only does he administer medicine and perform surgery when needed, but he also encourages his patients to develop a quiet philosophy of life. This has had excellent results in improved physical conditions. He says: "I believe that doctors in the future will need a deeper understanding of the mental and emotional problems of their patients in order to help them."

Another effective method for gaining peace of mind is the practice of what I call "memorized peacefulness." By this is meant the mental storing up of peaceful impressions to draw upon as needed.

I discovered this procedure, quite by accident, during a stay at Atlantic City. I looked out at beach and ocean while working at the desk in my room. It was an overcast day with alternate cloud and fog and sunshine. Circling seagulls were crying in their hoarse manner. The ocean was washing languidly upon the sand. Now and then the sun would break through and a great streamer of light would pass across the water. Then it would fade as the mysterious fog closed in again from the sea. I found the scene quite restful and closed my eyes in a moment of relaxation.

While so doing I realized, of a sudden, that I could "see" this scene just as plainly with my eyes closed as with them open. I was, of course, beholding it in memory. But, I reasoned, if I could visualize it plainly one minute after actually viewing it, why could I not do the same one year or even ten years afterward. So, I began to use the technique of memorizing peacfulness, storing up in memory scenes of peace and quietness. In times of stress, I bring them out and they pass as pictures across my mind with healing effect.

Carl Erskine, famous Brooklyn Dodger baseball pitcher and my good friend, who has developed skill in relaxation and inner quietness, uses this interesting and successful method of "memorized peacefulness."

It helped him to achieve the all-time record for strikeouts in a World Series game, when he struck out fourteen New York Yankee batters.

When I commented to Carl upon his distinguished pitching career, he made the interesting remark that he had learned much in church that had helped him to arrive at Big

League success. He says, "One sermon has helped me overcome pressure better than the advice of any coach. Its substance was that, like a squirrel hoarding chestnuts, we should store up our moments of happiness and triumph so that in a crisis we can draw upon these memories for help and insipration.

"As a kid I used to fish at the bend of a little country stream just outside my home town. I can vividly remember this spot in the middle of a big, green pasture surrounded by tall, cool trees. Whenever tension builds up both on or off the ball field, I concentrate on this relaxing scene, and the knots inside me loosen up." This practice of "memorized peacefulness" is an extraordinary technique for relaxation and mental peace.

The practice of quietness in the physical body is also important. Your mental state and your muscle tensions are closely related. Note the many evidences of muscle tension within yourself: restless movement of the hands, drumming of the fingers, stroking the cheek, chair squirming, even nail biting. Some years ago, I became convinced that reduction of muscle tension would help reduce mental tension. So I began experimenting with bodily-stillness techniques in connection with spiritual practice.

One method I employ is to use the words: "Be still, and know that I am God," (Psalm 46:10) as a practical physical relaxation formula. In bed, ready for a good night's rest, I get into a comfortable position and then say: "Be still, my muscles, and know God's relaxation. Be still, my nerves, and know God's rest. Be still, my heart, and know God's quietness. Be still, my body, and know God's renewal. Be still, my mind, and know God's peace." This should be repeated several times.

John Masefield who used a somewhat similar procedure referred to it as "the getting of tranquility."

An amazingly effective method of *peacefulizing* the mind

is the getting of tension out of the physical body. Incidentally, it will help you go to sleep.

Of the many other techniques for creating mental peace and stimulating your power center, I wish to single out a practice which I like to term "aggressive activation." That is but another way of saying, "Stop fretting and do something constructive about your problem." When you face an upsetting situation do not work yourself into an emotional state, but ask yourself what you can do about it and then start doing the wisest thing you can think of. It is remarkable how quickly you will begin to experience peace of mind about the matter. This attitude will deepen your mental control and help bring about a constructive solution.

An illustration of this method is the case of a woman who telephoned me from her home in the far West. "I am distressed and almost desperate," she sobbed. "I have just discovered that my husband is having an affair with another woman. She is younger than I, and more attractive.

"This has come as a terrible shock. I never suspected anything. My husband and I have worked hard for all we now have. I suppose I have become rather old and, now that he has arrived, he wants someone with more glamour. But I must try to accept it. Please pray for me that I may bear it."

"Yes," I said, "I will, but why not go further and pray that you take over again?"

"What would be the use," she said dully. "It wouldn't be dignified and besides it's all over."

"I wouldn't be too concerned about dignity," I said. "He is your husband and you love him. And besides, you should save him from himself. As for it being all over, the election isn't always decided until the last precinct has been heard from. With God's help, I would get him away from that other woman."

"Tell me what to do," she asked meekly.

"I have never met you, Madam," I replied, "so would you

be kind enough to describe yourself to me? Are you a handsome person?"

"Why," she said with some hesitation, "they used to say I was one of the prettiest girls in this section."

"Don't they say that anymore?" I asked.

"Why, no," she replied. "You see, I am forty-five."

"What has being forty-five got to do with it?" I asked. "Go and take a look at yourself in the mirror. I'm sure your basic beauty is still there."

"I have lines in my face," she told me, "and I'm tired and right now, I am pretty bitter, too."

"Perhaps if you got the tiredness and bitterness out of your mind, the lines would be erased from your face, and the old charm would return," I said.

"Think of the advantages you have," I counseled. "You have a legal marriage to your husband. You have years of association behind you, and in that there is deeper sentiment than you think. You have an immense advantage over this younger person, for their relationship is not honest, but furtive, and so is on an unstable basis.

"Hold a picture in your mind of the restored relationship. Pray with compassion for this poor woman who is making the mistake of thinking there is something in this for her. Stand up to this problem.

"If it is just vitality that she has, you can have vitality too, only in a deeper sense. Pray those depressive thoughts out of your mind and attack this problem constructively."

After some weeks she wrote me, "Through God's help my husband and I are rebuilding our marriage on a strong spiritual foundation. Had we done that in the first place I don't believe this would have happened."

When this woman practiced aggressive activism and went constructively to work on her problem, she began to have mental peace. Her mind cooled from its hysterical state. And when the mind is cool it begins to function efficiently.

The purpose of the mind is to think, which it cannot do when overwrought. Thus, peace of mind is of practical importance for it releases that quality of mind-power which produces constructive results.

Having peace of mind may be as simple as cultivating unemotional common sense. Just make up your mind to stop being upset. You have enough potential will power to do that if and when you really want to. I had an interesting talk with one of the most famous baseball pitchers of all time, the late Cy Young. Even in the era of iron men in baseball he was a sensation. He started in eight hundred seventy-four games and won five hundred eleven, a record that has never been broken.

Also, his record of twenty-three consecutive hitless innings stands unchallenged. In fourteen seasons he won twenty or more games. In five seasons he won more than thirty.

"During your baseball career were you ever nervous or tense?" I asked.

Cy looked at me with genuine surprise. "Why, of course not," he replied. "I wasn't made that way. And besides, what sense would there be to that?"

I asked his opinion of today's pitchers as compared with his day. He admired some current pitchers but added, "In the old days managers did not jerk them out of the game at the first sign they were in pitching trouble. In my time we just stayed in there and pitched our way out of trouble."

That is a power-packed idea. And peace of mind develops that control with which you can "pitch your way out of trouble."

With peace at the center you can handle crisis situations efficiently. Not being emotionally motivated, you can think. The power of controlled thought is immense.

An example of a man whose peace of mind enabled him to deal with a great crisis in masterly fashion in my friend F. W. Delve, C.B.E., chief officer of the London Fire Brigade. Little did Mr. Delve realize the terrible responsibility that would come to him one tragic night when twenty-five hundred fires burned simultaneously in London. It was the first great incendiary bombing and it seemed that London, like ancient Rome, might burn to death.

"We looked the situation over, and it seemed a bit bad. But we spent no time telling ourselves how badly it looked. We just took things as they came and tried to do our job. The bombing and burning continued for one hundred and twenty successive nights. We had to save everything we held dear, and so we went ahead and saved it," was his very casual explanation of one of the most astonishing defense actions in history.

When seeking peace of mind remember the importance of aggressive activation. Instead of a purely emotional reaction, do something constructive about the situation.

It is important, also, to develop slower-paced emotional reactions in gaining peace of mind. This can be accomplished by practice. One way to do this is to picture yourself as reacting calmly under every circumstance. Since we tend to become what we imagine ourselves to be this practice will, in time, give you such a habit of mental peace that it will be very difficult to shake your composure. One man of impressive emotional control has the policy of "never getting mad until twenty-four hours later." He scientifically analyzes an annoyance and lets its heat simmer down, meanwhile mentally seeing himself as meeting it with control. He prays for guidance and considers all phases of the matter in an objective, dispassionate and scientific manner. He also applies to it a benign good humor. Almost invariably, within twenty-four hours he is able to handle the situation without anger.

We do not fully comprehend what we can do with our emotions. When we control them we have power. When they control us the results are often disastrous.

A friend says that his father, when irritated or provoked, instead of flying into rage, "flies into a great calm." To have peace of mind discipline yourself never to get mad or resentful. This, of course, is difficult. But then, as stated throughout this book, important emotional victories in life are never easy. But they are possible, and that is the vital fact. To aid in self-discipline hold this text in mind, "When he giveth quietness, who then can make trouble." (Job 34:29) This means that God will give you a depth of inner peace so that nothing or nobody can trouble you.

Many destroy their peace of mind by being grievance collectors. Even if there is adequate cause for such feelings, still, the nursing of grievance isn't worth the emotional effort. It can only create a prickly condition in your mind which will disturb your peacefulness and emotionally condition your reactions. Then you are so likely to do and say things which are bound to be ill-advised. The net result will be one of harm to yourself. Nobody can develop upper-level personality power who allows himself to collect and hold grievance. The only sane attitude to take toward a grievance, even injustice, is simply to forget it, skip it, let it go by. In this way you will handle yourself with dignity and skill and enjoy the benefit of peace of mind.

Moreover, by reacting to injury, injustice, and hostility in this spiritual manner and with emotional control, you will develop a power that your detractors do not have. Not only will you have the satisfying consciousness that you can absorb into the equanimity of your spirit criticism and the attacks of jealous and unfair individuals as they come, but gradually, by your powerful control, you will gain the understanding and esteem of all fair-minded people.

In attaining peace of mind the ultimate method is to establish a close contact with God. As you live in harmony with His teachings, gradually you will build up a very strong consciousness of His presence. When that occurs there will come to you a deep and profound peace that nothing can shatter. Then you will be able to handle your difficulties with greatly increased effectiveness.

Finally, many people are without peace of mind and therefore lacking in the power to live effectively because of their sense of guilt. This is so vital to peace of mind and power that I urge you to eliminate at once anything that is wrong. Have a spiritual operation on yourself and get all moral fester removed. Be absolutely honest and ask yourself the straight question, "Am I doing anything that is wrong according to the laws of God and the teachings of Jesus Christ?" Peace of mind and greater strength will come in as moral wrong goes out. It will be an exchange of great advantage to you.

One morning in a dining car the steward seated me at a table for two. A woman sat opposite. I was reading the morning paper, when of a sudden the train, which was traveling at a high rate of speed, gave a noticeable lurch and this woman cried out with real fear in her tone.

"Oh," she exclaimed, "that lurch. Don't you think this train is going awfully fast?"

"Well," I said, "it does go right along, but not too fast, I am sure."

"Many more such lurches and we will be wrecked," she said nervously.

"Oh, I don't think so. This train makes this trip every night and I never heard of it being wrecked."

"Maybe this will be the time," she said fearfully.

"Oh, I doubt it. The law of averages is with us."

Then she said, "I had a lower berth last night and couldn't sleep for worrying because I had read in the paper where a woman out west was murdered in a lower berth."

Next she told me she had to get home because she was worried about her children. "Oh, I am worried about so many things."

"You have already told me three things you are worried about—the lurching of the train, possible murder in a lower berth, and your children. How many more fears have you?" I asked.

"Oh, I've a lot of them." Then she asked, "Why do people have so many fears?"

"There are many reasons. Sometimes fears are projected on one by parents, unconsciously; or perhaps people with whom you associate infect you with their fears. Sometimes people develop fears from a sense of guilt, some wrong they have done. There are lots of reasons." When I mentioned the one about guilt, she immediately called the steward, paid her check and left without another word. I was troubled that I might have offended her in some way, but could not see how, so went back to my paper.

Later on my way through the train, I saw this woman crying bitterly. I passed her, then returned and said, "Madam, I hope I didn't say anything to hurt your feelings."

"Oh, no," she said, "I am just so upset."

"If I can help you in any way, I will be glad to," I replied.

She looked up at me and asked, "What are you? A psychiatrist, or some kind of a doctor, or something?"

"No, none of these. I am a minister of the Gospel. Here is my card, and when you are in New York I hope you will worship in our church."

"I no longer go to church. You see—I'm a—bad woman," she replied so quietly I could scarcely hear.

"That is all the more reason why you should go to church," I said. "The church is for bad women and bad men, as well as for good people. Why do you say you are a bad woman?" I asked.

"Why am I telling you these things?" she said.

"Perhaps God wants you to," I replied. "Maybe you had better get it out of your mind. Why do you think you are a bad person?" I persisted.

"Because I have been away with a married man, and it bothers me."

"Of course that would bother you. You see your actions are contrary to what you really are." Then I explained how moral lesion creates intense conflicts and fears. "You are suffering from an acute sense of guilt. And your guilt makes you afraid. You are sick and you need a physician. You need to be healed in your mind and soul."

"What can I do?" she asked. "I'm so unhappy."

"There is only one thing to do and that is to ask God's help. Start by immediately quitting your wrong-doing. Then ask forgiveness. Simply tell me as a pastor that you are sorry for your wrong-doing and that, with God's help, you want to live a righteous life. You have committed sin in an acute form but you are not really a bad woman. You are a woman who is thinking and acting badly. Essentially, you are a good woman, so you are in conflict between what you want to be and what you are. Through forgiveness, God will change you. Then your fears will gradually pass and you can have peace of mind."

I gave her the name of an understanding and competent minister in her city who helped her to find new life. He counseled her; she accepted his guidance, and she is now living on an entirely different basis; no longer is she filled with fear. She has found peace of mind. With it she has gained power over her weaknesses. She is another of those who know the meaning of living dynamically.

❖ ❖ ❖

I wish to conclude this chapter by giving you an excellent formula for having peace of mind. It was given me by an old friend, Fred Fuller, a prominent attorney of Toledo, Ohio. Mr. Fuller suffered a serious illness during which he had a struggle with tension and unrest of spirit. A thoughtful physician gave him a "Creed" which proved very beneficial. Mr. Fuller, who carries it on a card in his wallet, read it to me. It seems so wise and helpful that I want to make it available to you.

1. Conserve your energy, i.e. don't race your motor.
   a. Do not rush—work, eat, and play leisurely.
   b. Do not get overtired at work or play.
   c. Be moderate in eating, drinking, smoking, working—everything you do.
   d. Do not hesitate to refuse to take on unimportant, burdensome tasks.
2. Stay calm and serene. Do not fret or worry or allow yourself to become unnecessarily involved in situations fraught with emotion.
   a. The past is past.
   b. Do your best today and let it go at that.
   c. Do not be apprehensive of tomorrow—it will take care of itself—most worries never come to pass.
   d. Put your trust in God and forget all fear. He has a plan for you and in such a situation who can be against you?

You can have peace of mind and with it the power to live more effectively.

CHAPTER XIII

HOW TO FEEL WELL AND HAVE VIBRANT HEALTH

"Even as airplane engines must be tuned up before taking off, so must a human being have a tuning-up process. The body has many miles of blood vessels and nerves to stimulate, if you want to travel in high gear. And your mental and spiritual elements also require constant attunement to keep them functioning at full potential."

STOP DYING and start living. And live vitally all your life. Either you are growing or you are dying. That is the law of life. And the secret of growing may be as simple as making up your mind to put the accent on life as did the writer of the following animated letter:

Dear Dr. Peale,

I have been a victim of nerves and fear for over twenty years. My husband died about twenty-two years ago and I tried to take out an insurance policy, being then forty-seven years old. I was turned down. I went to my family doctor and asked him what was wrong with me, and he told me that there were a lot of things the matter, that I could expect anything, any time.

Well, I just gave up and have thought, every time I get sick, "Now I'm going to die." I have lived this dying-life for over twenty years. Finally, I remarried, thinking I should have someone to take care of me and bury me.

Now, at the age of sixty-nine, after reading your book* and memorizing the Scripture verses as you said to do, I feel wonderful and I am going to quit dying and start living all over again.

There is a woman who made up her mind to be alive and who took the first necessary step toward being alive, that of filling her mind with lifegiving thoughts. When her spirit came alive she began to feel alive and well.

One memorable night years ago I learned how faith helps in restoring life, for I saw one of the greatest laws, the law of health, in actual operation. It was two o'clock in the morning. The ringing of the telephone roused me from a deep sleep. The voice was that of a prominent physician who said, "I have a case that isn't yielding to my treatment. My patient is in a crisis and I need help. Will you come immediately?"

This request startled me. What help could I give? I remember standing at the door of that home before pressing the bell, and praying for guidance.

The doctor took me into the living room and I asked, "What can I say to a patient under these circumstances? Is she conscious or unconscious?"

"Intermittently both," he answered, "but I don't want you to say anything to the patient. Remember, the Bible says that where two or three are gathered in His name He is in their midst to help. So, you and I, a minister and a doctor—two, as in the Bible's formula—are going into that room and

* *The Power of Positive Thinking.*

fill it to overflowing with faith in the healing Grace of Jesus Christ.

"As her human physician, I have done all of which I am capable. But I am also an agent of the Great Physician. I treat the patient, but God must heal. Science now needs the help of the spiritual. And," he added, "you and I are partners because you, too, are a servant of God, and as such you also are charged with the responsibility of healing."

So, as a team, we entered the patient's room. The doctor sat on one side of the bed, I on the other, and each of us quoted Scripture passages. The patient was restless and feverish. I offered a prayer. The doctor prayed. I prayed again, and he prayed still another time until we both became startlingly aware of a Presence; *The* Presence. Apparently the patient did, too, for her restlessness stopped. She opened her eyes and looked at us with a very sweet smile; then she fell asleep.

We sat for perhaps an hour, praying and talking about God and His healing power. We focused an harmonious spiritual fellowship on the situation. We recounted the healings of Jesus. Presently I became aware that this spiritual conversation was actually being absorbed into the consciousness of the patient, for the change in her was marked, even to my unpracticed eye. Finally the doctor said, "The crisis has passed. She will get well."

This experience was also a turning point in my life. I was so moved that I could not sleep the remainder of the night, but walked the streets in great excitement. For the first time I began to see that I had been making a serious mistake in teaching only a highly ethical religion. I had seen a power actually at work that was beyond ethics or science. I had looked skeptically upon the supernatural. I had thought of religion, basically, as a system of ethics and theology, concerned with moral betterment and the improvement of social conditions, primarily the latter. I regarded medicine as concerned only with the cure of disease through materialistic processes.

That Christianity might have any important relationship to health had never gripped my thinking. I was a strict materialist and regarded as cranks those who related stories of healings where faith was claimed as a factor. My experience with the dedicated doctor, and other subsequent incidents, taught me that the Christian Gospel is dynamically applicable to sickness; that Jesus Christ is not only the healer of our souls, but of our minds and bodies as well.

So, for years now, I have taught that the practice of the principles of religion, in connection with medical guidance, can help you feel alive and well. Today we know that God works in at least two ways in healing people: through His servant the practitioner of medical science, and through His servant the practitioner of spiritual faith.

When we apply this joint therapy to human problems we discover that many people do not feel alive and well because their minds are poisoned by wrong thinking. They hate, they are resentful, they are tense and frustrated, they are filled with fear. That the body can be adversely affected by unhealthy thinking is generally realized today.

The Reader's Digest carried an important article entitled, "Stress—the Cause of All Disease?" in which Dr. Hans Selye, a prominent medical research scientist, outlined his theory that all disease is caused by a chemical imbalance in the body due, primarily, to stress. He bases his conclusion on the fact that the chemical balance within the body is governed, mainly, by three tiny glands: the pituitary and the two adrenals. The pituitary lies at the base of the brain and the two adrenals lie astride the kidneys.

"These three glands, together, weigh no more than a third of an ounce, and their principal job is to adapt the body to all manner of stress. If you are chilled, the arteries constrict and raise the blood pressure to product greater warmth.

When bacteria invade the body, the glands provide hormones to produce inflammation which walls off infection. In case of severe injury, they hasten the clotting of the blood, lower blood pressure to control hemorrhage, increase blood sugar to provide quick energy, decrease sensitivity to pain. It is the task of the pituitary and the adrenal hormones to combat stress and fight off any threat to the body's welfare."

But, as Dr. Selye points out, "in this hurry-up world we are subjecting ourselves to too many stresses. We hurry constantly and worry incessantly. The businessman drives himself at his office all day, then worries half the night. The housewife tries to run her home, maintain a social life, and participate in community activities and at bedtime is so jangled that she takes a sleeping pill.

"Glands attempt to adjust to the continual demands of constantly increasing stress. They pour out excess hormones, trying to keep the body going. For a while they succeed, but in the end the defense mechanism itself breaks down. As a result, arteries harden, blood pressure rises, heart disease develops, arthritis strikes. These and other diseases are all part of the stress picture."

Recently a nose and throat specialist said to me, "In your books and articles remind people of the harm they are doing to themselves by stress in the form of hate, vindictiveness, resentment, and frustration." This physician told me, further, that over one-third of his patients have ear, nasal, or sinus trouble, not for physiological reasons, but because of their resentments, anxieties and other conflicts.

He told of one man who came to his office whenever he caught cold, which was rather frequently. The doctor discovered the interesting and revealing fact that every such cold was preceded by a fight with his wife. The tissues were actually affected by changes brought on by intense emotional stress. (I am not saying that every time you have a cold you have been fighting with your wife!) The doctor declared, also, that dizziness, ringing in the ears, temporary deafness, nervous tension, and pressure may often be attributed to ill will, fear, anger, and other forms of wrong thinking. It seems that we are just catching up with the Bible which always linked disease with wrong-doing.

Dr. Karl B. Pace of Greenville, North Carolina, was recently honored as National Country Doctor of the Year. When I asked the chief cause of sickness his quick reply was, "Nerves and tension." He gave some worth-while advice: "Live each day as it comes. Don't worry about next week. Learn to live instead of trying to get rich. Never remain angry. Begin each day by liking everyone you meet. Take a siesta after lunch to help you relax. Marital quarrels can cause your ulcers, your headaches, or other pains. If either the husband or wife would try one-twentieth as hard to make a go of marriage as finding fault with each other, you would probably have no problems. Never go to bed angry with each other. Go to church, practice your religion, and live a quiet and serene life."

Another physician says: "Many patients could have good health if they would simply practice the therapy of their religion; really use prayer and faith in their daily lives." Another doctor states: "Many of my ailing patients could be well if they would have a real experience of God." A clinic examination was made of five hundred patients. It was found that the illness of some three hundred eighty-eight, or about seventy-seven percent was traceable to psychosomatic causes. The doctor picturesquely commented, "These persons are draining back into their bodies the diseased thoughts of their minds."

Another physician believes so profoundly in the unity of religion and health that on his waiting room table he places religious books and a copy of the Holy Bible. These books are well used, according to the office secretary. Still another physician with an apt gift of expression, said, "Beat wear and tear by prayer and care."

The dynamic effect of Jesus Christ in creating health and vitality is described in a dramatic scene. He stood on a plain by the sea, the waters sparkling like dancing diamonds in the sunlight. Snowy peaks grazed the sky in the distance. A vast multitude surrounded Him as He stood tall and erect, the picture of health and vitality. They were conscious of power flowing from Him, of the emanation of a vital force.

The multitude, which surged around Him, came bringing the lame and the blind and those that were "vexed" in their minds. These people instinctively knew they were in the presence of dynamic power. They had faith and healings resulted. The Bible describes the event in these words, "And the whole multitude sought to touch him: for there went virtue out of him, and healed them all." (Luke 6:19)

We are also told that "Jesus Christ is the same yesterday, and today, and forever" (Hebrews 13:8), which means that the same power is available now if, with similar faith, we ask help. Obviously you cannot touch Christ with your physical hand as they did long ago. But there is a more subtle way to reach Him: by sending out faith thoughts from your mind to His. The outstretched hand or the outstretched thought; each expresses faith, and it is faith that releases the healing force.

The experience of a man in Georgia is typical. He writes: "For some time I have had it in mind to write you a word of appreciation for a wonderful experience that came to me when I was in the hospital with a heart condition which had been brought on by stress and overpressure.

"I felt that I would never be able to work again, for all power and strength had gone out of me. That morning you suggested something in your radio talk that started me on the road to recovery and now I am able to do my work and

I feel better than I have felt for years. I still practice the thing you suggested.

"First, you asked the people in that hospital to get quiet; then to start thinking of God touching the feet and following with His healing touch over the entire body until it became a mass of the thought of God and His power to heal. I remember doing that, and I affirmed as you directed, 'Think of the hand of Jesus Christ as touching your feet and every member of your body and finally resting on your heart, and hear Him say, "Let not your heart be troubled." (John 14:27) Then feel His hand resting upon your head.' By the time I had finished that process I felt calm and confident about my condition. I got well, and ever since that time I have felt vigorous and strong." This man, in a hospital, no less than those long ago on the hillsides, reached out by faith and touched Christ and was healed.

A real cause of ill health is ill will. This malady is well named, for it is actually "sick will." Having allowed ill will to accumulate and its inevitable accompaniment of guilt to clog the mind, naturally your vital powers are depressed. Sick feeling results. The cure of this condition is good will, that is to say, "well will." This may be accomplished by a shift to the attitude of love and the healing qualities which it generates.

I was once asked to see a man who had every material thing that anyone could seemingly want in life. He had been so abjectly catered to by everyone that if any person had the effrontery to differ, even slightly, with him he would seethe in resentment. One associate had opposed him rather vigorously and this tycoon had developed what literally amounted to hatred for this man whom he accused of "double-crossing him," though this appraisal was not true.

He had dwelt upon this man's honest difference of opinion to such an extent that he could think only evil of his business associate. This ill will had gone on for some months.

At the time I saw him he complained of a small appetite and of not being able to sleep. His stomach was also causing considerable discomfort. Moreover, he had developed pain, particularly in his hands and fingers.

The doctor had diagnosed this trouble as a type that could be healed by treatment of his emotional state. "In fact," said the man, "the doctor says that I can get over it if I 'get myself straightened out.' "

"What do you mean, 'straightened out'?" I asked.

"I mean straightened out in my mind. But the worst thing bothering me most is my right arm. I can't seem to raise it higher than my shoulder, try as hard as I will, nor can I fully clench my fist. I can close it about nine-tenths of the way, but that is as far as I can manipulate it, and I feel a lack of force in my hand."

As we talked, a curious and repetitive emphasis came out in his speech. As he discussed the man whom he declared had double-crossed him, he fumed, saying explosively, "I would give my right arm if I could smash that guy." Referring to several other people whom he disliked, he kept coming back to that figure, that if he could only retaliate against them he would "give his right arm." Apparently in his mind the picture of giving his right arm was, for him, a sufficient characterization of the virulence of his ill will.

I do not wish to press this diagnosis too far. It is perhaps almost too apt and simple, but I made a long guess and said, "I think that right arm of yours might actually be inhibited by hate. To feel well and vital, maybe you'd better empty out the poisons and acids of antagonism through the curative force of love."

"How in the world do I do that?" he asked.

"It's just this simple," I said. "Pray for that man you hate until you actually pray out the hate and pray in love. You will have to forgive and forget and attain for that man good will—well will—if you hope to be well."

This man was a very forthright individual, and it was with great difficulty that I persuaded him to employ the suggested cure. But he is one of those strong characters who goes all out for anything, whether it be hate or love; so when he finally decided to practice love he gave full cooperation. I told him that the way to get rid of hate and substitute love was, while praying for the disliked man, to try and see the good in him rather than the bad. I encouraged him to adopt an objective and scientific attitude toward his hates, thinking of them as symptoms of an illness that required treatment.

When he was convinced that he could eliminate the ill will that was making him suffer physically by praying for his enemy he began practicing this healing formula. I asked him to pray out loud to be sure he had the right approach. It was a bit amusing because halfway through the prayer he stopped and addressed the Lord, colloquially, though not without proper respect, "Lord, I'm a fourflusher and I don't really mean this prayer. I'm only doing it because I'm told to."

But I interrupted and said, "But you've got to mean it, and you must pray until you do mean it."

"O.K.," he said, "let's start praying again and I'll make myself mean it." Note that he did not qualify his intention by even saying he would try, but would make himself mean it. If I know the Lord at all I'm sure He likes honest and forthright men like this one.

He finally got to the point where he could actually pray for the other man. And then things really began to happen. Power came through. I cannot report that all of a sudden, miraculously, he raised his right arm. He had a lot of deep-lodged sin and spiritual sickness in him, and it took many weeks of this stiff curative process to drain it out, but drain it out he did.

Recently I saw him, and with a grin he said, "Look at

that arm." He raised it full above his head. He chuckled and declared as he demonstrated, "I can clench my fist, too, and I could sure hit that bird now, but do you know, the funny thing is I no longer want to hit him because I really like him. We have come to understand each other. I like that fellow because I always know exactly where he stands." (That characteristic was what originally caused his dislike.)

This industrialist became a man of vital energies. He feels well and is very alive. Moreover, he has brought to his new spiritual interest the same thoroughness that gave him success in business. He reads and studies the Bible and other religious writings meticulously. He applies Christian principles in business and has become extraordinarily service-minded. He explained his reversal of attitude from his former self-centeredness by explaining: "You must share God's blessings, for you cannot keep them unless you also give them away." How right he is. People who seek God's power only for what it can do for them will be frustrated unless they become a medium through which the benefit is conveyed to others.

Still another illustration of the strange manner in which unhealthy thinking and attitudes conspire to reduce aliveness, is a case history which was reported to me by a pastor who conducts healing services with considerable success.

To a healing service came a middle-aged woman who walked with a noticeable limp. She waited for the pastor afterwards and said, "Of late this limp has developed and my doctor says there is apparently nothing he can do for me, that it must represent some hidden injury to the muscles. Will you please pray for me?"

"No," was the surprising answer of the pastor. "I will not pray *for* you, but I will pray *with* you. We will make the prayer a cooperative spiritual enterprise, not primarily to ask relief for your trouble, but to ascertain what has happened within you, spiritually and psychologically, that has manifested itself in this physical condition. We must probe for possible psychosomatic and spiritual ills." He then prayed that the woman might receive insight, and she went away. She returned to several successive healing services, and each time the pastor had a private exploratory prayer with her, asking for guidance. But still the limp continued.

Finally, after one prayer session, she said, slowly, "An idea keeps coming to mind in my prayers. It is this: my daughter and son-in-law formerly lived with me and I simply could not abide my son-in-law. I detested him, and not long ago we had a big row. My daughter took his part against me. It was a terrible experience and it left me limp in my mind and spirit. And it was not long afterward that the limp developed in my leg. It never occurred to me that there could possibly be a connection between my physical condition and my feeling toward my son-in-law and daughter. The notion is preposterous, isn't it?"

"One way to find whether there is any connection is to remove the barrier between the young couple and yourself and then see what happens in the physical problem," the minister replied.

The woman decided to go to her son-in-law and daughter and tell them she was sorry for her attitude. She said, in reporting to her pastor, "I hesitated at first, fearing they might not receive me, and I did not want to be humiliated. I continued to pray and finally, I went to their house. They were surprised and cool at first, but when I told them how sorry I was, that I hadn't acted right and wanted to correct my attitude and have their forgiveness, they were very kind. We had a genuine reconciliation and," she added, "I'm surprised at what a nice person my son-in-law really is; and he seems to like me, too, believe it or not."

As the pastor watched the woman walk from the church he had the impression that she was improved, but was hesitant to expect a seemingly miraculous result. But, after some weeks, the woman became aware that she was walking normally again. The minister tells me that physicians authenticate the case and, in fact, one remarked, "People limp in and out of my office whose basic illness is in the emotions; yes, perhaps in the soul."

Do not conclude from this that everybody you see limping around your community has had a fight with someone in the family or is filled with hate. I only cite this as an illustration of the apparent relationship between unhealthy thinking and feeling.

You can stay dynamically alive by flushing out of your mind the unhealthy attitudes which act as depressants and then by filling your mind with those creative thoughts which faith stimulates. Aliveness depends upon the penetration into the personality of a stimulating, transforming, and vitalizing faith.

Aliveness and a sense of dynamic being do not come easily. Values of this importance cannot be achieved without spiritual "blood, sweat, and tears," to use Churchill's famous phrase. It is hard to change a wrong mental cast developed over many years. Sometimes a person may have such a tremendous spiritual experience that he is changed very quickly and dramatically. But, for the most part, we must painstakingly work and practice our way to vital well-being.

An excellent suggestion for practicing aliveness was given me by a dynamic and energetic friend, Melvin J. Evans. An expert in management engineering, industrial relations, and marketing, Mr. Evans likes to describe himself as a "human engineer." His achievement in the field of personality rehabilitation through industry is outstanding. Mr. Evans maintains an almost incredible schedule of speeches and conferences in addition to regular business activities.

I asked the secret of his energetic and joyful aliveness of body, mind, and spirit. He believes it possible to develop a daily rhythm that stimulates energy and vitality. He described a recent schedule: "I have been out on conferences and lectures for two days straight. I came in on the plane at seven o'clock tonight and leave by plane again at eight tomorrow morning and for the next three days will be busy from early morning until late at night. I have been able to develop zest and energy for this activity through the following routine.

"First, every morning breathe very slowly and deeply, stretching meanwhile.

"Second, repeat the Twenty-third Psalm slowly and prayerfully, stopping after each phrase to express thanksgiving."

That is a quite interesting technique. For example, the first phrase in the Twenty-third Psalm is, "The Lord is my shepherd." After saying that, meditate on the way God has watched over you and taken care of you. The next phrase in the Psalm is, "I shall not want." After repeating those words, reflect, thankfully, that you do not lack food or shelter. Since hearing of this technique I have practiced it myself and find it amazingly effective and stimulating.

"Third, make a similar use of the Lord's Prayer, briefly stopping to be thankful after each phrase.

"Fourth, turn on the radio to a marching tune and really step out for a few moments." Mr. Evans says he used to be hesitant about suggesting this procedure until he read that Winston Churchill uses it. He puts on his bathrobe, a cane over his shoulder, and really prances around every morning.

"Fifth, stop several times every day for two minutes of prayer." Consider the potential value of this. It means twenty to thirty minutes a day of prayer, and a different kind of prayer at that, the thanksgiving, joyful type. Contrast this with your usual, depressing thoughts, not for thirty minutes, but for several hours a day. They take the life out of you. These brief prayers of thanksgiving and joy and faith will have a powerful tonic effect on you.

"Sixth, whenever an interruption comes, fill it by taking a half dozen breaths and saying a quick prayer."

This daily tune up of body, mind, and spirit may be effectively aided by spiritual reading and meditation. Supply yourself with books or booklets that are scientifically constructive in spiritual practice. I have prepared two booklets, *Thought Conditioners* and *Spirit Lifters,* which may be helpful.

Even as airplane engines must be tuned up before taking off, so must a human being have a tuning up process. The body has many miles of blood vessels and nerves to stimulate, if you want to travel in high gear. And your mental and spiritual elements also require constant attunement to keep them functioning at full potential.

When you contemplate the bad effect of years of unhealthy thinking on your mental and emotional nature, you can understand why the verve and spring goes out of you. To feel alive and well, daily revitalize your entire being with dynamic spiritual thinking, with exercise, and with the observance of the laws of health.

No one needs to go drooping and crawling through life. Jesus Christ teaches a method that makes people come alive, makes them joyous and vibrant.

When you live contrary to the truth which Christ teaches, you actually siphon off your own dynamism and drain your basic vitality. Wrong thinking and living can so undermine personality that, in effect, it may give up completely and produce nervous breakdown. It can even kill you. Dr. Charles Mayo is reported to have said, "I never knew a man to die of overwork but I have known them to die of doubt." It appears that faith is more even than creed or thought; it is life force. When faith declines and wrong thinking dominates, the personality sickens.

❖ ❖ ❖

The following suggestions may help you to feel alive and well:

1. Send for your minister even as you call your doctor when illness comes.
2. Believe in the healing Grace of Christ and affirm that it is operating in you.
3. Think of your body as the temple of the soul and treat it with respect.
4. Empty out all resentment and hate.
5. Pray for your doctor that he may have healing skill as a servant of the Great Physician.
6. Keep body, mind, and soul spiritually tuned up by daily periods of exercise and thanksgiving.
7. Visualize health and wholeness and entertain no sick thoughts about yourself or loved ones.
8. Believe that God, who creates, can also re-create, and think of the re-creative process as operating within you at all times.
9. Study and practice the spiritual rules of health contained in the Bible.
10. Remember the famous statement of Ambroise Pare, one of the most noted physicians of Europe, "Je le pansay, Dieu le guarit"—"I dressed him, God cured him."

CHAPTER XIV

SELF-CONFIDENCE AND DYNAMIC ACHIEVEMENT

"Many people, perhaps most people, never utilize the potential strength within their own personalities. There is resident in you an immense reservoir of force; the power of the subconscious mind. Faith releases this power. Then, mental, emotional, and spiritual strength emerges which is more than enough to override your defeats."

FROM INFANTILE PARALYSIS to world champion high-jumper, that is the thrilling story of Walter Davis. It was said that he could not walk again. But his minister planted creative faith in his mind. His mother nurtured that faith, and lovingly worked over his weakened legs until he could walk and, presently, even run.

One day he saw a boy high-jumping and thought this a sport he would like to try. He did quite well at it, so decided he would become the best high-jumper in the world. What audacity faith puts into our minds!

But his legs were still weak. When he married, his wife watched his painstaking efforts to strengthen them and she said, "Walter, you must have power in your mind, too." Then she coined a wonderful phrase: "The strength of belief; with that you will have the strength you need in your legs."

Walter Davis put his wife's suggestion into practice and, eventually, it brought him a world record. In a championship field meet he cleared the bar at six feet, eleven inches, then at six, eleven and a half. The bar was raised to six, eleven and five-eighths. On his first jump he knocked the bar down; on the second jump, the same. He lay on the ground for a moment's rest and repeated to himself, "The strength of belief." He painted a mental picture of himself clearing that bar, propelled by the strength of belief. Then, before a hushed stadium, he jumped and went over the bar at six, eleven and five-eighths! The boy they said might never walk again was champion high-jumper of the world!

The strength of belief is your key to self-confidence. It will more than help you meet and overcome your difficulties and obstacles.

There is a text in the Bible which is fundamental in attaining self-confidence. It is so powerful that if driven deeply into your consciousness, it can change your life.

"If God be for us, who can be against us?" (Romans 8:31)

Personalize those words so that they apply directly to you, say "If God be for *me*." Then bring to mind a picture of all the things you think are against you. Now bring a picture into your mind of God facing your obstacles. Can they stand against God? Practice the strength of belief.

No hazard, obstacle, or difficulty need defeat you. Accept that as a fact, hold that confidence firmly in mind until it becomes reality, and you will have mastered one of the greatest secrets in this life. But this must be a humble faith in God and not bumptious faith in your own power. Every day fill and refill your mind to overflowing with that kind of faith until your thinking is thoroughly reconditioned.

Faith, the greatest power in this world, moves mountains and hurls obstacles aside. It overrides so-called impossibles. It crushes fear. It makes life vital, dynamic, and joyful. The answer to all your struggles, to all your defeats, and to all your hopes as well, is faith—wholehearted, all out, enthusiastic faith.

One of the most powerful, most valuable, most practical truths ever stated is described in the following three sentences. "If ye have faith . . . nothing shall be impossible unto you." (Matt. 17:20) "According to your faith be it done unto you." (Matt. 9:29) "If thou canst believe, all things are possible to him that believeth." (Mark 9:23)

The words of the Bible can condition your mind so that confidence and faith may develop within you. Having spent several summers in Switzerland, I have come to know that one of the great personalities of that country was the late Friedrich Frey. From peasant beginnings he became a leader in the Swiss power industry and developed a uniquely beautiful summer hotel enterprise on the famous Burgenstock. In these hotels he placed his own magnificent collection of paintings, tapestries, and antique furniture.

His son, my friend Fritz Frey, the dynamic head of these enterprises, in explaining the strong personality of his father, said, "In his early life my father was ill for a year. During this period he read the Bible through many times. What he read profoundly affected him. I believe he could walk a ridge with a precipice on either side and have absolute confidence."

It cannot be urged too forcefully that successful living depends upon acquiring confidence and this is best accomplished through the consistent and persistent practice of faith. To an amazing degree this practice will free you from your weaknesses and fears, give you a consciousness of your untapped resources, and make possible the releasing of your hidden abilities. It will activate the deeper powers of your personality, and help you to develop a more effective grasp on life.

So, do not attempt to cope further with life without learning and perfecting the techniques of dynamic and creative confidence.

I make these assertions because of the great number of people who have developed confidence through the suggested techniques. They took seriously the Biblical statement, "The Lord is on my side, I will not fear." (Psalm 118:6) What more do you need than that? Only your own cooperation. So shift your thoughts from the things that are against you and focus them on the vast power that is for you. Think obsessively of difficulty and it will grow to enormous proportions and may defeat you. Change your thinking to a confidence-obsession and you will be made bigger than your difficulty. It will require a very great deal to defeat the person who actually attempts to do God's will at all times. And certainly God wills that you shall be victorious over your weaknesses.

In this book I can tell about only a few of the many whom I have known who have found the key to self-confidence. One is my friend Dr. Alfred P. Haake, an outstanding public speaker. But he was not always eloquent for, as a boy, he was so badly afflicted with stuttering that he could scarcely form a complete sentence.

I asked him how a boy who stuttered so pathetically became a competent speaker. His answer was, "When we adapt ourselves to God's laws, changes occur within ourselves that seem miraculous, but which are simply the working of spiritually scientific principles."

As a boy his stuttering made school very difficult. The boys would sometimes call him "out" in baseball games when he was actually safe, just to hear him stutter. He knew well enough what he wanted to say, but the words piled up below his throat and he was unable to organize them. He was the butt of the unthinking cruelty of his schoolmates.

One Sunday afternoon he went to a meeting at the YMCA in Chicago to hear the late Senator Albert J. Beveridge of Indiana. The Senator was himself a celebrated orator.

"Until this very day," says my friend, "I can close my eyes and see Senator Beveridge standing there with his finger seemingly pointed straight at me as he said, 'Young man, there isn't a thing in the world you cannot do if you believe you can.' "

To this unhappy, nervous, stuttering lad it seemed that the words were meant especially for him. For the first time he actually accepted the incredible possibility that he might overcome his handicap.

He told his mother about his great new hope. She was a wise woman and knew something of the heartbreak that results from over-expectation, so she cautioned gently, "Be patient, my son. If we have faith and never stop trying, some of our dreams are bound to come true."

The boy, deeply stirred, knelt by his bed that night with the first real feeling he had ever had that God does understand. Then, to his astonishment, he started to pray out loud with scarcely a stutter. It was a tumultuous outpouring of deep, inner feeling and, he says, "I felt then, and I feel now that my prayer went straight to the heart of God."

This first release gave evidence that complete victory could and would come. But no miracle happened. He still stuttered a great deal and the boys and girls continued to laugh at him; but now he was different inwardly and his mental attitude was becoming more confident. Next day he stood bravely and answered a question in class, struggling hard, but not giving up. Through all his painful efforts to speak he heard the voice of the Senator saying, "Have faith," and the voice of his mother adding, "Be patient."

He read about Demosthenes who was said to have overcome a speech impediment by speaking with stones in his mouth. For days after that the boy went to the shore of Lake Michigan, filled his mouth with stones and practiced speaking as Demosthenes did. He tried this again and again with fewer stones each day. Then he would fall upon his knees, crying out piteously, "Oh, God, please let me talk."

"God must have listened to my words and known the pain and hunger in my heart, for one day as I knelt by the Lake shore a calm came over me, and I knew I would win this battle. I was certain that my dreams would come true if I continued to believe in God and in myself."

Lots of trying followed. He took lessons in public speaking and worked and struggled, prayed and believed, and then one day he made a complete speech without hesitation, receiving applause from his audience. That was the happiest day of his life. From then on he made speeches whenever opportunity offered, and always told people how they can overcome every difficulty if only they will believe in God and so have confidence in themselves.

Many people, perhaps most people, never utilize the potential strength within their own personalities. There is resident in you an immense reservoir of force; the power of the subconscious mind. Faith releases this power. Then, mental, emotional, and spiritual strength emerges which is more than enough to override your defeats.

In the subconscious God presides with His illimitable power. If you are allowing yourself to be defeated, practice thinking confidently and focus your thoughts upon God. This inward power, this power of God within you, is so tremendous that under stress and in crises people can perform the most incredible feats. Such demonstrations should make us realize that we can overcome every difficulty in life.

A newspaper tells of a farmer's wife, a woman of only average strength, who was in the farm garage where her husband was working under a jacked-up automobile. Suddenly the car slipped off the jack, leaving one wheel resting partially over his body in such a manner that he was unable to extricate himself. No one was near to help her. Ah, yes, there was! There was God and His immense untapped power within herself.

She prayed and was guided to draw upon this vast power which emerges from within us under extraordinary crises. As this inner force flowed up within her she lifted the car almost imperceptibly, just the barest fraction of an inch, but nevertheless enough so that her husband could wiggle free.

When, later, she attempted to move the car, of course she could not budge it at all. No doubt nature sent a tremendous shot of adrenalin through her system in that moment of crisis. But beyond that chemical assistance, where did she get this power? Was it from the outside? Obviously not. That extra power came from within herself; from God within. It was a super-strength which she did not know was stored up within her. She was able to draw upon it through the combined dynamics of crisis and affirmative faith.

Another case is that of a man who was an invalid, or who thought he was, which may be quite as bad, for if you are an invalid in your mind, the consequent reactions and result are often not dissimilar to physical invalidism. One may slip into an invalid state from psychological as well as from physical reasons. At any rate, this man sat helplessly in his wheel chair, a psychological invalid.

One summer day his sixteen-year-old son wheeled his father to the beach and then went in swimming. Presently, too far off shore, he was stricken with a cramp. No one was near to respond to his cries for help. The father, terrified by his son's danger, looked frantically about for assistance. Realizing the situation, crisis freed him. He sprang from the wheel chair, rushed to the water, threw off his clothes, dove into the sea, and brought the boy safely ashore.

Then he was aghast at his own action. But when no ill effect immediately occurred, the possibility began to dawn upon him that he was not an invalid at all except, perhaps, in his thoughts. He never returned to the wheel chair and ultimately became a normal person.

Whence came this sudden access of strength? From outside himself? Not at all, but rather from within where it had been waiting all the time. It is very important to emphasize to yourself that there is an enormous reservoir of power within yourself, but it is God-power and must be used spiritually and in harmony with the laws of Christ. You may draw upon this power by practicing faith in God and by humbly conditioning your life to His will. You may then be confident that the "impossibles" of life are not impossible at all. As the Bible points out "The things which are impossible with man are possible with God." (Luke 18:27)

It is also expressed in another significant statement, "For, behold, the kingdom of God is within you," (Luke 17:21) meaning God's mighty power is deep within your subconscious waiting to come to your aid when faith releases it. When you realize your inner power supply and live upon it, you will experience one of the most thrilling discoveries in this life. You will know that you have adequate ability to handle life successfully through the power of God within you.

The dramatic fact is that the very moment you decide positively that nothing shall longer defeat you, then from that instant of decision *nothing can defeat you.* If your decision is a real one, and truly God-centered, in that flashing second you take power over circumstances. You will grow in your new strength through the deepening of your faith.

As a boy I was afflicted with extreme shyness, and for

years I suffered actual mental pain and agony. My shyness was so bad that I was acutely self-conscious and shrank from meeting strangers. Then, in some manner, I got the idea that I wanted to be a public speaker, probably out of a desire to compensate for my defeat feelings. While I wanted to be a speaker, yet I hated speaking, for whenever I forced myself to appear before people I suffered excruciating misery from my shyness and embarrassment.

Near the end of my freshman year in college, a professor rendered me a very great service although in the process he gave me a rough time. "Norman," he said, "you might conceivably amount to something, but never as long as you are such a pathetic victim of shyness. What is the matter with you? Have you no manhood?" he asked. He really let me have it. His comments were what you might term uncomplimentary, to use profound understatement. "In fact," he said, "I am disgusted with you. You are afraid of everything. Try making a man of yourself. Use the faith you have been taught. Do something about yourself."

That sort of talk made me so mad I stomped out of his office. He was only trying to rouse me and knew he had to hit me hard to bring me out of my self-consciousness. But I walked down the hall enraged, saying to myself, "I'm going to leave this school, but I shall come back and tell that professor a few things." What I was going to tell him would make your blood run cold.

Then I started down the steps of Gray Chapel. Strangely, I recall that I came to the fourth step from the bottom and there I stopped short, for a new and revolutionary thought hit me. I can remember even yet how it struck with almost a physical impact. It was "Why don't you quit this shyness now? Why not stop it right this minute? Get through with it, and do it immediately."

And so, on the fourth step from the bottom, I asked the

Lord to help me, and the Lord seemed to say, "If you really mean it, I will help you now."

And I answered, "Yes, I really mean it." The combination of prayer and faith, and being none too gently prodded by that professor, brought this decision to focus at that precise moment.

I moved down from that step across the campus, and can even yet remember the feeling of exultation which swept over me. I knew that I did not need to be a frightened, shy person any more. I realized, for the first time, that I could conquer my inferiority. Of course, I did not get over it immediately. In fact, I had plenty of struggles with it for a long time, but the process was started which led to control over this unhappy personality difficulty. In that moment of spiritual experience I gained the confidence that, with God's help, I could master my failure.

So, I say you do not really need to be defeated by anything if you make up your mind that you won't be, and if, at the same time, you do these four things. First, decide you are now through being dominated by an inferiority complex. Second, start filling the mind with an affirmative faith in God. Third, believe humbly, but strongly, in yourself. And fourth, start living in the belief that God is with you, helping you.

Lack of faith in yourself is one of the greatest barriers to the full expression of your personality. Carlyle says "Alas! the fearful unbelief is unbelief in yourself." Actually it is an affront to God when you have a low opinion of yourself, for He made you, you know.

Put your problem in the present tense. Affirm that God is *now* helping you. Affirm that you are *now* doing and acting efficiently. Affirm that, since God is *now* guiding you, your ineptitude and failures are *now* being superseded by a new keenness of mind and by a calm confidence. This may not happen in one dramatic moment, but even the gradual unfolding is dramatic.

Several years ago I met a young man who had just been made a junior officer of his company. The president of his organization is a famous businessman whose facial expression and demeanor give somewhat the impression that he is forbidding and difficult, although actually, he is a kindly person. His extraordinary physical size adds to this overpowering impression of sternness.

The young man was required, by his duties, to report personally to this president every day which made his job a painful problem since he was an acute sufferer from inferiority and shrinking. This daily consultation with the "great" man presently assumed the proportions of a crisis, so much so that he contemplated resigning.

He explained that the effect the older man had on him was "overwhelming." "Frankly," he continued, "that man frightens me so that I find it impossible to think clearly when in his presence. I become inarticulate and awkward. If only I could overcome this terrible shyness, I believe I might handle my job satisfactorily; but otherwise, I may be forced to quit."

The answer, of course, was to start developing within his thought rational, reasonable, belief in his own abilities. He needed to hold the thought that he had been appointed to his important position because his superiors had respect for his ability. Beyond that he should think of his new position as an opportunity for constructive service. Here again was that old bug-a-boo of thinking too much about yourself.

I made the following specific suggestion: "When your president summons you to his office, before you enter, stand for a moment outside his door and silently pray for *him*. Do not pray for yourself. Actually, all shy people are egotistical, their thought being painfully self-centered. To be healed, the shy person must master self-forgetfulness.

"Then," I continued, "send out good will thoughts to the man behind that door. His very reserve and pompous attitude may indicate his need for understanding, even affection. He may also need someone who is not afraid of him. Pray that you may be of help to him, believe that you will be, then enter his office with confidence and with a desire to serve." He promised to follow these directions.

Some months passed before I saw him again and then I met quite a different person. He revealed a new and quiet confidence. "How are you getting along with the boss?" I inquired.

His face lit up as he replied, "He is a wonderful person. When you get under that rough exterior he is a kindly man. I followed your suggestions and, for a while, nothing happened. But presently I began to realize that I was feeling better about the problem. Then one day the boss said something that nearly bowled me over. 'Bill, I have come to depend upon you. You are a great help to me.'

"That was the finest compliment ever paid me. For the first time I felt that I mattered in the business, that I was actually important to its success. That really did something for me. Now I get a big kick out of the job and," he added, "it is a privilege to work with that man." I noted that he said "with" rather than "for," denoting an identification and growing confidence in his own value to the enterprise. This man's attitude changed from one of self-consciousness, fear, and tension to one of relaxation, confidence, and assurance.

Every person who is now defeated by situations or circumstances, or by any feeling of inferiority or inadequacy, or any other personal weakness, must come to a precise releasing moment when, in this thoughts, he resolutely decides that he is going to have confidence.

When your conscious mind definitely accepts this thought it is then passed to the subconscious where, if firmly emphasized, it will become determinative. There must be present, however, a positive spiritual force to activate your decision. That force is a humble faith in God. It may be deepened by using such an affirmation as, "I believe that God *now* gives me strength. I believe that God is *now* helping me. I believe that God is *now* releasing my hidden powers."

Continue to affirm in this manner until your subconscious mind fully accepts that which the conscious mind passes to it. Then it will become a fact. As you maintain and strengthen faith in this manner your problems, instead of appalling you by their difficulties, will become increasingly easier of solution. Instead of being controlled by your weaknesses you will assume control over them.

Two of my most inspiring friends are Roy Rogers and his charming wife, Dale Evans Rogers, who are beloved by young Americans and older ones as well. At dinner in our home Roy told of his painful struggles with his inferiority complex, especially about talking in public. As a boy he says he was so shy that "the thought of saying anything before a class or just a few people would make me take off across the cornfields. But Dale is a mighty smart woman. My biggest triumph came when I used her suggestions about talking in public. The music part I handled without any fear, but when it came time to say a few words, I felt the same old nervous symptoms. Then I closed my eyes for just a moment and said silently, 'Lord, I'll just make a mess of things on my own. Help me to relax a little so that what I say to these people will really mean something.'

"I started to talk and found myself saying things I'd never said before. And they came out as naturally as though I was just standing there and someone else was talking. From that time I've never had more than the normal amount of nervousness."

I write so certainly about these matters for, as previously indicated, personal convictions concerning the power of faith developed out of my own painful experience with inner defeat. At the risk of making this chapter too biographical, I should like to relate another of the determinative incidents out of which this philosophy evolved. I feel justified in so doing since the point of view presented in this chapter and throughout this book developed out of hard, difficult, personal experience. And, if by recounting my own sufferings and struggles I can help other people overcome their own, the purpose of this book will be achieved. I, personally, know that the techniques of faith work, and have no doubt about it at all, for I tested them in my own experience. Thus, in urging my readers to become practitioners of creative faith, I am advocating a formula of living, the soundness of which I have good personal reason to know.

At age twenty-eight I was suddenly called to head a church situated in a large university community. Its membership consisted of professors and their families, as well as leading business and professional people. Some learned and distinguished men were regular worshippers at that church.

I came to this responsibility young and with little experience. Furthermore, I was still struggling with self-doubts, a holdover from my earlier battle with shyness. These conflicts are hard, but fortunately they do die. In my heart I agreed with the many people who prophesied my early failure. But I stubbornly determined not to fail. Unfortunately, however, I did not attack the problem in the right spirit which was to forget self and go ahead and do the job in a natural manner. Instead, I worked ceaselessly, day and night, with tense effort, my nervous activity being largely based on fear of personal failure rather than on a humble desire to serve God.

Due to the kindly cooperation of the people and the efficiency of my associates, and perhaps to some extent to my own unremitting activity, the church program went along fairly well. But the strain of my feverish attempt to keep pace with the job began to tell. The haunting fear of failure drove me on. Soon I found myself in a highly nervous state. These hectic efforts were undermining my reserves of strength. Not only did I derive little satisfaction from my work, but I began to have a feeling that, despite all good intentions and sincerity of purpose, something fundamental was lacking. There was no lift, no spiritual power within me.

So, driven by necessity, I began to experiment with prayer in real earnest. I prayed for illumination and guidance, and presently found the solution. It came about as follows:

During this period of unhappy conflict, while traveling on a train running between Toledo and Columbus, Ohio, I was working on a sermon for the following Sunday entitled "The Secret of Power." Suddenly the thought came that the title was highly incongruous, for what did I know about any secret of power? Though I was completely sincere yet, actually, I was using only words without personal experience.

Then, strangely, I felt an overwhelming urge to pray. This proved to be one of the greatest prayers of my life. James Russell Lowell describes my experience as well as his own:

> I, who still pray at morning and at eve . . .
> Thrice in my life perhaps have truly prayed,
> Thrice stirred below my conscious self
> Have felt that perfect disenthrallment, which is God.

In my prayer I told the Lord that I was tired of my fear of failure and of being everlastingly concerned about myself. I told Him I was fed up with struggling simply to justify the confidence some people had in me, or to prove my worth to others, or to have good results for mere personal satisfaction. I told the Lord I wanted to be honest and sincere. And I deeply meant every word of this prayer.

Then, suddenly, I discovered one of the greatest of all spiritual laws, that of complete surrrender. Driven by the intense pain of my conflicts, I went the full limit of surrender to God and told the Lord that if it was best for me to fail, I was willing to fail. I stated that God was free to do anything with me He wanted to do, expressing only the hope that He would get it over as quickly as possible. I told God that I put myself completely and unreservedly in His hands and would try to follow His will as He might indicate; that my desire was only for spiritual peace and strength. It was a sincere and complete outpouring of deepest desire.

I learned in that moment that when we really mean our prayers, not fractionally or halfheartedly, but completely and wholeheartedly, we receive accordingly.

The result was overwhelming and amazing. I had no sooner finished this prayer than I became conscious of deep and complete peace. It is difficult to describe the serenity that came. It was one of the few unforgettable moments of my life. Then I began to feel a strange, quiet confidence. For the first time in my whole existence, I experienced personally, the meaning of spiritual victory.

I knew, then, that we may live victoriously, not because we have any power within ourselves, but because when we give ourselves to God, He gives Himself to us. It was a most ecstatic feeling of joy and wonderment.

Yet, coupled with this new and victorious feeling of release was the recognition that this was no power of my own, but was something given me. It was God's strength as He bestows it upon weak human beings. Many times since then my personal power has been very low, but that experience reminds me that, when I continue to surrender myself completely into God's hands and practice faith, I am sustained.

It is with some hesitation that I relate this experience lest pride be read into this narrative. I assure my readers that this type of experience does not lead to pride, but rather to humility, emphasizing as it does a profound recognition of one's dependence upon a power greater than himself. I tell of this experience only to say to you that whatever your condition in life, whatever difficulties you may be facing at the moment, this procedure is an absolutely certain way to gain strength and peace and victory. Practice wholeheartedly giving yourself to God, and God will, with equal wholeheartedness, give Himself to you. This is your great key to humble self-confidence.

❖ ❖ ❖

4 Keys to Self-Confidence

1. Cultivate "the strength of belief."
2. Shift your thoughts from the things that are against you and focus them on the vast power that is for you.
3. The very moment you decide that nothing shall defeat you, from that instant *nothing can defeat you.*
4. Surrender yourself to God.

CHAPTER XV

LIVING ABOVE PAIN AND SUFFERING

"We live in a world full of wonders. Indeed, we have seen so many marvels that scarcely anything now excites our incredulity. Can we, therefore, believe that wonders may not also occur in the area of spirit? Can they be as exactly governed by law as phenomena in the materialistic realm? The fact that we do not completely understand these laws does not indicate that such laws do not exist. Spiritual healings do not always occur; but they do occur, and one may always have the hope that he may be granted this great blessing by God."

LIVE DYNAMICALLY, enthusiastically, and with vitality, is the message of this book. But some face the problem of pain and suffering and to them this type of life may seem difficult. Life can indeed be a tough, hard road when one must walk with pain. But, even so, you can make of it a creative experience.

As difficult as it is, pain is not without value. Du Noüy discerned its purpose: "Without . . . suffering . . . man does not really humanize himself nor liberate his spiritual aspirations. It is because of this that pain is fruitful . . ."

In this chapter we will discuss effective techniques for the enduring of pain and suffering. But, on the more positive side, I want to plant the creative thought in your mind that you can rise above pain and, perhaps, even eliminate it altogether. The way you think has a great deal to do with the way you feel. And faith is the healthiest form of thought. So, instead of thinking sickness, weakness, and disease, try thinking in terms of vitality, energy, and well-being. This will require effort, of course, but many have demonstrated that such constructive thinking tends to tone up the system and greatly increase well-being.

Always hold a mental image of yourself as healthy and vigorous. Such an image, held in the mind, has a strong tendency to develop into actuality.

Also, when you pray for the well-being of others it is important to hold optimistic thoughts. While voicing the words of faith, if you visualize that person as sick instead of well, your real prayer, then, becomes an affirmation of sickness, not health. And the result is that you get what you see and believe. "According to your faith" [that is, according to the image in your mind] "be it unto you." (Matthew 9:29)

The Reverend A. H. Durham relates an incident illustrating how faith projected upon a condition of sickness sets vital forces in motion.

"About three years ago I was requested to visit, immediately, a young member of my church who was critically ill.

"I went at once and found the most frightened person I had ever seen. She held my hand in both of hers and kept repeating through her tears, 'Oh, Reverend Durham, I don't want to die.' I told her that she was the only one who was talking about death, and asked her to repeat for me the opening phrase of the Twenty-third Psalm. She replied at once, 'The Lord is my shepherd; I shall not want.'

" 'Now,' I said, 'if you could say that from your heart, and not just merely with your lips, you would not be the frightened girl you are, for you would be sure that your Shepherd is here, and that He will supply your wants.'

"Then, for about ten minutes I told her of all the comfort those words of faith could bring to a believing heart, and thus succeeded in calming her and preparing her for the prayer for her complete recovery which I then offered. Before leaving her I administered the 'laying on of hands,' using the form found in *The Book of Common Prayer* of the Episcopal Church.

"The next morning I was back at the hospital shortly before nine, but had to wait outside her room as the nurses were busy with her. Her doctor came up to me while I was waiting and said, 'Reverend Durham, some wonderful physical change has happened overnight to that patient . . . I can't understand it.'

"I replied, 'Oh, Doctor, I think she was just a very frightened girl last night.' But the doctor insisted that I was wrong, because she was having convulsions when they put her in that private room. It then occurred to me that they had taken her out of her ward and put her in that room to die without disturbing the other patients. I was glad, then, that I did not know the night before that the doctors had given her up.

"A week later as she left the hospital for her home, the nurses said, 'Well, we have seen a miracle, for we never expected her to walk out of this ward.'

"I do not believe I would have succeeded in awakening her faith in God that night if I had known what the doctors thought of her condition. Today she is well and hearty."

Had the minister known about the convulsions before he went into the patient's room he might very well have transmitted to her an image of death. Not having that knowledge to make him negative, he surrounded her with a positive faith image. That vital force turned the tide.

The problem, however, is to hold an image of health when you have full knowledge of the situation. The method then is not to concentrate mentally upon the sickness, but to see the person, or yourself, as in the flow of God's health and vitality. All creative energy in the universe flows from God and, through faith, we may draw upon it to combat sickness.

But the fact must be faced that pain and sickness may remain with one until the end of earthly life. In that event, one prays for strength to meet the inevitable with courage. Then faith becomes an instrument for getting insight into the fundamental meaning of suffering and for bearing it. Even as pain may be removed by faith, so it may be endured by faith.

This truth was brought home to me by the experience of my own uncle, William F. Peale. My affection for him is unbounded. He was a successful oil producer, a keen thinker, a strong yet kindly personality.

In his sixty-eighth year he contracted cancer of the throat and his larynx and tongue had to be removed. He suffered indescribable pain. All resources of modern medical science were employed, together with the techniques of prayer and faith.

But God's answer was that his life on earth should end. And that answer will come to each of us in due course. We must develop within ourselves the philosophy, the faith, and the courage to meet it and see it through, knowing that God never lays a burden or a pain upon us that He does not give us equivalent strength to bear it.

My uncle was not a regular church-going man, though a sincere believer. He talked very little about his religion. He had deep sentiments, but he concealed them well. His main sign of affection would be to thump you heavily in the chest, or give you a clap on the back, or do something nice for you, minimizing it at the same time. Under a rather brusque exterior, was the kindest and tenderest heart in the world.

As he lay on his bed before the operation I sat by his side.

I told him how sorry I was for all that he was compelled to endure. And then I said to him, "I would like you to know, Uncle Will, that my admiration for you is more than I can ever express. Some of us talk a great deal about God and faith and the things of religion, and you say very little. But I shall always remember you as one of the greatest human beings I ever knew. I would like to ask you how you are able to stand up to this thing as you do?"

He turned to me with a very peaceful look on his face and said, "There is nothing else to do, is there? I just have to take it as it comes."

We sat in silence for a moment and then he added, "But with the Lord's help I think we can see it through."

"Would you like me to pray?" I asked. He nodded and said, "Pray like Mother used to pray long ago when she put me to bed at night."

I remembered my grandmother so well. She had a simple faith in Jesus. So, in my prayer, I prayed to Jesus: "Dear Jesus, be with Uncle Will in this operation. Help him to put his hand in Yours and not be afraid. Help him to know that You will stand by him every minute of the time. Help the doctors, too. And give Uncle Will the strength, the comfort, the patience he needs. This we ask in Jesus' name. Amen." That was the way Grandma would have prayed and he looked at me with a wonderful smile.

Then, before I left the room, I did something I had never done with him before: he was not the kind for whom you showed affection in this manner, and it wasn't the way I usually did things, either. I leaned down and kissed him on the forehead. In that hospital room I had a wonderful experience of the Presence of God in a time of pain and tragic suffering. By simply putting your faith in Him, you can get through your pain and suffering as Uncle Will did.

Also, I have known others who were not claimed by death, but whose disability became permanent and who learned to live with it in a victorious manner. In the last analysis the secret of life isn't in what happens to you, but what you do with what happens to you.

There is my friend Harry Doehla. He was a bright lad making a good record in school when, at seventeen, he was taken with rheumatic fever. He was told that he would never walk again and could never use his hands.

The word "useless" drummed itself into his consciousness. The hurt in his mind was worse than the pain in the muscles. He was in black despair.

While his parents worked in the mill he sat at home in a handmade wheelchair. One day he fell onto the floor, and lay hopeless and helpless until a passing mail carrier put him back into the chair. Then, one day, a man gave him a Bible text, "If ye have faith, and doubt not, yet shall . . . say unto this mountain, Be thou removed . . ." (Matthew 21:21)

"Well," said Harry, "mine is a big mountain, but one thing is sure, while I may be crippled in hands and legs I am not crippled in mind or soul. And I can live, not by leg power, but by mind power; not by hand power, but by faith power."

Then he "got" the idea that he might sell greeting cards. So, with his gnarled hands he painfully made his first greeting card. It took him weeks and he sold it for a nickel. That was the greatest day of his life. Later he built a successful greeting card company. "I discovered I had something in my brain greater than any deficiency in my body. I had mind-power through faith."

He wrote his unforgettable story for our magazine *Guideposts* under the title "By Wheelchair to the Stars." Harry Doehla is the fastest man in a wheelchair I have ever known. He whirls it up to his automobile, slides into the seat of his car, and drives with skill.

You see, it isn't all-important what the condition of your body is; the important factor is the condition of your mind and soul. With mental power and faith power you can weave pain and suffering into a great life. Harry Doehla did; so can you.

Another example is my friend Harry Moore. One tragic day he was told that he would be blind. Standing at the window of his room on the sixteenth floor of a New York hotel the thought came that in less than a minute he could end all of his troubles; he need not live with the agony and frustration of blindness.

But instead of throwing himself out the window he fell to his knees and prayed, "Dear Lord, I need You. I cannot get along without You. Help me and show me what to do."

He prayed for a long time. "All of a sudden," he said, "I seemed to feel a Presence and to hear a Voice saying, 'I am with you always.' " (Matthew 28:20)

In the succeeding years he has had a successful career of service. He is one of the best storytellers south of Mason and Dixon's line, which is saying a great deal for any storyteller. He is a radiant, victorious person bringing inspiration to all. He stood up to his pain and suffering and did something constructive about it. You never think of him as blind, at all.

Such human experiences as these I have described prove several things about life. One is that sometimes we simply have to live with our pain and suffering and physical disability. Another is that in living with it we can overcome it.

The man with arthritis may go to a doctor and be told that there isn't much that can be done about it, medically speaking, and that he will just have to live with his arthritis and get along with it the best he can. And, if he stops fighting it, and cooperates with it, the chances are that it won't bother him too much and he can live a very satisfactory life with it. That is the way life is; we have to get along with arithmetic, and with arthritis, and with other things as well.

There is an enormous power in the human spirit to rise above pain and suffering when the spirit is determined and when you plumb those deeper resources of power which have been inherently built into your system.

William James brilliantly discussed the second wind that enables us to forge past the first and even second barrier of fatigue.

Your normal energies carry you to the first barrier of fatigue. You feel that you cannot go further. But, if you project your faith and energy beyond the first conscious barrier of fatigue, you emerge into an area of consciousness where fatigue drops away and you have what Professor James called a second wind, or new access of power.

People who do the great things in life, who overcome enormous odds and difficulties, are those who go not only beyond the first conscious barrier of fatigue, but perhaps beyond even a second, as well. There is released within them what seems to be a superpower so that they perform the most astonishing feats.

An illustration is the experience of Enrico Caruso, the famous tenor, who was so ill that it was felt he could not get out of bed to sing. But he said that he must sing, and that he was determined to sing. Seven-thirty came and his manager said, "Senor, the last moment has come; you must go to the opera house."

Blinded by pain, he dragged himself from his bed and was taken to the opera house. He lay on a couch as they dressed him for his role, being too ill to stand.

Eight-thirty came and the manager said, "Señor, you must go on the stage." He pulled himself up, went to the wings. Then he forced his great will beyond the first and second barriers of fatigue and, when the cue came, rushed on stage, pouring out unforgettable melodies.

Charles A. Lindbergh, in his historic flight through the lonely vastness of the Atlantic skies, amidst drifting fogs and winds, kept his little plane going hour after hour until he became overwhelmed with the desire to sleep. If he could only close his eyes for just one delicious moment! His description of his struggle against sleep is a classic. He knew that if he gave in it would mean certain death. So, he pushed his spirit past the first barrier of fatigue, then past the second barrier, and then he became aware, all at once, of a second self. It was the emergence of power from within.

Real champions force through these barriers by sheer faith and courage. Alice Marble, former tennis champion of the world, on the day preceding the championship match at Wimbledon, strained a muscle. She suffered such excruciating pain that when she tried to raise her arm to practice her serve, she cried out in anguish. The doctor told her she might permanently harm herself if she insisted upon playing.

But Alice Marble was there to play so she went into a little room off the stadium and prayed for strength. Before beginning the game the players were supposed to curtsy to the Queen. Her opponent gave a beautiful curtsy while Miss Marble was able only to nod her head. But the Queen smiled pleasantly, nonetheless. It was with great agony that she served. At that moment she came to a pain fatigue barrier where it seemed she could go no further, but by her faith she forced beyond the barrier and lost her pain. When Alice Marble became champion she used an interesting phrase, "Prayer is my racquet."

No discussion of pain is adequate that does not consider the possibility that pain, either of spirit or body, may be a manifestation of disharmony.

One form of disharmony is ill will. I have indicated elsewhere how appropriately named is such feeling, for the will is indeed sick. This can create a form of pain quite as intense as physical pain.

Dis-ease means ease discounted. Ill will is dislocated harmony. So, when you live on a basis of ill will, your will is actually dis-eased. But your will can be made well by the healing power of good will (healthy will).

Dr. James Dale Van Buskirk, in *Religion, Healing and Health*, recounts a case history from Dr. Walter C. Alvarez of Mayo Clinic about a man who killed himself with ill will. The patient was in good health, when his father's death precipitated a dispute with his sister over their parent's property. The sister contested the father's will and won. From that time the patient could think or talk of nothing else.

It became an obsession. He detested his sister with a malignant hatred. At length he developed symptoms of illness. His breath became foul and stayed so. He began having difficulty with his heart and blood pressure. Then followed various bodily deteriorations, and before many months he was dead. "It seemed obvious," was the doctor's startling comment, "that he died of bodily injuries wrought by powerful emotion. The profound ill will generated in his system over a period of time had actually killed him."

The powerful effect of spirit on the body is generally recognized today. If the soul is sick, the body may become sick. It appears, then, that to be healthy you need, also, to be holy. The word "holy" does not mean super-pious, but derives from "wholth," an Anglo-Saxon word meaning the entire being or whole person. Spiritual harmony is a powerful resistance to that disharmony known as disease. Faith greatly helps in alleviating pain, especially psychic pain.

One way that Christ heals is by restoring spiritual harmony, both within and without the personality. And harmony is so vital to well-being that it cannot be overstressed. Harmony has a powerful influence in establishing health which may have been undermined by vindictive attitudes.

A pastor told me of a girl in his parish who took twenty-eight sleeping pills and was at the verge of death. The doctor considered her chances for recovery as slight, for she had a profound will not to live. Her father, it seems, was a mean, dominating person, and the house was filled with a spirit of tension and ill will. The girl was sincerely religious and she had a strong sense of filial obligation to her father.

But she had hate feelings toward him and, consequently, developed a deep sense of guilt. The inharmonious situation finally became intolerable to her. This, coupled with neurotic feelings of unworthiness, stimulated deep depression which resulted in the suicide attempt.

The pastor, in counseling with the family, made clear the necessity for spiritual harmony among them. Through prayer, self-examination, and forgiveness the members of this family were fused into a feeling of unity between themselves and with God. Hate was washed out and love, the most creative of all emotions, began its salutary operation. This made them ready for the act of healing faith. They surrendered the sick girl to God. They affirmed that, being God's child, His healing Grace was even then touching her. They asked for her recovery but, with love and faith, surrendered her to God's will.

Then the pastor took that formerly inharmonious family to the church. He had them kneel at the altar and pray for a deepened harmony in their hearts and in their home.

The father, who had never before prayed aloud, now offered a simple, but curative prayer. "Lord, I am a mean man. I ask You now to take all the meanness out of my heart and fill me with the harmony of Christ."

The pastor reported that the turn came in the illness of the girl at that precise moment, and in a short time she was well again. This was corroborated by the physician. "That father," declared the pastor, "is now one of the best Christians in my church. And," he added, "the home is a place of harmony and peace."

Thus, healthy thinking helps bring about healthy feelings. Never forget that there is a close relationship between faith and physical and emotional health.

A fact of comfort to the pain sufferer is that he can actually lose his pain, at least temporarily, by becoming more interested in something else. A professor who had a severe chronic sinus condition discovered that during the three hours a day he spent teaching, he was without pain. In other words, his teaching was more pleasant than pain was unpleasant.

Another man who suffers constant pain has his own method of relief when it hurts more than usual. "My back hurts," he says to his wife, "so I guess I'd better wash the car and put up the storm windows."

My own father lived with the pain of arthritis. His philosophy of pain always impressed me as extraordinarily sound. "Learn what you can about your disease," he said. "Know what to expect. Learn to do what you can about it. Beyond that, just get along with it." One should learn, he advised, to be aware of corollary symptoms and not to worry about so-called "new symptoms," as in arthritis, for example, in which many reflex pains occur. The fact that you know what these pains are removes alarm over symptoms and actually lessens their effect. "The thing to do," says my father, "if you have arthritis, is to say, 'Well, it's arthritis, and that's the way arthritis is.' Take pain, like people, as it comes," he advised. And then he adds, "You can live a great life within your limitations."

All of which leads to the proposition that, as tough as it is, one of the most practical solutions to the problem of pain is simply to make up your mind to live with it. The effect of pain is great, very great indeed. But the power of mind, the power of soul, is greater.

Not only can the mind be made philosophical with regard to pain, but by discipline some have also cultivated stoicism (the ability to take pain without evident reaction). People who were reared from childhood to be overly conscious of pain suffer to a greater extent than those who were taught as children to minimize or ignore pain.

A neurosurgeon, who is conducting advanced research into controlling pain with supersonics, is reported to have explained that "ultra-high frequency sound waves are used to destroy pain pathways in the brain." Perhaps prayer and faith may also set in motion spiritual high-frequency waves vibrating from God to the believer to destroy "pain pathways" in consciousness.

The basic way to cope with pain is simply to pray. You have the right to ask God to take away or reduce your pain. That is what you honestly want, and any forthright and honest desire may be expressed to God. Believe that He will grant your request.

Put the pain in God's hands and leave it to Him. If it is His will that you are to bear it, God will fortify you with sufficient understanding and strength to endure it. Also, pray for the healing of other people who suffer pain. Develop the attitude of compassion toward all sufferers. As sympathy and love flow out from you, curative forces will flow in toward you.

The following letter shows with simplicity and sincerity the effective use of prayer in the experience of pain.

Dear Dr. Peale,

Eight months ago I suffered a coronary attack. I am fifty-one years old and for the past twenty years have been an athletic coach. Although I have a wonderful wife who is a good Christian, my own spiritual salvation was sadly lacking. During my illness I read your book. Then I started to read the Bible. I did a great deal of thinking, and for the first time started praying. Curiously, I found I was praying for others as much, if not more, than for myself. I continued to read your book and the Gospels and to pray.

One night, as I lay in bed, I was having a bad spell of pain. Then I decided to put everything in God's hands. As I lay there quietly praying I suddenly found myself weeping. Then a sense of warmth and light, prevailing peace and joy, seemed to flood my being, and the pain was gone.

Such complete giving of the self to God is the most effective way of gaining that inner peace and sense of Divine love that takes pain away.

In dealing with pain and suffering one needs, as I have indicated, to practice spiritual acceptance. If, after deeply spiritual prayer, the pain and suffering remain, one must then draw strength from God to live with it and to be creative about it. Never forget, however, that there is within you potential power to rise above pain and gain victory over it. And, do not neglect the possibility that through deeper and more intense prayer and faith you may finally find release.

I was impressed by a phrase used by Captain Raoul de Beaudean of the *Ile de France* when that ship arrived to help the sinking *Andrea Doria*. There was heavy fog as the *Ile de France* came up to the scene of the disaster. The Captain of the French liner said, "I gave an intense mental prayer for a clearing of the fog. In truth the fog did start lifting." The phrase used by the Captain is of utmost significance: "an intense mental prayer." Intensity of effort, intensity of faith, intensity of longing, intensity of self-giving, these are basic factors in healing by faith.

A friend told me of the following prescription written by a physician for a woman patient suffering from a severe throat and chest condition. It read "Rx—More vigorous prayer."

"Did she follow your prescription?" my friend asked.

"She did indeed," said the physician. "She was in true pain, had definite congestion and symptoms, but I could not reach the seat of her trouble for it was of the spirit."

"Did your prescription restore her to health?"

"Of body, mind, and spirit," the doctor answered.

The late Dr. Alexis Carrel who won the Nobel Prize in Physiology and Medicine gave many clinical reports on spiritual healing and significantly stated, "The only condition indispensable for the occurrence is prayer."

A thought is a force, and a good thought is a more powerful force than an evil one. Hold the following thought for it contains power: "The one who created my body will care for its failings and failures. If need be, He will heal me physically or mentally through a doctor or nature, and when doctors or nature fail He can heal me through His own power."

It might be well to define our terms. Physical healing is bodily healing through the application of medical knowledge and skill. Mental healing is healing of mind or body through the therapeutic use of psychology or psychiatry. Spiritual healing is that type of healing which is effected through other than the recognized methods of medicine, psychology or psychiatry, that is healing wrought directly through religious faith.

A minister who has had outstanding success in the field of healing through religious therapy is the Rev. Alfred William Price, Rector of St. Stephen's Episcopal Church, Philadelphia. People began coming to him with their troubles, mental, emotional, spiritual, and sometimes physical. He did his best to help them, but there always seemed some whom he could not reach. He remembers particularly one man badly crippled with arthritis and filled with bitterness, because he had been passed over for promotion in his job, a promotion he felt he deserved. Dr. Price tried to make him see that there was a strong relationship between his illness and his bitterness.

The clergyman sat one day in the pew in his church which was occupied years ago by the famous Dr. S. Weir Mitchell, great neurologist and pioneer of psychosomatic medicine. He remembered Dr. Mitchell's famous words, "It is not the body that is ill, but the mind." He turned to a Bible passage and read, "Is any sick among you? let him call for the elders of the church; and let them pray over him . . .

"And the prayer of faith shall save the sick, and the Lord shall raise him up; and if he have committed sins, they shall be forgiven him." (James 5:14-15)

Dr. Price rose from that prayer to take up the great work of healing in the name of Christ.

He says, "God is on the side of health. Remember that God always answers every genuine prayer according to the measure of our faith. If we create the proper conditions His power will flow through us, healing every fiber, every tissue, and every drop of blood. With your spiritual imagination create in your mind a picture of the perfection in your body or mind which you crave."

"In our healing ministry," Dr. Price says, "our primary effort is to have the sick person healed in the area of the mind and soul. When this is accomplished the healing often comes as a by-product."

Gertrude D. McKelvey says that some few receive instant healing, others gradually over a longer period, and some are not healed but write of new courage to face their maladies with peace of mind.

For example, there was Mrs. J. whose hands had been so badly crippled with arthritis that she could not even move a finger.

"While I knelt at the altar a doctor's name kept coming into my mind," she told Dr. Price. "I had seen so many doctors, but I felt a strong urge to see just one more; this was God's leading."

"Did you know the doctor?"

"No," answered Mrs. J. with an expression of wonderment. "To my knowledge, I had never heard of him, and I didn't know where to find him, either. When I came out of St. Stephen's Church onto the street I realized that Jefferson Hospital was just around the corner and, strangely, I knew I must go there and ask for him.

"To my amazement I learned at the hospital that he had just finished his lunch and could see me for a few moments. He said he was glad I had come because he thought I had the kind of arthritis that he could cure with a new serum he had just learned about. He asked if I was willing to try it. I agreed, and in five weeks I was completely healed. Since then I have dedicated these hands to God's service," she concluded, holding out hands with no trace of the knotty, twisted mass they had once been.

We live in a world full of wonders. Indeed, we have seen so many marvels that scarcely anything now excites our incredulity. Can we, therefore, believe that wonders may not also occur in the area of spirit? Is it not as exactly governed by law as phenomena in the materialistic realm? The fact that we do not completely understand these laws does not indicate that such laws do not exist. Spiritual healings do not always occur; but they do occur, and one may always have the hope that he may be granted this great blessing by God.

The power of faith and prayer, taken together, constitute the greatest power available to human beings.

A sound demonstration of this power is related in this moving story written for *Reader's Digest* by Elise Miller Davis and Edward S. Zelley, Jr.

"Speeding more than 1,000 travelers homeward from New York City, the Broker, crack Jersey-shore commuter train, jumped the track, plunged down a 25-foot embankment. Coaches piled up in a tangled mass of grotesque wreckage. Here is the amazing story of one man among the injured, Bob Stout, of Locust, New Jersey.

"The Rev. Roger J. Squire, pastor of the First Methodist Church of nearby Red Bank, New Jersey, had many parishioners on the Broker. He went from house to house, lending sympathy and offering what help he could. He came to the Stout home as Mildred Stout was kneeling by the crib of her child.

"The Rev. Mr. Squire offered a brief prayer for Bob and his family. Then he went on to others. Mildred felt a little better. Tall, lanky, red-headed, Bob was beloved in the church.

Both Stouts sang in the choir, and Mildred remembered that she was to sing a solo on Sunday.

"Not until 12:30 A.M. did she find him. His chart in the Perth Amboy General Hospital read: 'Possible skull fracture.' And then: 'Last rites given at 10 P.M.' Some kindly priest had done all he could.

"Next day Bob Stout sank deeper and deeper into unconsciousness. He responded to no stimuli, no tests. His condition was too critical to permit X-rays, but severe brain injury was suspected.

"Mildred stayed in his room, praying almost constantly. Wednesday passed. And Thursday. Every feeble pulse beat, every faint breath could have been the last. But, incredibly, Bob hung on.

"On Friday an eminent neurosurgeon was called in. He scheduled an exploratory operation for Sunday noon. He didn't mince words: the risk was great, chances were slim.

"Sunday morning the nurse telephoned Rev. Mr. Squire, 'Mr. Stout's wife is the only person in the world who is sure he will live. She just keeps saying, "I've put my trust in Him." '

"As the pastor began the 11 o'clock service, a line from the order of worship, mimeographed days before, caught his eye: Solo—'Trust in Him'—Mrs. Robert Stout. What he did then seemed to be dictated by a Power beyond himself. Stopping in the midst of the service, he left his pulpit and faced his congregation before the altar rail.

" 'It is 11:15,' he said. 'Bob Stout is critically ill at Perth Amboy General Hospital and soon will undergo an operation. I think Bob and Mildred would like to know we are praying for them.'

"He asked each member of the congregation to concentrate on Bob Stout, to surround his hospital bed with love and faith. Then he turned and knelt at the altar as every head bowed in prayer.

"Picturing Jesus as long ago He had gone about on earth

touching the sick and healing them, Mr. Squire prayed, 'We beseech Thee to go with us now, O Master, to the hospital at Perth Amboy, to walk up the stairs, down the hall to Room 248, to enter and stand by the bed.

" 'Now, Master'—the pastor's voice faltered . . . 'lay Your hand on Bob Stout's brow and heal him!'

"An unreal moment of vast silence hung in the air.

"Then Mr. Squire rose, returned to his pulpit to continue the service. The prayer had seemed long to him, but when he glanced at his watch it was only 11:20.

"After the service Roger Squire sat alone in his study when the phone rang. Answering he heard Mildred's voice, husky with tears. 'There's no medical explanation for what happened,' she said. 'His pulse and respiration were almost nonexistent, and then . . . he just opened his eyes.'

"Instructed to report to the doctors even the slightest change, the nurse had run from the room. When she returned with a doctor, Bob was unconscious again. He was then wheeled to the X-ray room.

"There the specialist re-examined Bob. 'I honestly don't know what made me do it,' he commented later. When he gently pinched Bob's shoulder the patient responded, 'Ouch!' It was Bob Stout's first word in five days.

"The surgeon turned from the table. He sent word to Mildred that the operation was being called off. Bob's pulse and respiration improved unbelievably. He had passed a crisis and the results of trauma were receding.

"As Mildred's voice came over the wire, Mr. Squire recreated vividly the scene at the hospital. What had actually come to pass? Who could say? Perhaps miracles do happen.

"Just one thing more," the pastor said, recovering his voice. 'Does anyone know what time it was when Bob first opened his eyes?'

" 'Yes,' said Mildred, 'it was 11:20.'

"Mr. Squire hung up the receiver and bowed his head."

❖ ❖ ❖

To Live with Pain

1. Even as pain may be removed by faith, so it may be endured by faith.
2. Hold a mental image of yourself as healthy and vigorous.
3. The secret of life isn't in what happens to you, but what you do with what happens to you.
4. God never lays a burden or a pain upon us that He does not give us equivalent strength to bear it.
5. As difficult as it is, pain is not without value.
6. It isn't all-important what the condition of your body is; the important factor is the condition of your mind and soul.
7. There is an enormous power in the human spirit to rise above pain and suffering when the spirit is determined.
8. You have the right to ask God to take away or reduce your pain.
9. Complete giving of the self to God is the most effective way of gaining that inner peace and sense of Divine love that takes pain away.

CHAPTER XVI

LIVE FOREVER

"Current scientific investigation seems to lend support to our intuitions and faith. Recently an eminent scientist expressed his personal feeling that the soul theory has been proved according to the minimum standards of science. His studies indicate that 'the soul survives the barriers of time and space.'"

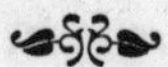

WHEN MY FATHER and my brothers, Bob and Leonard, and I returned home after the funeral services of my mother we felt, as do all families, a deep sense of loss and loneliness. We sat in my minister father's study in the parsonage home at Canisteo, New York and talked about the old days when we were little boys. Our talk was about the dear old homey things, the tender experiences that bind families together by ties that not even death can shatter. We alternately laughed and cried, for life is a patchwork of smiles and tears, each emotion fertilizing and enriching the other.

Then Leonard, the youngest brother, and a capable pastor, took up the old Book, the Book that she had taught us to love and believe. He began to read aloud some of those great and eloquent passages:

"Let not your heart be troubled: ye believe in God, believe also in me. In my Father's house are many mansions: if it were not so, I would have told you. I go to prepare a place for you. And if I go and prepare a place for you, I will come again, and receive you unto myself; that where I am, there ye may be also." (John 14:1-3)

"For we know that if our earthly house of this tabernacle were dissolved, we have a building of God, an house not made with hands, eternal in the heavens." (II Corinthians 5:1)

"For this corruptible must put on incorruption, and this mortal must put on immortality. So when this corruptible shall have put on incorruption, and this mortal shall have put on immortality, then shall be brought to pass the saying that is written, Death is swallowed up in victory. O death, where is thy sting? O grave, where is thy victory?" (I Corinthians 15:53-55)

Suddenly Dad leaped from his chair, pacing the floor in great excitement. With profounder emotion than I ever heard him show from the pulpit, and he had rare power to move men and women, he cried, "If these things are true and I know they are, this message of life and joy should be shouted from the housetops."

So that is what I am doing now, "shouting from the housetops" the greatest of all messages, the glorious truth that you and your loved ones live forever.

When I told my great friend, Dr. Daniel A. Poling, about this book, its title and message, he declared, with his usual keen understanding and glorious faith that the last chapter must be called "Live Forever." And so it is.

I have not the slightest doubt concerning the truth and validity of immortality. I believe absolutely and certainly that when you die you will meet your loved ones and know them and be reunited with them, never to be separated again. I believe that identity of personality will continue in that greater sphere of life in which there will be no suffering nor sorrow as we know them here in the physical sense. I hope there will be struggle, for struggle is good. Certainly there will be ongoing development, for life with no upward effort of the spirit would be incredibly dull.

Nor is this immortality given to us cheaply. To be worthy of living forever, your soul must be cleansed and you must be in harmony with God. In the teaching of Jesus Christ death does not refer to the body but rather to the soul. "The soul that sinneth, it shall die." (Ezekiel 18:20) But the soul that has been forgiven and cleansed, will live forever.

The sign of Christianity, the cross, is a plus sign. It is not a minus sign. The Bible itself says that Christianity is a process of addition, not subtraction. "But seek ye first the kingdom of God, [that is everything that is described by the cross, the plus sign] and his righteousness; and all these things shall be added unto you." (Matt. 6:33) When life is finished here, it is not subtracted from you, but immortal and eternal life is added to you.

Some seem to want proof of this positive faith. There are few out-and-out disbelievers yet remaining in these more enlightened days. And what tremendous difficulty faces a disbeliever in immortality in having to prove his negative position.

Many years ago I read a statement by a scientist who said dogmatically, "At death the life of man is snuffed out like a candle flame." When he made that statement he was listened to with some respect because materialistic science was still riding high, wide, and handsome. But now, he would simply be asked to prove his statement. How does he know? How can he prove his remark? The answer is, he doesn't know, and cannot prove it.

On the positive side we do not believe in immortality because we can prove it, but we try to prove it because we cannot help believing it. Indeed, the instinctive feeling that it is true is one of the deepest proofs of its truth. When God wishes to carry a point with men he plants the idea in their instincts. The longing for immortality is of such universality that it can hardly be met with indifference by the universe. What we deeply long for, what we deeply feel must surely reflect a basic fact of human existence.

Such great truths as this are not believed because of proof and demonstration, but by faith and intuition. Intuition is an important factor in the scientific perception of truth. As Bergson pointed out, scientists often come to the end of verifiable knowledge, then, by a leap of intuition, arrive at truth.

Current scientific investigation seems to lend support to our intuitions and faith. Recently an eminent scientist expressed his personal feeling that the soul theory has been proved according to the minimum standards of science. His studies indicate that "the soul survives the barriers of time and space."

Exciting scientific investigation is proceeding in the field of extrasensory perception. Years ago a number of eminent scientists, among them Wallace, Myers, Royce, and James, began psychical research studies.

Later McDougall and Rhine and others developed parapsychology. This study of the "psyche" or "soul" included those phenomena with which psychology did not deal. These scientists raised the question, "Is there a spiritual factor to men?" Using the most exact methods they examined precognition (the ability of the mind to see something which has not yet happened) retrocognition (the ability to see again that which has happened in the past) and finally clairvoyance and telepathy. After innumerable experiments competent authorities have declared these findings sound from a mathematical point of view. That is they occurred more times than the mathematical percentage of chance would justify. Such investigations seem to have come close to proving scientifically that there is an aspect to man distinctly of greater permanency than his physical attributes.

One of the most significant facts about modern thinking is the new conviction that the universe is spiritual. The old materialistic and mechanistic conception is fading. Sir James Jeans declares that, "All the world is in vibration." Einstein told us, "Matter and energy are interchangeable, one and the same." Scholars, it seems, are recognizing the deep spiritual something that lies at the core of life.

I have quoted Jeans and Einstein. Now I am going to quote a cowboy. The philosophers and the scientists are not always the wisest; sometimes fishermen, farmers, cowboys, men who live with the stars and the earth may have the subtlest wisdom. This cowboy writes as follows under a San Antonio, Texas date line.

Dear Sir,

What is the thing that is spoke of as subconscious? I have used that thing all my life and I know there is something about that thing I don't understand. I have read all I have gotten a chance to on the subject. I strongly believe that it is something we can use. I believe that it has saved my life many times.

I was raised in West Texas and I spent much of my life breaking wild horses. And I know something that is called the subconscious will work on horses. I know that something travels from man to horse, and from horse to man. I have felt it on the bridle reins. That same thing will tell me which trail to take when I am lost in the mountains or on the plains. It guides me through the darkness of the night.

You may think I am crazy to make such statements, but I won't try to do anything without first asking that thing about it. And I then act quick when the answer comes.

Now, if you can see any sense to this question and these statements, will you please answer me in very simple language.

Your friend,

I like that cowboy. Living with the stars and the plains, with the mountains and with God has made him a philosopher of depth. On the trail he felt this "thing." And what is this "thing?" It is God in contact with that deathless "thing" within man.

This is a mysterious universe and within its outward forms is indestructible life. The Bible reminds us that what seems to be death isn't actually. It describes how the Lord, whom they thought dead, was alive and appeared to many. He would be seen; then He would vanish to reappear again.

These manifestations of disappearing and reappearing were designed to emphasize that while He seemed to be gone, He was not gone, but is ever near to us. Then comes the astonishing statement that we shall know the same aliveness after the experience called death. "Because I live, ye shall live also." (John 14:19) The mere fact that we can no longer see our loved ones in the flesh does not at all mean that they are not alive. They still live in this dynamic, mysterious universe even as we too shall live forever.

The day I received the news that my mother had died I went to the Marble Collegiate Church and sat in the pulpit. I did that because she had always told me, "Whenever you are in that pulpit I will be with you." I wanted to feel her presence.

Then I went into my study. On the table lies a Bible. It lay there that morning and it has been there ever since. It is old and tattered now, but that Bible will remain there as long as I am connected with the church, and then I will take it with me wherever I may go. I never give a sermon that I do not, first, put my hand on that Bible.

On that morning of her physical death I placed my hand on the Bible, in an instinctive desire for comfort, and stood looking out toward Fifth Avenue, when all of a sudden, I distinctly felt two cupped hands, soft as eiderdown, resting very gently on my head. And I had a feeling of inexpressible joy.

I have always been afflicted with a questioning kind of mind and, even then, I began to deal factually with this experience, reasoning that it was hallucination due to grief. But I did not believe my own attempt to reason it away. Then the idea dawned that I should lift my thinking to the spiritual level and realize that in this dynamic universe, what we call death is but the change in form of deathless spirit. From that moment I never doubted my mother's spiritual aliveness.

I once wrote of this incident in a magazine article, and received scores of letters from people who told of a like experience. One physician wrote: "I was attending a man in his last illness. Of a sudden, a look came over his face that can only be described as out of this world in its beauty. He began to call by name his mother, father, brother, sister. Then he said, 'Why, Frank, I didn't know you were there.' And, closing his eyes, his spirit took flight.

"The daughter of the man," the doctor continued, "told me that mother and father, brother and sister, had been dead for years. But about his mentioning Frank, she could not understand. Frank was not dead.

"An hour later came the message that Frank, a cousin, had been killed in an accident some hours before."

They live and they will live forever as you will, also, in this dynamic universe. The conviction that this is true first gripped me years ago in a little country cemetery in Ohio. I was standing by my father's side as the body of my beloved grandmother was lowered into the grave. I felt very sorry for him that day for he was sad and so was I. I can see the preacher even yet, standing by the grave and, in memory, hear the strong, sure tone of his voice as he repeated those immortal words, "I am the resurrection, and the life: he that believeth in me, though he were dead, yet shall he live.

"And whosoever liveth and believeth in me shall never die." (John 11:25-26) Suddenly, I had one of those flashing experiences of intuitive perception and instantly, deep in my heart, knew that immortality is a true belief.

Only a short time ago, on a sun-kissed day, I came to the place where those words were first spoken. We rounded a turn in the road that winds up to Jerusalem and there on the shoulder of the Mount of Olives was the village of Bethany just as it appeared in every Biblical picture book. We came to the grave where once rested the body of Lazarus and descended to the spot from which he came forth. Later, emerging into the brilliant daylight, we stood by the open tomb and read aloud the great words. The place where we were standing must have been almost the exact spot where Jesus made that immortal statement to those grieving people.

You never know when your greatest experiences are going to come. When least expected an unforgettable moment flashes across your life with inexpressible meaning. It is difficult for me to recall without deep emotion the feeling of absolute certainty that burned into my mind at that moment that the words spoken there nearly twenty centuries ago are absolutely true. I turned to my wife and said, "On the spot where we now stand was uttered the greatest statement in the history of the world. Think," I said, "of all the grieving millions of people down the centuries who have been comforted by the words spoken here." And again I had that overwhelming feeling of their truth. "I am the resurrection, and the life: he that believeth in me, though he were dead, yet shall he live."

So, God's answer to death is life. In fact, the Bible is filled with emphasis upon life. It preaches a faith based on life, not death. The Bible constantly talks about spiritual experiences, flashing intimations, being surrounded by shining ones, the glory of a Presence, all of which is to tell us that what seems to be death only seems so, that the real fact is life eternal.

Our conception of death as a horror is surely unrealistic. Robert Louis Stevenson said, "If this is death, it is easier than life." Somewhere I read the statement of a great thinker: "Life is the dull side of death." No doubt death is only a process of passing to the other side through a very thin barrier. We need not fear it. Socrates, one of the earth's wisest men, said, "No evil can happen to a good man either in life or after death." The Biblical Book of Revelation in a marvelous passage tells us not to fear death, "And he laid his right hand upon me, saying unto me, 'Fear not . . .' " (Rev. 1:17)

It would be incredible, that a good God, acting as Creator, would make anything as horrible as the death we have traditionally pictured. Basically, all natural processes are good, and death will be but another experience of God's kindness.

The unborn baby, tucked up under its mother's heart, must feel very secure. Suppose somebody might come to him and say, "You are going to leave this place and pass into another world. In other words, you are going to die." The baby might say, "But I don't want to leave, I like it here. I am comfortable. I know this place. I am secure." So he might express his dread of what, to us, is known as birth, but to him is death, or the end of his present existence.

But there comes the day when the baby "dies" out of that prenatal world, or, as we say from our side, he is born. For him it means passing from a known form of life to an unknown and it might very well seem death, since it is the end of that existence as he knows it.

Then what happens to him? Immediately he finds himself in loving arms. Looking down at him is the kindliest and most loving face in all the world and everybody hovers around and rushes to do his bidding. Surely he must say,

"What a wonderful place this is." How foolish I was to dread and fear it and to doubt God's provision.

So he begins to love this new world which he once feared. Then the years add up until he becomes an old man. One day the thought comes, "I must die and leave this world, which has been my home for so long. I love its sunlight which warms my body. I love its starlight which lifts my soul. I love its dear old human ways. I am secure here. I do not want to leave loved ones. I do not want to die out of this world into another." He resists it and again he is afraid.

Then comes that final moment when he "dies" as we call the process. But who are we to say that it is not, instead, simply another birth? What will happen to him when this change takes place? All of a sudden he is young again and surrounded by love and beauty. Twice he "died" and twice he was "born." It is all very reasonable to believe that when your time comes to die you will simply be born into a more wonderful world.

The observed experience of men and women as they pass the so-called valley of the shadow of death indicates, I believe, conclusively that the other side is a place of life and beauty. Sometimes, of course, there is pain in sickness and the passage of a human being through physical death may be a pathetic and seemingly difficult one. But at the moment of death, as a great physician described it, "A great wave of peace seems to come over one and all human suffering ends."

A nurse who told me that she had seen many people die said that never had she noted terror in any face at the moment of death, except in one woman who had cheated her sister. She died with fright written on her face. "Many patients," said this nurse, "have given expression, at the moment of death, of having 'seen' something, and often they spoke about wondrous light and music. Some spoke of seeing faces which apparently they recognized. There was often a look of incredulous wonder in their eyes."

A friend tells of a man who submitted to an operation under local anesthetic. But the strain was greater than anticipated and during the operation he sank alarmingly. Heart action practically ceased, but the patient was finally brought through the operation. Afterward, he reported that at one point he had a strange desire to go further into a state of being which gave the impression of being more appealing than anything he had ever known. The deeper he sank, the less he wanted to return. That was the moment when the physician noted a definite sinking. What he saw as he ventured farther and farther across the river, apparently was something so wonderfully beautiful that it lured him deeply.

Then there was another friend, a meteorologist or weather man. I was with him when his time came to die. As the mist of the valley came over him, suddenly he said, speaking to his son who was sitting beside him, "Jim, I see beautiful buildings. And in one of them is a light, and the light is for me. It is very beautiful." Then he was gone.

Jim said, "My father was strictly an intellectual and in his scientific work never reported anything that was not a proven fact. The habit of years could not change. He was reporting what he saw."

I talked with the late Mrs. Thomas A. Edison about her husband's view of the after life. He was working on a project to determine the weight of the soul. He believed that the soul is an actual entity that leaves the body at death. By weighing the body before and after death he hoped to get some idea of the soul's substantiality.

Edison was one of the few greatest minds in this country. When he was close to the moment of death, the physician saw that he was attempting to say something. He bent over him and distinctly heard Edison say, "It is very beautiful over there."

When Edison invented the electric light he performed hundreds of experiments before he reported that he had an incandescent bulb. Can we believe that the habit of a lifetime of scientific exactitude would disappear at the moment of death and the man of science would suddenly begin to talk poetry? Definitely he saw something, or he would not have said that he did. He sent back to us the reassuring word . . . "It is very beautiful over there." And you can believe it is so.

I was asked to call upon a woman who was very ill in the hospital. Upon entering her room I asked her how she felt and was startled by the directness of her answer. "Mentally and spiritually I am fine. Physically I may as well tell you that I am going to die."

The level and unfrightened look in her eyes made me realize here was a person able, imperturbably, to meet that which frightens most of us. With serene objectivity she approached the event that holds terror for so many. She was like a person making ready to go on a long journey, a beautiful journey. There was no sense of fear, only sublime trust.

She said, "I wanted to see you, not because I particularly need comfort, but to urge you to keep on teaching Christ's message of hope and faith. You must continue to tell people that Jesus Christ has the truth about life and death; that He will help them throughout life and then guide them across to Heaven at the end." A lovely smile crossed her face. "As I have faced my inevitable death I lay here thinking of all the spiritual truth I had read and heard. I determined to put myself completely into God's hands. A deep conviction came that it would be all right. He is so close to me." And she added another sentence which rings like a bell in my mind. "I have no fear of life; I have no fear of death."

Before leaving, I stood at the foot of her bed and said, "I

salute you as a very great lady, one of the greatest I have known. You have no fear of life; you have no fear of death. You have won the greatest of all possible victories. Wherever you go in the vastness of eternity Jesus Christ will be with you."

How good God is. The Bible, His Book, promises the most astonishing blessings. Personally, I believe the Bible makes good on every promise, as extraordinary as they are. And so superlative are these promised blessings that even the Bible sometimes runs out of words to describe them. It simply declares, . . . "Eye hath not seen, nor ear heard, neither have entered into the heart of man, [that is, even to imagine] the things which God hath prepared for them that love Him." (I Cor. 2:9) So, have no fear of life, no fear of death.

Dr. Leslie D. Weatherhead, of London says: "Let me tell you as one who has witnessed many deaths, that in my experience I have never seen one that was unhappy. Sometimes there is fear beforehand, and pain, too, but the end is either sudden and over before we can register any emotion, or else we enter the complete painlessness of sleep, or else it is one of the most joyous experiences we can undergo.

"I sat once on the bed of a man who was dying and his hand lay within my own. I must have gripped his hand more tightly than I thought, for he said a strange thing to me. 'Don't pull me back. It looks so wonderful further on.' And when my own sister was thought to be dying, she overheard the doctor say to the nurse, 'She won't get through the night.' The patient heard it as the best news in the world. When later, the nurse said, 'She is going to pull through after all,' my sister told us afterwards that she heard the words with regret."

Dr. Weatherhead also quotes Dr. William Hunter, a distinguished physician who, on his death bed said, "If I had strength enough to hold a pen I would write how easy and pleasant a thing it is to die."

Of course, the instinct to live is very strong and we resist death to the end. That is part of our human nature. Resistance to death is built into us by a wise Creator. If we did not have resistance we would often give up in the presence of life's difficulties and take the easiest way out. Therefore, we are so constructed that no man will take his own life unless reason has been, at least, temporarily disenthroned. But God who has built this resistance to death into us has also built into life another great truth in the form of instinctive faith that when we must die we go from life to life, from mortal life on earth to eternal life with God.

Since God never did anything badly, but has arranged good for his children (the bad is man-made), all evidence points to the fact that when we pass over to the other side, this death that we have feared for so long will hold no terror at all.

My father died at eighty-five years of age. I never knew a man who wanted so to live. Everytime I saw him he would say, "Norman, I am going to live to be one hundred." And the only weakness I ever saw in my father was a fear of dying. But about three months before he died I noticed that he seemed no longer afraid of it.

My stepmother, who was with him when he passed to the other side, said that as he came to the last he looked at her enquiringly (he could no longer speak), as if to say, "Is this it?"

And she said, "Yes, Clifford, this is it." She said that a wonderful smile passed over his face as if to say, "How foolish I have been."

My stepmother, Mary Peale, is a very factual, sensible woman. She is a wonderful person. Some months after my father's death she told me, "I had an experience with your father. You won't think I am foolish if I tell it to you, will you?"

"Why, of course not," I replied.

"The other night he seemed to come to me," she continued. "I seemed to hear him; there was no sound, but the hearing was by an inward ear, and it was with exactly the old time inflection and tone of his voice.

"This is what he said, 'I would be willing to die again if I could only make you understand how beautiful it all is and how all right I am.' And then he said, speaking of death, 'There's nothing to it.' "

Now that is precisely the way my father would dispose of a matter once he knew the facts. That was his characteristic way of speaking. When he reached a conclusion and saw the facts he expressed his opinion forthrightly and positively. If he found, "There's nothing to it," he would say just that and in that manner.

Of course, when he said, "There's nothing to it," he did not mean that death is not a profound experience. He did not mean that those who are left behind do not suffer great sorrow. He would not minimize it. But what he did mean was that when we come to that final moment when God receives us from one world to another, it is nothing to fear. I am sure that my father now knows what he could not know while in mortal life, that God takes us to that other side where we are reunited with loved ones and live forever in joy and peace.

In Syracuse, New York, I was told that I should talk with Dr. James H. Bennett who was selected by the Medical Society of the State of New York as the General Practitioner of the Year. Dr. Bennett who practiced for many years in Baldwinsville, New York, had contracted an inoperable disease at age forty-nine.

I was told that everyone knew about his sickness and that he would talk quite freely about it. And it was further stated that he had a wonderful philosophy of life. So, I telephoned and had a half-hour talk with him over the phone. He mentioned his illness quite naturally, and without hesitancy, telling me that his time on earth was very short.

"How do you feel about that?" I asked.

"I have learned to take things as they come," he said. "All my professional career I have been dealing with life and death."

"Are you afraid?" I asked of him.

His answer was direct and forthright. "What is there to be afraid of? My conscience is clear. And besides, God is good."

"When your time comes to die," I asked, "do you feel that you will still be in life on the other side?"

His answer was equally forthright, "I have no doubt of it," he replied.

So, neither do I and neither should you. Therefore, be glad and live with faith, as is fitting of those who never die.

Develop deep confidence in the eternal future of your own life and that of your loved ones. Keep believing until you know with certainty that you are an ever alive and deathless part of a dynamic universe. Learn to know that faith in immortality is completely reliable and absolutely true. Immerse yourself in the Bible, in the deathless faith which it teaches. Learn to know, not only by your mind, but by the intuitive perception of the spirit that the great assumptions of continuing life are true.

Life is filled with uncertainties; fogs of doubt, dismal and shadowy fears sometime obscure the landmarks of our faith. Simply put your trust in God and in the deep instincts of your own nature. Read the Bible, pray, and fill your life with love and goodness. Have faith in the accuracy and dependability of your spiritual instruments. They will guide you through the overcasts of this life to a perfect landing in that beautiful land beyond.

Some time ago I flew in a United States Navy plane with an officer who is one of the best pilots in the service, into Floyd Bennett Field, Brooklyn. He told me several hundred miles out that the ceiling at Floyd Bennett was very low. "Are we going in?" I asked.

"I think we'll go in there, but if we don't then we'll go in some place else," he replied nonchalantly.

I do not know what the ceiling was at Floyd Bennett when we came in because the pilot did not tell me, but I knew we were descending rapidly. Down, down, down, we went, but still we did not break through the heavy overcast.

Then, peering out the window, I saw a sandy beach. I estimated we were one hundred feet above it, perhaps more; it was hard to tell. Then water. I knew there were sandy beaches and inlets around Floyd Bennett. Then another sandy beach, and then . . . out of the mist, the runway . . . lights dimly illuminating it in the fog.

When the pilot came from his cockpit I said admiringly, "That was a marvelous landing. That required skill."

"Ah, no; maybe a little experience. Really, it required faith more. I must have faith in my instruments and not deviate on my own. If I become doubtful and think 'These instruments could be wrong, they could be deflecting,' then I could go very wrong indeed. But if I put full trust in my instruments, we make good landings."

We have our instruments, too, precise, exact instruments; prayer, faith, the instinct of God and immortality. They are trustworthy and will take you through the fogs, the drifting winds, the storms, and the uncertainties of life. Trusting those instruments of faith you will come in, finally, to be welcomed by the lights on the eternal runway. And there will be your loved ones to meet you with the same old smile on their beloved faces. Believe . . . and live forever.

About the Author

NORMAN VINCENT PEALE is one of the most widely read inspirational writers of all time. He was coeditor and copublisher (with his wife of over sixty years, Ruth) of *Guideposts* magazine and senior minister of the Collegiate Reformed Protestant Dutch Church of the City of New York. He was the recipient of many awards throughout his long and illustrious career, including the Presidential Medal of Freedom.